Whatever
Happened
to
Madison Avenue?

Whatever Happened to Madison Avenue?

ADVERTISING IN THE '90s

by Martin Mayer

LITTLE, BROWN AND COMPANY

BOSTON   TORONTO   LONDON

First Edition

Excerpts from *And Hearing Not . . . Annals of An Adman,* by Earnest Elmo
Calkins, copyright 1946 Charles Scribner's Sons, copyright renewed © 1974
Walter E. Beer, Jr. are reprinted with permission of Charles Scribner's Sons,
an imprint of Macmillan Publishing Company.

Excerpts from "What Forces Shape the Future of Advertising Research?," by
Leo Bogart, *Journal of Advertising Research,* Feb./Mar. 1986 are reprinted with
permission.

Parts of chapter 5 appeared in *Forbes* magazine in a different form.

Library of Congress Cataloging-in-Publication Data
Mayer, Martin, 1928–
    Whatever happened to Madison Avenue?: advertising in the '90s /
by Martin Mayer. — 1st ed.
        p.   cm.
    Includes index.
    ISBN 0-316-55154-6
    1. Advertising — United States.   I. Title.
HF5813.U6M32   1991
659.1'0973 — dc20   90-24150

10 9 8 7 6 5 4 3 2 1

RRD VA

*Published simultaneously in Canada
by Little, Brown & Company (Canada) Limited*

Printed in the United States of America

For
Britta and Mike,
Julia and Amelia

Contents

Preface

THE READER should know the provenance of what he has begun to read.

A generation ago, Cass Canfield, a J. P. Morgan partner turned publisher after the bank had to bail out the old house of Harper & Brothers, commissioned me to write a book with the title *Madison Avenue, U.S.A.* This title was, I believe, Canfield's own choice. He was confident a book on the advertising business, under that title, would sell. I learned later that he had proposed it to other writers, but had not convinced them. He convinced me, and he was right. The book sold well in five languages.

Among those I consulted in the early phases of work on *Madison Avenue, U.S.A.,* was Jack Hirshleifer, a friend from college days who had gone on to get a Ph.D. in economics and was teaching at the University of Chicago Business School. (Later he would move on to the Rand Corporation and U.C.L.A., and become a leading light of the profession.) He couldn't help me. "Well, you know," he said, "economic theory assumes that everybody acts rationally, and that rules out advertising right from the start."

Not having a Ph.D., I was more vain about the possibility of applying the economics I had learned to whatever I was writing about. Philosophically, too, I wanted to believe that most of the people are indeed rational most of the time. The 1950s were a period when the intellectual community (especially but not exclusively its left wing) was fearful of what were assumed to be the immense persuasive powers of advertising. Sloan Wilson had written a novel centering on "The Man in the Gray Flannel Suit" who knows he is unworthy of the influence at his command. The sociologist-journalist Vance Packard had successfully warned Americans about "The Hidden Persuaders." A smart cookie named James Vicary, who had a little research company, had roused fears that the movie and TV screens were being contaminated with "subliminal" advertising that in effect hypnotized people, who thereupon bought this bar of soap rather than that.

For the 1952 presidential election, Rosser Reeves of the Ted Bates agency wrote vulgar one-minute spots of Dwight Eisenhower answering questions Reeves had written for men-in-the-street to ask him. Eisenhower had made all the recordings in a couple of hours in a single afternoon, not concealing his distaste. ("To think," he said at one point, "that an old soldier would come to this!") There was much learned comment at the time about the contribution those damned spots made to the Eisenhower victory.

As an apostle of the rational, I was insistent that this stuff about the overwhelming power of advertising simply made no sense. The governor of Illinois was never, no way, going to beat the supreme commander of the Allied Expeditionary

Forces in the largest war America had ever fought. Subliminal advertising would be as invisible in its effects as it was on the screen. Advertising unquestionably "worked" — it sold goods and services — but mostly it influenced consumer decisions that were of very little importance to the consumer. Advertising that led someone to switch from Bayer aspirin to Anacin was hugely important to Sterling Drug (which owned Bayer) and American Home Products (which owned Anacin), but not to the people who switched. Most such advertising influenced what the psychologist Milton Rokeach called "Type E" beliefs: "inconsequential beliefs. If they are changed, the total system of beliefs is not altered in any significant way. . . . The more competitive the advertising, the more it seems to address itself to changing psychologically inconsequential beliefs."[1] Moreover, much advertising did not "work." I wrote a chapter about the planning for the Edsel campaign, which was A-1 professional work; and the car bombed like something in Lebanon.

If you could get far enough away from advertising to see it in the round, what was happening most of the time, I thought, was the attachment of a quality to the product itself. When advertising "worked" — and even when it failed — the reason had to be that it changed the product. Because of the advertising attached to this brand of this product, people perceived it differently — and received different benefits from its possession and consumption. "It is remarkable," I grumbled in 1958, "how many people who readily see that a new package or a new brand name will change a product fail to see that advertising inevitably has a very similar effect."[2] In this focus, one could indeed apply economic analysis to the phenomenon of advertising. The central purpose of advertising had to be the creation of partial monopoly rents for the proprietor of the advertised brand. As the result of his advertising, he could charge more for the same quantity of his product, or sell more of it at the same price. Advertising, in short, "added value" to the branded product. This idea was not as original as I or all but a handful of my readers thought. As long ago as 1921, the great Chicago economist Frank Knight had written: "[N]early every manufacturing and mercantile business has a monopoly on *some feature* of its product: its good or service is differentiated from others in some manner and to some degree. . . . [T]he presence of partial monopoly is a qualifying factor in determining short-run price. . . . [Therefore there is a] striving after the greatest possible degree of real or fictitious uniqueness in a product."[3] Even in 1921, the establishment of uniqueness through communications was what paid for the advertising; that's what always pays for the advertising.

What sold *Madison Avenue, U.S.A.,* was not this philosophy, of course. Probably the most important element was the first public prominence the book gave to four figures who were then talked about in the industry but not generally known — Bill Bernbach, David Ogilvy, Norman B. Norman, and Rosser Reeves, whom I took as the exemplars of different attitudes toward advertising. But some remembered the last chapter, among them Peter Georgescu, now president of Young & Rubicam, the largest American agency.

In 1988, Georgescu was chairman of a "Value of Advertising" committee in the American Association of Advertising Agencies. When we met in his office at his invitation, he asked if I still believed what I had written more than thirty years before, and I said I did — keeping in mind, as I had written then, that these values are not necessarily socially desirable. They may be trivial (lemon-scented dishwashing soap), or anxiety-inducing (if you don't eat the high-fiber cereal we are advertising you are more likely to get cancer, and your wife will be depressed), or even harmful (the identification of cigarettes with masculinity or with pleasure). But to the extent that advertising attaches to a branded product a quality for which consumers will pay, manufacturers and suppliers have reason to advertise rather than incur costs for the more striking but less durable sales results of price-cutting, in-store promotions, the bribery of retail dealers ("slotting fees" is the polite term), and other more direct means of moving merchandise.

Georgescu said the advertising industry was in deep trouble, largely because expenditure on such short-term promotions had been displacing advertising budgets in all the big packaged-goods companies. Assuming the industry had to be defended, he asked, what were the best defenses?

I said I thought there were three easily defended positions. Brands as major assets were the result of years of investment in what Burleigh Gardner of the Harvard Business School had called "image," in papers written almost forty years ago, what David Ogilvy in his heyday had called "personality," and Hal Riney, guru of contemporary advertising creativity (his Frank and Ed, earnest, aging bumpkins supposedly the producers of the Gallo wine coolers, had put an entire product class into a category very different from where it would otherwise have been), likes to call "tonality." Building these brands was among the last high time-horizon activities of American business in the age of the corporate takeover. Advertising forced management to contemplate a longer term, which was in itself healthy for the corporate planning process. Advertising was also an activity that increased incentives for product improvements, or at the least the maintenance of product quality, while selling by price promotion or trade deals created incentives to cheapen the product for the sake of maintaining profit margins.

The second line of defense for advertising lay along the nation's sudden obsession with "competitiveness." It is an article of faith in Washington that the United States can satisfy its appetite for foreign oil and foreign automotive and electronic products by exporting "services" — banking, insurance, software development, architecture, business consultancy. Georgescu's phone call had come to me soon after I had served my time as part of a panel on international trade in services established to advise the Office of Technology Assessment of the Congress on the feasibility of policy changes — and the desirability of various bargaining positions at the negotiations in the Uruguay Round of the General Agreement on Trade and Tariffs — to help American service providers make sales abroad. As we panelists contributed our bits and pieces of knowledge, it emerged that the United States was far from sure to benefit by free trade in services. European banks are closer to the frontier of electronic consumer banking than ours are, and in the reinsurance game the British and Swiss are the leaders. A growing fraction of the work associated with the development of computer software is moving out to the Indian subcontinent, where a well-educated middle class that speaks English looks upon U.S. minimum wage as a princely income. Used tickets on American Airlines are being bundled into giant packages and flown to Barbados, where Bajans better educated than the average New York City high-school graduate key in the information to be transmitted by satellite to the company's data processing center in Tulsa.[4]

But the creation of perceived value through advertising — that is an American specialty. Foreigners own many large American agencies now, but the revenue flows from the sale of services go much more heavily to the people who work in the process than to the owners of the operation. The income stream from branding still goes primarily to Americans. To use economists' lingo, advertising is one of the few areas where the United States enjoys "comparative advantage." As such, its domestic health is a significant contributor to our foreign economic relations.

The third argument grows from the first two. If the United States must compete with the rest of the world as a producer of manufactured commodities, it will lose to Korea, Taiwan, Thailand, Singapore, and Brazil. And probably others, too. The American standard of living is threatened by what Georgescu calls "commodityness," and not many American businessmen understand the danger. Not long ago, a young man applying for a job said to Frank Stanton of Simmons Research Corporation, "When I was at the Harvard Business School, sales was an expense item." Such attitudes are as widespread as they are foolish. Looking ahead into the next century, then, the price advantage that comes to the branded product is significant far beyond the confines of the advertiser and his agent.

From this conversation with Georgescu grew an arrangement between the American Association of Advertising Agencies and Little, Brown, whereby the publisher was subsidized by means I do not know to commission a book from me about the advertising business a generation after *Madison Avenue, U.S.A.* The A.A.A.A. gave me the run of its library, and A.A.A.A. president John O'Toole called some of his members to tell them I would be calling. When the manuscript (or, more properly, disc) was finished, the printout was read in the usual way by some friends of mine, by people in the industry, and by Debra Roth, the perceptive and hardworking editor put on the case by Little, Brown. I took some suggestions from column A, some from column B, most from column C. Copyeditor Elisabeth Gleason Humez then created a thoughtful and sympathetic column D of technical comment, and I took some suggestions from that one, too. The book and its errors continue, of course, to be mine.

1.

Even aficionados of this subject will find much of the one-third or so of this book that has a historical focus as unfamiliar as any of the new material. Some of this is just a benefit — yes, Virginia, there are benefits — from my having been around a long time. But the novelty of much of the history has been drawn from two long unpublished manuscripts (and the notes for one of them), written respectively in the mid-1960s and the early 1980s.

The 1960s manuscript is a history of the Ted Bates agency, and thereby hangs a tale. That book was a pet project of Rosser Reeves, a forceful copywriter from Virginia, inventor of the "Unique Selling Proposition" and author of *Reality in Advertising*, who had by threatening to quit got himself installed as C.E.O. of Bates. Reeves had come after me to write a history of his agency rather soon after the publication of *Madison Avenue, U.S.A.,* and I had declined. There was in those days a restaurant on East Fifty-third Street called Baroque, where Reeves ate every day at a table placed in a bulbous nose of second-story floor space cantilevered out over the bar, giving him a perfect view of everyone who came in or went out the door. He would invite me to join him once every few months, and up the ante on the history project. Finally, the money became just terribly tempting. I said in some anguish, "Rosser, why do you want this thing so much? Your people will never let you publish it."

"Martin," Reeves said in his idiosyncratic growl, "I'm going to be fifty years old. I'm going to retire to my place at Half Moon, in Jamaica. I'm going to be stretched out on a chaise longue beside the pool, looking out over the bay. There will be a Tom Collins on the table. I am going to take a sip of the Tom Collins, put it back on the table, and reach out my hand for a book. I want it to be a book about *me*." This was irresistible, and I signed on for what proved to be a fascinating year's work. Bates himself, very skeptically (he was an immensely intelligent man), had approved the project and instructed people to answer every question I asked, and to give me access to clients as well as to files.

But when the manuscript was finished, my initial warning to Reeves turned out to be completely correct. The members of the executive committee of the agency all read the book, and all (except Reeves) voted to bar its publication. Indeed, the agency's lawyers demanded that every copy of the manuscript and every page of my notes be destroyed. If they could have put me in solitary confinement in a penal colony, they would gladly have done so. I had no complaint: I had been paid in full, and if the agency wished to suppress the manuscript, that was part of what it had paid for.

Shortly after Rosser died, in 1986, his widow, Betty Joy, got a call from the University of Wisconsin library, asking whether it was now permissible for the library to make the Mayer history of the agency available to students of advertising. She was bewildered, and explained to the librarian that all copies had been destroyed — her husband hadn't even been allowed to keep one for his own amusement. And then it turned out that without telling anyone, Reeves had asked his secretary to take my manuscript home for the weekend and type a copy. He had then taken that copy to Madison in his own large hands, and given it to the library to keep under seal as long as he lived. With Betty Joy's collaboration, then, the prodigal book returned to me after twenty years in the grave. Carl Spielvogel, who now runs the conglomerate agency that includes Bates, read the manuscript, expressed enthusiasm, and kindly made extra copies for me. Everyone significantly involved in the Bates history is now, I think, dead — certainly, none has any continuing involvement at Bates. So I have felt free to poach from it.

The other unpublished document that surfaced as I rummaged my files for this book was a twenty-thousand-word article I wrote in 1981 for *New York* magazine. This had been in retrospect a mistake for both the magazine and me: we see the world, it is fair to say, on different focal lengths. Reading my notes on the several-score interviews that had gone into that article, I was surprised at how many people had been prescient about the onrushing troubles of the industry — and how little I had made of it at the time. These interviews, too, fed into what follows.

Other sources for historical material included my book *About Television* (1972) and the notes for it, which covered the advertising as well as the broadcasting corners of the subject. And from 1976 to 1981, for Hollis Alpert, I wrote a monthly column on television for the magazine *American Film.* Though I did most of my reviewing in screening rooms (not wishing to waste evenings watching television), I necessarily kept an eye on the commercials that supported the programs.

One last stroke of luck for this book was my discovery in the A.A.A.A. library of the advertising executive Earnest Elmo Calkins's memoir . . . *And Hearing Not,* a delightful, beautifully written piece of Americana I had never read before. I have run away with half a dozen pages of it here, quite gleefully, and I hope that this contact with a book that has been out of print for more than forty years will persuade someone somewhere to reissue it.

Martin Mayer

New York

Whatever
Happened
to
Madison Avenue?

CHAPTER ONE

Madison Avenue Revisited

For all the marble in the lobbies and the elegant offices in the towers — for all the nine-figure deals in which one advertising agency purchases another — the advertising industry in the United States is troubled as the century of its efflorescence dies, more insecure than usual, with more reason for insecurity than ever. Through the decade of the 1980s, the relative importance of advertising to American industry steadily declined as expenditures on other sales techniques steadily increased. Consolidation of store chains greatly increased the bargaining power of the retailer. New technologies for gathering and processing information cast doubt on the effectiveness of advertising as a sales tool. The mass audiences that had made advertising efficient began to fragment with the spread of cable television and the arrival of the VCR, the splintering of the magazine business, the growth of suburban newspapers. In 1980, advertising absorbed something like two-thirds of all marketing expenditures by manufacturers; by 1990, advertising's share was no more than one-third.

Elephantiasis on all sides of the advertising relationships meant that the advertising man who was larger than life (as most great salesmen are) could no longer dominate the field of his activity. Hal Riney, an eternally young, now middle-aged, advertising writer with a bushy mustache, who operates out of a skylit room in the center of the top floor of a San Francisco warehouse, argues that advertising has become "a business run by businessmen who have no real interest in advertising. They think they do, but they don't." He says, "I don't think any of them cares about long-term brand images. They don't sell advertising, they sell services. They're M.B.A.'s." The market researcher Larry Light blames the decline of the industry on the rise of the business-school graduate. "There's not a business school in the country that teaches a course on branding," Light says. "M.B.A. can stand for 'Managers of Brand Assets' or 'Murderers of Brand Assets.' Right now, the murderers are winning."

In fairness, the heads of the agencies have big operations to run, worldwide. "The boss has to come around and show the flag at least once a year," Bruce Crawford, chairman of Omnicom, says wearily. "And we're still in an acquisition phase. If you're going to buy an agency in Seoul, someone has to go and kick the tires first." But even if he were a genius and a true acolyte of the god of advertising, and devoted all his time to client contact, the head of a major agency dealing with major corporate clients might have trouble getting heard where it counts. The Albert Laskers and Stanley Resors and Raymond Rubicams and Ted Bateses of earlier generations had met with the George Washington Hills and Lord Leverhulmes and Neil McElroys and E. H. Littles, not perhaps as equals, but as experts whose advice in the areas of their expertise was considered important. Today only a handful of the C.E.O.'s at the nation's biggest advertisers will even look at the new campaigns before they run, let alone take time at meetings to discuss strategies and approve tactics. Advertising agencies now deal with middle managers meeting assigned short-range goals, who have little flexibility and less inclination to use what flexibility they have. The chief financial officer wears several more bars on his shoulder than the executive vice-president for marketing.

Indeed, the marketing function for packaged goods is fragmented among divisions that deal separately with coupon and premium and price promotions, store displays, distributor liaison, conventions and public relations campaigns, and advertising. More than ten years ago, Young & Rubicam, the largest American advertising agency, began a campaign for "integrated marketing," offering a variety of services through its owned subsidiaries, which would work in a coordinated manner. This approach was and is marketed under the slogan "The Whole Egg." Some clients buy it; most don't. "When you talk about an agency coordinating all these activities," says the head of a large rival agency, "the heads of all these divisions in the client companies begin worrying about who is going to take them to lunch." Charles D. Peebler, Jr., of Bozell, Inc., who agrees with the Y&R approach, says that clients will eventually drive integrated marketing: "Agencies are not drivers." Alex Kroll of Y&R says, "Well, that leaves open the question of which comes first, the chicken or the Whole Egg. Clients can't demand it if it isn't available."

With the decline in the status of advertising has come a loss in recruiting power. "When I got out of the Harvard Business School right after the war," says James Burke, who ran Johnson & Johnson through the 1980s, "advertising got the brightest people. I didn't go into advertising myself, I went to Procter and Gamble, but I used to say to people that the brightest people I knew were in the advertising business." Burke has lost none of his faith in advertising itself — "I've always started with the premise that the added value of advertising in a brand was extraordinary, so large it wasn't measurable." On his retirement from J&J, he accepted a full-time job as chairman of the Media-Advertising Partnership for a Drug-Free America. "But I can't say I think advertising got the brightest people in the 1980s. They went off to investment banking, where the rewards were so much bigger."

And it was the habits of mind in the financial markets of the 1980s that put the skids under advertising. It is not that Wall Street failed to appreciate the value of brands — indeed, much of the takeover activity in the latter part of the decade was designed to profit by what the raiders considered undervaluation of brand franchises in the market price of corporate securities. But there was a contradiction in the logic of the buy-out artists. The true value of the brands was their longevity, while the "corporate restructuring" contemplated in the takeover deals was designed to capture such values for current shareholders without concern for the future. The combination was destructive: "brand extensions" that placed old names on new products damaged established franchises, while other brands were cannibalized or used as "cash cows" to beef up quarterly earnings figures and help the restructurer sell out at an inflated price. Cashing in on brand equities, to quote the very precise reference of Rena Bartos, who ran communications research for the J. Walter Thompson agency in the 1970s, "kills the goose that lays the golden eggs."

The receding tide of takeovers left behind immense swamps of debt. Stockholders historically have been willing to accept low dividends now in return for plausible growth strategies and the reinvestment of current earnings. And the tax code encouraged such attitudes by rewarding the patience that converted today's earnings into tomorrow's capital gains. Debtholders, unfortunately, can be satisfied only with cash flow — and quick payouts come from price promotions, not from advertising.

Meanwhile, the growing concentration in retailing — in 1989, five chains accounted for half of all sales of nonfood, nondurable consumer goods in the United States — had returned to the stores the strategic advantages over manufacturers that advertising had been invented to reverse. "To the manufacturer who advertises," Earnest Elmo Calkins wrote in 1905, "it makes no difference what jobber or what commission man buys his goods. All of them will have to buy them in the end. Just as soon as a retailer finds that a certain line of goods is so strongly demanded that he must have it, he will go where he can get it. If a given jobber doesn't handle it, he will go to a new jobber."[1]

Roy Bostock of D'Arcy Masius Benton & Bowles, an amalgam of three great names into one $4 billion agency, looks back fondly on "the old days when I'd say, 'I'm introducing Scope or Cool Whip. There's a giant advertising budget, and you'd better carry it.' Now it's, 'We'll help you with the trade promotions.'" The market power is on the other side. "Once the stores were 'outlets,'" says Mike Koelker of Foote, Cone & Belding, who creates the advertising for Levi's jeans (dressing for work, naturally, in Levi's jeans). "Now they're as powerful as consumers. If these retail conglomerates decide to dump you in bins under the escalator, you're dead whatever the advertising does."

Market power problems are even more severe in Europe, where agencies see much of their future. In 1988 at a conference at the University of Texas, a rather grim study was presented by Jean-Noël Kapferer and Gilles Laurent of HEC (Hautes Etudes Commercial, one of the French *grandes écoles* and the closest equivalent in Europe to the Harvard Business School). In France, they reported,

> retailers have developed strong private brands (including generics but also higher-quality brands) and are putting strong pressure on price and margins of national brands. They are able to influence demand by:
> • Over-allocating shelf space to their private labels.
> • Under-allocating shelf space to national brands.
> • Pricing national brands relatively high.
> • Pricing private labels relatively low . . .
> • Fostering an "anti-brand" communication policy implying "unbranded" equals "freedom."[2]

The path of least resistance is to cooperate with such market power rather than to fight it. David Ogilvy was himself the image of advertising in its postwar heyday — the elegant Englishman who tooled around in a Rolls-Royce (but left it parked overnight on the street), who had sold door-to-door in France and designed questionnaires for George Gallup and written "The Man in the Hathaway Shirt." In 1986 he complained bitterly at an industry dinner that "manufacturers of packaged goods are now spending twice as much on below-the-line deals as on advertising. . . . Manufacturers are buying volume by price discounting, instead of earning it the old-fashioned way — using advertising to build strong brand franchises. . . . [T]hey are *training* consumers to buy on price instead of brand."[3]

Supermarkets advertise long lists of sale prices, and make money not only on the discounts that finance the price reductions, always greater than the reductions themselves, but also, often, on the advertising. "Co-op" payments by the manufacturers who own the brands frequently exceed the actual cost of the ad. The introduction of the new models of the great brand-name cars was once one of the rituals of fall, like the World Series, trumpeted with spreads in the newspapers, color extravaganzas in the magazines, specials on television. Now the cars come off the assembly lines with rebates attached.

Some advertising agency executives see the beginnings of a reversal in fortunes. Procter & Gamble, which had led the flight to coupons and sampling and price promotions and in-store deals, is reputedly coming around to greater use of advertising. The Wall Street houses that led the merger-and-acquisition race are mostly, as Y&R's Alex Kroll says, "wrecked or on the beach." And while they abused the insight, the Wall Street operators did call many people's attention to the importance of the brand franchise. There is a plus for the image of advertising even in negative attention, like the new Treasury Department revenue-raising proposal that advertising be capitalized rather than expensed (which would temporarily increase the taxes corporations with heavy advertising budgets would have to pay) and the British accounting proposals that would compel British purchasers of corporations with branded products to amortize the "goodwill" thus added to their balance sheets. Most significantly, the marketing business has seen advances in the technologies underlying market research and in its ability to deliver selling arguments closer to where the sales happen. Some of these advances promise striking improvements in the efficiency of the advertising system. Such promises have been made before, but "before" was a time without computers that could massage billions of bits of information.

Still, there can be no question that for all the apparent prosperity of the giant agencies, the mighty have fallen a great distance. Which raises Thomas Huxley's comment about the sex of a hippopotamus: is the question of interest to anyone but another hippopotamus? To which the answer, I think, is "Yes." What happens to advertising is nontrivial on both practical and symbolic levels. However much one may dislike specific ads or commercials or even advertised products, a continuing decline of advertising as a factor in the American economy would be harmful to the national interest. The subject deserves continuing and thoughtful examination.

1.

Consumers choose the brand they perceive as delivering the values they wish to find in this kind of product. William Moran, an Irish philosopher turned social researcher, who at various times headed the research function for Lever Brothers and Young & Rubicam, likes to deny the conventional proposition within the industry that brands find their customers; the truth, he says, is that customers find their brands. Advertising informs the consumer that the brand is there and attaches to the brand certain attributes and values. And the consumer picks it off the shelf for its "added value." DDB Needham, an agency that spends something more than $4 billion of its clients' money, has run consumer studies in which people are told, "Look. Salt is salt. Morton's also packs the store brand, and it's eight cents less." But people still want the little girl with the umbrella, and "When It Rains, It Pours."

That such values are created by advertising has been

demonstrated repeatedly through the last forty years. In the 1950s, Philip Morris had consumer panels of smokers take alternate puffs of two different unmarked cigarettes, one their own brand and one another brand, and found that without the name they could not tell the two apart. The researchers then showed people ads and commercials for two different brands, gave them two cigarettes that were really the same brand, identified one cigarette as one of the advertised brands and the other as the other advertised brand, and asked after the alternate-puff test which of the two "tasted better." Everyone had an opinion, and the source of that opinion, that preference, had to be the advertising. Later even more "scientific" work was done. John Philip Jones, an English market researcher turned American college professor, describes an example of this conclusive research in his book *What's in a Name:* "A leading breakfast cereal was preferred to two competitors in a blind test in the ratios 47:27:26. When the test was repeated with identified packages, the preferences changed to 59:26:15. The . . . difference of twelve percentage points . . . can only have come from the added values in the brand that were not in the product alone."[4]

William LaPorte built American Home Products from a minor to a major factor in the drug and household products businesses during his twenty-one years as its president or chairman. "He had an almost childish belief in the power of advertising," says Frank Stanton, who runs Simmons Market Research. "And he's probably the most successful entrepreneur since Adam Smith — for more than two decades, his company grew ten per cent a year, and profits grew ten per cent a year." LaPorte, still a director of American Home Products (where he took his first job, in 1938), recently made a compendious statement about the value of advertising: "If you have the customer coming in and asking for it, you're in pretty good shape."

When the value attached to the brand catches a social or demographic trend, the advertising can "work" very forcefully. Keith Reinhard's "You deserve a break today" filled the airwaves for McDonald's at a time when more and more women with children under ten were in the labor force. They didn't want to cook when they came back from the office, but they also didn't want to get dressed up to go to a restaurant — and they didn't want to feel guilty about not taking care of their families. Stunningly executed, the McDonald's commercials made it absolutely OK on all counts for the family to head off to the fast-food counters when Mom and Dad came home from work. "The place wasn't *quite* as nice as we showed on the screen," Reinhard recalls affectionately from his present status as chairman of DDB Needham and of the American Association of Advertising Agencies, "but it was within the bounds of reality. The commercials became part of what people experienced when they went to McDonald's." One can even argue that advertising increased the sum total of happiness (or reduced the sum total of misery), because the women were going to go to work and refuse to cook when they got back whether or not they felt good about going out for "dinner." What can't be argued, of course, is that more women went to work *because* they felt good about McDonald's: the power is in the trend, not in the advertising.

Outside the industry, the conventional proposition is that the customer is cheated by advertising because he pays more "for the same product" than he might have paid if there were no brands, no asserted "uniqueness." Max Beerbohm expressed this view perfectly in the 1920s, offering an entry to an industry-sponsored contest for the best slogan about advertising: "Buy advertised products and help pay for the advertising." Defenders of the business who stress "communication" and "persuasion," placing the changes wrought by advertising in the consumer rather than in the product, play into the hands of such critics. N. W. Ayer, the oldest continuing advertising agency in the country, confirms the critics' case by announcing in a video-tape presentation in its waiting room: "We create your wants! We create your desires!" We have not, after all, asked N. W. Ayer to do any such thing.

When it is understood that advertising changes the product, the argument moves to a different plane. The aspirin cures the headache faster because the sufferer who takes it believes in it. The value the consumer receives from buying this brand rather than that one is perfectly real. ("It may not be *tangible*," said Alexander Biel at The Ogilvy Center for Research in San Francisco, "but it's always *real*.") A woman who feels herself prettier in a red dress may also feel herself more appealing in the olfactory aureole of Chanel No. 5. "August Busch understands," Keith Reinhard says gratefully of this client, "that we put the night into Michelob."

Frank Knight, in 1925, defined economics as "the science that deals with the satisfaction of wants," and added: "Human beings act not on the basis of fact and reality as such, but on the basis of *opinions* and *beliefs* about *facts*. . . . [O]ne who aspires to explain or understand human behavior must be, not finally but first of all, an epistemologist. . . . Wants are culture products, to be judged by culture canons. . . . Even our food and clothing, in all their concrete content, and by far the larger part of their money cost, represent social and aesthetic and not biological values."[5] The copywriter James Webb Young gave the perfect example:

"Nobody ever criticized the advertising which has made Steinway 'The Piano of the Immortals' and gives pride to every owner of one."[6]

Perhaps the clearest of these abstract values is confidence that the proprietor of a branded product will maintain the quality of what he sells the public: the slightest hint that a product is not what it was can demolish a brand: namely, the U.S. automobile industry. As branding proliferated into new product areas — fast-food restaurants, hotels, insurance, stockbrokers, chickens, banks, traveler's checks, real estate brokers, airlines, tax preparation, medical services, child care — the significance of confidence became increasingly obvious. The economist George Akerlof argued that branding is "an institution which counteracts the effects of quality uncertainty."[7] The lesson has been internalized in Japan, where manufacturers will say they learned from Edward Deming that the reputation for quality has less to do with the level attained than with the consistency achieved — and that this was the greatest lesson Deming taught them. "IBM," says the marketing researcher Larry Light, "doesn't stand for International Business Machines. It stands for 'If I recommend this product, I won't get fired.'"

And it is far from certain that advertising raises the price the consumer pays. The great Hungarian-British economist Nicholas Kaldor (later Lord Kaldor) argued in 1950 that advertising reduced competition by eliminating the wholesaler, who had compelled manufacturers to compete by choosing among the brands he would carry,[8] but in fact sales operations that bypassed wholesalers eliminated a source of expense. To the extent that Kaldor's wholesaler had been able to pressure the manufacturer into lower prices, he had kept the extra margin for himself: for reasons associated with the relationship between the wholesaler's "drummer" and the retailers he serviced, there wasn't much competition among wholesalers. Branding, which is virtually synonymous with advertising, makes possible open-shelf distribution, eliminating from most transactions the alleged expertise of the storekeeper (which must be paid for, whether the allegation is true or false). And the knowledge that the advertiser is pulling the goods through the stores enables retail chains to dispense with the local and regional wholesalers who had to be paid (ultimately by the consumer) to take the risks and expenses of warehousing.

It is hard to work up much sympathy for the neoconservative argument that the information advertising provides the consumer is worth its cost, an argument that Judge Robert Bork has put into judicial opinion; the products most heavily advertised are those for which the consumer least wants more "information." But there is certainly a case to be made that the consumer receives much of the benefit of the economies of scale advertising permits. Paul Farris and Mark Albion state in its simplest form the argument that advertising tends to lower prices: "As the most efficient marketing method for many products, advertising allows the price of a product category to be lower than if less efficient marketing tools are employed." High levels of advertising by manufacturers do in fact correlate with low margins for retailers. People who come in to buy the brand they have seen advertised impose fewer costs on the sales staff in the store. The discount-store phenomenon, of course, was made possible by the existence of nationally advertised brands of white goods (washing machines, refrigerators, and the like) the customer felt he could trust even if he knew none of the Eight Jewish Korean War Veterans who pioneered the business under the acronym E. J. Korvette.

On the manufacturing, as distinct from the marketing,

level, it can be argued with strong empirical backing that companies with a hot brand will profit more by increasing production at reduced unit cost rather than by increasing prices at the same level of sales. And they will have a strong trope in that direction, because taking the profits in increased sales rather than increased prices discourages competitors who would be drawn by unusually fat margins.

Moreover, like the patent and copyright system, branding facilitates innovation. (One notes in passing that patents and copyrights expire, but a trademark is an intellectual property right in perpetuity.) The advertised brand becomes an instrument for what Joseph Schumpeter called the creative destruction of capitalism. When the double-edged blade arrives, the price of the straight razor falls; when the twin blade comes, the double-edged razor (still the same quality) sells for less. Advertising that can permanently tie an innovation to a brand name gives producers incentives to create product improvements.

Someone who worked on the original campaign for Glad sandwich bags remembers the speed and secrecy required while everyone held his breath in disbelief that Baggies, which had been first with the little plastic bag and owned the market, would not see that the first company out with a bag that folded closed would take the business. One of the great contributions of the advertising agency in its glory days was to push the client into product improvements, because they were promotable. Mobil Oil put detergent in its gasoline after the Ted Bates agency, which had just acquired the account, asked the company's scientists to enumerate the elements they would hope to find in an ideal gasoline and compare the company's existing product with that standard. Advertising can make some product attributes more important, which means that others become less important. The attributes remain in the product. Among the handicaps agencies have to carry these days, says Simmons's Frank Stanton, is that "people are no longer willing to invest so much in making their brands different. Or better."

Meanwhile, advertising facilitates the spread of innovations by alerting competitors to the product features that are moving someone else's product ahead of their own — and the need to build something a little extra into that product improvement to erode the advantages the originator had gained by getting there first. "Active awareness of and response to the competition," writes John Philip Jones, "are among the most salient characteristics of oligopoly."[9] The advertising that announces one manufacturer's novelty may or may not blunt the leader's edge, and may or may not supplant the previously advertised feature as the prime value of the brand. In Jones's example — Pepsi-Cola's introduction of Slice, a soda with 10 percent real fruit juice content — competitor Coca-Cola's Minute Maid was able to claw back for its own new if rather similar products some of the billion-dollar market Pepsi-Cola had invented for Slice.

Acceptance of such approaches to advertising now stretches across the political spectrum. Lester Thurow, head of the Sloan School at M.I.T. and adviser to the left wing of the Democratic Party, writes that "brand name corn flakes must be yielding some psychic utility or brand name corn flakes would not be sold. Consumers may have been convinced of this psychic utility because of advertising, but so what? . . . [M]onopoly rents are inherently limited in an economy full of large conglomerate firms. . . . [O]ligopolistic firms may be able to extract a small price premium from their customers, but this ability is inherently limited by . . . a set of large firms that scan a wide range of

products and markets to search for profitable investments. . . . [P]rice is clearly only one of the many competitive
weapons. . . . Nonprice forms of competition are just as useful and valid as price competition."[10]

2.

Partly because the people who know best have their lips
sealed for purposes of commercial secrecy, most of what
gets written about advertising is too solemn, too trivial, or
too . . . well, too unintelligent. The solemnity is natural,
because the expenditures are enormous: in all, counting the
radio, television, newspaper, direct mail, magazine, bill-
board, packaging, and in-store displays, American producers spend something like $120 billion, more than 2.5
percent of net national product, on selling and promotional
activities, and about a third of that goes to advertising. From
the point of view of a company committing money in eight
figures or more, the effectiveness and efficiency of advertising are nothing to joke about. Few decisions a C.E.O. can
take are so important as a go/no-go choice for a new product. A "line extension" — the use of a brand name for a
product not previously associated with that name — can
lead to a quick and profitable introduction, or to the dev-
astation of the old established franchise. It's embarrassing
and irritating to be told that apart from your employees and
stockholders and competitors, nobody in the world — not
even the supermarket chain, for which your new product is
one of some 27,000 "SKU's" (Stock Keeping Units) — cares
in the least how your decision turns out. But that's the truth.
     In the minds of those who pay for it, the images associ-
ated with advertising are necessarily images of war. Adver-

tising is a weapon in the battle for share of market and share of mind. Though the industry has a trade association and everybody joins together to solicit Congressmen, in the advertising context competitors are enemies, and the agency must enlist in the war. When I first came visiting in the mid-1950s, every channel in every cigarette machine on every floor of the Madison Avenue office building that housed Batten, Barton, Durstine & Osborn offered the same brand (Lucky Strike: the bulletin board had a sign, "Confucius Say: Advertising men who use product advertised by rival agency should draw paycheck from rival agency"). One of the most famous stories in the industry told of Albert Lasker, proprietor of Lord & Thomas, finding one of his employees at a conference table smoking something other than the brand his agency advertised. Noting the boss's gaze, the employee muttered something about picking up his wife's pack by mistake, and Lasker said, "Your wife, I assume, has an independent income?"

Most "negative" advertising, casting discredit on a rival brand, derives from the tendency of advertisers and their distributors to take this war imagery seriously. Explaining (not defending) some commercials that had taken Coca-Cola's side of the war against Pepsi-Cola, a high executive of Lintas, which does Coke's advertising, noted that those commercials had been designed to meet the needs and desires of the company's bottlers, independent companies that actually produce the product, from syrup supplied by the proprietor of the brand. "You go before a bottlers' convention and you put on the screen a commercial that says, 'Pepsi-Cola is SHIT,' and you'll have them all on their feet cheering."

From an agency management's point of view, of course,

advertising is mother's milk. People are exalted or cast down by small changes in the market share of the products they advertise, in reported sales, in Return On Investment. They post o'er land and ocean without rest to seek out the right people at accounts that are supposed to be up for grabs. They have mouths to feed. Though the average account stays with the same agency for nine years, and some remain set for generations, advertising is an insecure occupation. A good fraction of the longevity of brands that is the glory of advertising can be explained by inertia, and inertia can be bought for cheap.

N. W. Ayer & Son, a Philadelphia agency selling advertising space in newspapers around the country, started in the advertising business in the 1860s, and in 1886 began promoting the virtues of advertising with the slogan "Keeping Everlastingly At It Brings Success." Rosser Reeves of the Ted Bates agency told me in the 1950s, "Given identical products, identical budgets, and identical sales forces, I will let you have a brilliant campaign every six months, provided you change it every six months — and I'll take a less-than-brilliant campaign and beat your tail off with it because I'll run it ten years." There are self-reinforcing processes at work here. People note and remember the ads and commercials for the products they already buy and use much better than the ads and commercials for other products in the same category. In a sense, absorption of the sales arguments for the products you buy is a defense of habit, and people cherish their habits. Spreading out to other businesses, General Electric told the world that it wanted to manufacture only those products and services in which its brand was first or second in the market. The economies of scale in distribution are greater than those in production.

Still, it takes something to remain true to the values

advertising has implanted in the product. Habit is boring; the reinforcement of habit reinforces boredom. Rosser Reeves used to tell a nice story about John Fox, proprietor of Minute Maid orange juice, who had taught Reeves, among other things, how to race sailboats. One day when they were cruising on Reeves's yacht, Fox suddenly said to Reeves, "You have forty-seven people working on my brands, and you haven't changed the campaign in twelve years. What are all those people doing?" To which Reeves replied, "They're keeping your people from changing your ad." But it isn't that easy. Watching the same commercial the fifth, sixth, seventh time is not great entertainment; the researchers speak of "wearout." As Bill Wells of DDB Needham in Chicago puts it, "[P]owerful campaigns stay powerful only when they remain true to what made them powerful when they were first exactly right."[11]

The persistence of brand identities and brand values is much stronger than most practitioners realize. John O'Toole, now president of the American Association of Advertising Agencies but then chairman of Foote, Cone & Belding, once had occasion to put together a reel of commercials for Dial soap spanning the years 1951 to 1976: "The overall impression of continuity was astonishing, despite dramatic changes in color, cinematography, editing, clothing, models, and even modes of speech over twenty-five years. Dial clearly had an identity that constantly adapted to the times but never fundamentally changed."[12] John Rindlaub of Young & Rubicam likes to talk about the Betty Crocker figure developed and improved for General Mills by his mother, Jean Rindlaub, when she was a pioneer senior copywriter for Batten, Barton, Durstine & Osborn more than fifty years ago. (Ads were directed to women, but this was not a woman's world.) There never was such a person as "Betty Crocker," and the ad campaign is long dead, but the name still ranks in the top ten when the pollsters ask people to name the American women they admire most.

Advertising agency people are torn between the desire to claim credit for the success of a brand and a need to insist that it's really the quality of the product that makes the success. This flatters both the manufacturer and the consumer, and the advertising man wants to be on the best of terms with both. The late Bill Bernbach made the classic statement: "I think the most important element in success in ad writing is the product itself. And I can't say that often enough. Or emphasize it enough. Because I think a great ad campaign will make a bad product fail faster. It will get more people to know it's bad."[13] And that's mostly true. James O. Peckham of the Nielsen Company advised manufacturers that if their new product did not get at least a 60–40 preference in blind tests against what was already on the market in that category, they shouldn't attempt to introduce it.[14]

What sells anything best — automobiles, books, laundry soap — is word of mouth. (This is why advertising that gets talked about probably has more value than practitioners think, and why agencies show off their trophies for "creative" work despite the received wisdom of the business that the ads and commercials practitioners alike achieve a less-than-average record as generators of sales.) And brand reputation can be built most effectively by the product itself. Not the least of the advantages the Japanese have had in competing for American markets is their understanding of the need for consonance between advertising and product. When Honda first sold cars in the United States, it told dealers that they were never to charge more than $35 to anyone who brought in a car for repairs. The company would pay the rest. Ease and inexpensiveness of repair was part of the message of the ads Stephen Kessler of Chiat/Day wrote for Honda ("In one year, many new cars depreciate as much as our new car costs"), and the underlying theme of the great "We Make It Simple" campaign by Needham, Harper & Steers a few years later.

It's repeat sales that make advertising profitable, and the history of the business is replete with products that took off like a shot — Teel liquid dentifrice, Kentucky Kings cigarettes, soft cookies — and fell back because so high a fraction of their early customers decided not to buy again. If the values implied or asserted by the advertising are not there, in an area of perception where the customer in fact knows what he's getting, the brand goes rapidly over the cliff.

Perhaps the best story of how the product let down the ads grows out of Ed McCabe's brilliant campaign for a New York restaurant chain called Horn & Hardart. The chain had been proprietors of the Automat, a gleaming-clean self-service system in which the customer went to a booth to acquire nickels and quarters and then put them in slots beside individual glass-doored refrigerated servo units to take out the sandwiches and salads and "glace cakes" (the equivalent for a New York child of Proust's madeleine) displayed behind the doors. Like much else in New York, the Automat had come upon hard times in the 1960s, and Horn & Hardart was using advertising to make a comeback. The ads, mostly in subway and bus car cards, showed vegetables and fruits in luscious colors, just themselves, very simple, but beautifully arranged.

Among those attracted to Horn & Hardart by the ads, the copywriter and eventual agency president Jerry Della Femina reported in his memoirs, was a young agency employee from the part of North Carolina where the accents are deepest South. He called her Betty-Sue: "One

Monday morning she comes up to me and she says, 'Jer, I bin reading those Horn and Hardart ads, the ones which say, "It May Not Be Fancy, but It's Good. ... And I decided to go to Horn and Hardart, and I had some of their beans and the beans were gooooood, and I had some lemon-mrang pah and it was gooooood, and then I had some coffee and it was gooooood. And then the man sitting across the way exposed himself.' "[15]

That sort of thing the consumer experiences and understands. But there are many areas where the consumer in fact cannot judge, and he may accept the attribute advertising attaches to the amorphous envelope of the product, even if it's not so. Through the years when Subaru posted the worst record in Consumers Union's annual survey of trouble in the previous year's cars, the brand kept its heavily advertised reputation for sturdiness. Keith Reinhard, whose agency advertises Volkswagen in Britain and the United States, reports that the repair rates for that brand are roughly the same in the two countries. "But if you ask people which cars have lower repair rates, they rank VW very well in the United Kingdom, very poorly in the U.S. Because year after year in the U.K. we advertised, 'Don't You Wish Everything Worked As Well As a VW?' "

Bill Bernbach, who devised the original Volkswagen ad with its stress on quality (a picture of the car with the word *Lemon,* illustrating that this particular beetle had been rejected as inadequate to the mark), made splendid use of consumer ignorance in one of his most famous campaigns. His partners had accepted the Levy's Rye Bread account, and like a good copywriter he tried the product. Now, in the New York of Bernbach's childhood (and mine), there were Jewish bakers on every avenue. Bernbach knew rye bread, and it was not this beige loaf with a soft crust and spongy insides. "You'll never get a Jew to eat this stuff," he said, and from that observation grew a great ad. Most people, after all, even in the New York of the 1960s, did not know Jewish rye bread. Bernbach put pencil to paper and wrote "You don't have to be Jewish to enjoy Levy's Rye Bread . . . ," and the art department added the appropriate Chinese, Italian, American Indian, Irish, and black figures to illustrate the slogan.

Sixty years earlier, Claude Hopkins, the greatest copywriter of his time, who dominated the advertising output of Albert Lasker's Lord & Thomas from 1907 to 1924, found that the executives of Van Camp's couldn't tell what came out of their cans of pork and beans from what came out of competitors' cans. So he ran big newspaper ads urging consumers to "Try Our Rivals, Too." Hopkins wrote a slim volume called *Scientific Advertising* that is still one of the most interesting discussions of the adman's problem (though much too optimistic, as a good adman is likely to be), and it may well be that he understood on a gut level why this ad would be effective. For if there was no perceptible product difference between Van Camp's and the other pork and beans brands, then the chances were strong that every user of the product category who tried Van Camp's as a result of the advertising would be pleased with what he got. All the more profound goods from advertising — perceived value, assurance of stable quality, leadership role — were reinforced by the slogan. And there could be no bads from it — the aspects of the advertising that persuaded users of other brands to switch could not possibly give existing loyalists reason to believe "their" brand was being taken away from them.

Even at its best and most responsible, there is an element of hype in this business, and most of the time there's no harm in it. A nice recent example of "branding" is the

Marriott hotel chain's response to the pizza boxes travelers left behind in their rooms. Marriott management couldn't see why hotel guests should have to send out for pizza, so pizza was added to the room-service menu. Some people ordered pizza from the menu, but the incidence of pizza boxes in the rooms did not noticeably diminish. So a card was added to the informative documentation in the room, advertising "Napolizza," available through an outside number. When the guest called that number, saving himself the work of looking up another number in the Yellow Pages, he got a voice with an Italian accent, which took the order. In the hotel kitchen downstairs, a waiter took off his Marriott jacket and put on a Napolizza jacket, put the pizza in a Napolizza box, and took it upstairs to the room. Within days, nearly all the pizza boxes left behind in the rooms were Napolizza boxes.

Quite a lot of advertising is designed to appropriate for one brand alone qualities that are in fact common to all brands of the product. One of the most famous of the Hopkins stories tells of his work on the Schlitz account. A thorough and serious man, he went out to visit the brewery, where he was particularly intrigued by the bottle-washing process. This was in the early years of the twentieth century, when Frank Norris and Upton Sinclair were scaring the American public about how unsanitary our food processing businesses were. Hopkins prepared a campaign around the fact that Schlitz beer came in bottles that had been "washed in live steam." The Uihlein family, which owned the brewery, was surprised: all beer bottles were washed the same way in all breweries. Hopkins patiently explained to them that what mattered was not what the industry *did* but what brewers *advertised* that they did. The campaign brought to national prominence a brand that remained a major factor for more than half a century.

But you have to watch out: not all trivial features can be successfully advertised as valuable discriminators, and some can be harmful. Braniff Airways did not benefit over time by painting its aircraft in fluorescent colors. Charles Peebler, Jr., of Bozell remembers from his early days the chairman of a brewery company who came back from a trip and said he'd learned that you could toast the malt and it wouldn't change the product, so he wanted to advertise that his malt was toasted. "We said, 'No,'" Peebler recalls, "but it was his company. So we wrote the ads, and sales went down. You went out and asked people, and they said the beer tasted burnt."

3.

What gets left out of most analyses of advertising, scholarly or popular, friendly or hostile, is the amount of fun this business is for the people who are good at it. "If you seek his monument," says the Latin inscription on the gravestone of Sir Christopher Wren in the ambulatory of Saint Paul's, "look around you." Modern man, said Ogilvy's Alex Biel, lives in a world of "brandscapes." People involved in an advertising campaign find the results of their work all around them, in what they watch and read and see. They look at both people and products rather differently from the rest of mankind. Advertising is indeed an occupation in which the best practitioners change the world. They don't change what's important in the world, unless your Weltanschauung says that the relative fortunes of Procter & Gamble and Colgate and Lever pose an important question.

And they don't really "manipulate" people, or "create wants." The wants are already there; it's just that until the product was made *and advertised,* consumers had no notion that these wants could be validated.

No small part of the economic impact of advertising derives from the fun its creators have while doing it. "In my opinion," Leo Bogart, who spent a generation as director of research for the Newspaper Advertising Bureau, told a University of Illinois audience at the James Webb Young lecture in 1988, "fun is what makes advertising successful."[16]

As a normal matter, the value added by advertising is simply a careful playback of what the consumer wants to find in the product, and the advertising most often "works" not because it has any special quality but because the right pressure is applied in the right places. But even in the routine situation, part of that value is something personal from the copy group, the art department, the filmmaker, even (sometimes especially) the researcher.

In summer 1990, the Copy Research Validity Project of the Advertising Research Foundation (ARF) published the results of a study that matched five admittedly successful and five admittedly unsuccessful new commercials, tested under controlled conditions over cable TV in test markets, for pairs of established brands seeking to expand their share of the same category. Broached in 1977, and approved and budgeted in 1982, it was one of the most elaborate social research activities carried on in the United States in the 1980s. "Successful" and "unsuccessful" were defined by sales measurements for the brand in the local markets. The owners of the brands cooperated (indeed, they were sponsors of the study, having much at stake) by withholding the national introduction of the successful commercials for a year, so they and the matched unsuccessful commercials could be run in other markets and tested by the procedures employed when you *don't* know which is a successful and which is an unsuccessful commercial. People were asked whether they bought this brand, thought it was the best or one of the best, remembered the commercial, remembered the argument made in the commercial, could identify what that argument was, and believed or disbelieved it.

At the insistence of Rena Bartos, one of the founding members of the A.A.A.A. committee on the image of advertising, a senior vice-president of J. Walter Thompson when the study started and a communications consultant when it finished, the "subjects" were also asked whether they had liked or disliked the commercial. And it turned out that liking or disliking predicted the sales results as well as the belief that the product was the best or one of the best in its category. In the words of a researcher, Russ Haley of the University of New Hampshire, who supervised the analysis, "If you like the product and you like the commercial, you buy it." That did not strike him as surprising, but it was very controversial in the trade, where the origin of wisdom is recognition that the purpose of advertising is to make people like the product, not the ad — and that failure to get the customer's attention means nothing can be accomplished. The fact that the test ran for a whole year, which is more time and more money than advertisers are usually willing to devote to a testing process, may have had something to do with the results. It makes sense that the durability of the values created by advertising, the longevity of the brand franchise, should have something to do with how the creator of the added values relates to the product, to the people who use it, to his daily work and to the advertising that results. Whether, in other words, he's having fun.

On the evidence of his memoirs, nobody ever had more

(clean) fun in advertising than Earnest Elmo Calkins, a major figure in the first thirty years of this century, whose accomplishments were all the more remarkable in that he was deaf. Calkins enjoyed the act of writing advertising, the rough-and-tumble with clients and the owners of the media (who were then in the trenches with their grunts, not on Wall Street or in Beverly Hills), the evidence that the ads sold what Calkins was being paid to sell. But he wanted his memoirs, he wrote, to be mostly about "the Everyman and Five Wits, the Harlequins and Pantaloons." He said, "There will be no statistics and no pie charts, and especially no histories of successful accounts, but descriptions of how accounts are lost rather than how they are kept and fattened. If your taste runs to success stories, you might read Claude Hopkins' *How I Made $1,000,000 in Advertising*." Advertising, Calkins thought, was a major social artifact. "These humbler adjuncts to literature may prove more valuable to the future historian than the editorial contents [of the magazines]. In them we may trace our sociological history, the rise and fall of fads and crazes, changing interests and tastes, in foods, clothes, amusements and vices, a panorama of life as it was lived, more informing than old diaries or crumbling tombstones."

Even more can be said. Like any artwork, a rare piece of advertising can acquire a life of its own, informing subsequent generations in ways that would amaze, sometimes scandalize, its creators. Calkins made one of these when the Lackawanna Railroad came to him to do more with its claim that travel on the Lackawanna saved passengers the annoyance of soot on their clothes: other railroads burned dirty soft coal, but the Lackawanna burned clean hard coal. The railroad had been using car cards in streetcars with a parody of the "House That Jack Built," featuring a drawing of a girl

in white, the "maiden all for lawn," whose dress stayed spot-
less through her travels. "Taking our cue from the girl in
white," Calkins recalled, "we gave her a name, had an artist
create a type for illustration, and produced an endless series
of new jingles. . . . The form of the verses was suggested to
me by an onomatopoetic rhyme in *The Humorous Speaker,*
one of the elocution books so numerous when I was a
boy — 'Riding on the Rail.' Its jigging meter was supposed
to suggest the song of the rushing train. This was the first
verse of the series:

> 'Said Phoebe Snow
> About to go
>   Upon a trip to Buffalo:
> "My gown keeps white
> Both day and night
>   Upon the Road of Anthracite."'

"An amusing story could be made," Calkins continued,
"of the manner in which the higher criticism has been
applied to the apotheosis of Phoebe Snow. One of the
Lackawanna officers learnedly explained (after the fact) that
Phoebe was the one woman's name that had the right psychological appeal, that the perfect name was not hit upon
until after experiments with other names, that Mary was
tried and failed to click, that when Phoebe was adopted the
public responded one hundred per cent. All of which was
vastly entertaining to the man who created Phoebe, who
named her without giving a moment's thought to the laws
of mental science, mnemonics, or the subtle influence of
association of ideas. And he realized that thus are legends
made.

"Phoebe Snow had her day and became a proverb, a
symbol, and a simile in her time and had her tribute of

burlesque, parody, cartooning and allusion that was evidence of a world's familiarity, and is now gathered into the limbo of outmoded advertising techniques. . . . Advertising styles share with theatrical productions," Calkins concluded, "the fate of disappearing without a trace once their brief moment is over."[17]

Then, to his amazement, after he had finished these paragraphs but before the book could be printed, in 1946, he found in The New York *World-Telegram* a story headlined "Phoebe Snow Is Back." The Lackawanna Railroad was reviving the forty-year-old campaign — "not," said the news release, as "the pin-up pretty of the Floradora days but a lovely luscious granddaughter worthy of the fair name of Lackawanna Girl in American advertising's hall of fame." Calkins noted gently that the revival was indeed an abstract tribute to the advertising itself, for the premise of the advertising was no longer true: "As the Road of Anthracite now burns soft coal, Phoebe will no longer be played up as the girl in white, but instead will represent the feminine influence that is beginning to penetrate railroad travel."[18]

The year these words were written, 1946, was also the year that Talley Beatty, a young black ballet dancer, left the Katherine Dunham dance group to form his own company. Thirteen years later, he would choreograph a ballet, *The Road of the Phoebe Snow,* to music by Duke Ellington and Billy Strayhorn. Beatty, the notes for the ballet explained, had been brought up beside the Lackawanna tracks (really he had been born and raised in New Orleans, and had moved to Chicago, two places the Lackawanna did not serve). Blacks lived beside the tracks. The grand lady, very white, passed by. "Somehow, after the manner of folklore," John Martin wrote in *The New York Times,* after the work's premiere at the Ninety-second Street Young Men's and

Young Women's Hebrew Association, "she seems to have got herself personified to the youngsters who live and play along the tracks as a particular train, 'The Phoebe Snow.'"[19] Beside these tracks play out what Anna Kisselgoff of the same paper, fifteen years later, called "the very American tensions of urban and ghetto life."[20] To the flashing red and green lights of the signal system, a black gang stomp a black young man and rape his black girl friend, who commits suicide. "Virtually a slate of related dances," John Martin wrote, "almost like some Negro folk 'Sylphides.'"

All good things, said the poet, are thus confused to ill. But it's an excellent ballet, with a long life of its own. The Alvin Ailey group performed it at a black tie gala for the benefit of the company some thirty years after its first performance. One way or another, in the minds of people for whom Earnest Elmo Calkins never existed, Phoebe Snow is still around. What advertising does reverberates far beyond the sales statistics.

CHAPTER TWO

The Tasks of Advertising

THERE IS no definable task called "advertising." The thing itself is too complex, involving all the social sciences and the literary, visual, oral, and musical arts. Moreover, the purposes of advertising vary enormously from brand to brand, from product category to product category, from place to place.

Campbell Soup owns soup products, tomato juice, and canned mushrooms that it sells under its own name. Standard "condensed" soup is an all but monopoly product for Campbell in the United States, and pricing is ad lib, because each kind of soup has its own price and nobody remembers what the ratios were last week between tomato soup, Homestyle chicken noodle, Manhattan clam chowder, pepper pot, and split pea. No product benefits more from inertia. There are no competitive products, and virtually no possible substitutes on the shelf, against which the price of a Campbell's soup can be compared. As might be expected from a company in Campbell's position, the standard condensed soup products are almost never the subject of manufacturers' price promotions. Profit margins for the stores are something the stores can decide for themselves, which guarantees sympathetic eye-level shelf space and lots of it.

The company is among the world's most sophisticated advertisers, though it has never achieved market dominance outside the United States. (Timothy Joyce, later head of MediaMark Research in New York, remembers from his time at the research arm of J. Walter Thompson in London a remarkable day when Campbell admitted that from the point of view of the British consumer, "There's something wrong about the tomato soup.") The "Campbell kids" go back to the beginning of the century, and logos and print styles have been changed very slowly. The same advertising agency has worked for the soups for longer than anyone now working at the agency has been alive. Advertising pressure has always been heavy. In the days when magazines presented a text "sandwich" of stories and articles, with the first part of every major feature printed in a section kept clean of commercial messages, Campbell bought the first page of advertising, facing the last page of that section in every issue of almost every general-circulation magazine. This was known in the magazine business, even in those special-interest magazines where another advertiser had the page, as "the Campbell Soup position."

The strength of the brand rests on the quality of the product. I once wrote a long article on the Campbell Soup company (for *Cosmopolitan* magazine, yet), and visited the plants. The oldest were the most impressive, one in Camden, New Jersey (the company's headquarters), the other in Chicago. They were organized around rail transportation. Boxcars brought in the ingredients, which were hoisted to the top floor, cleaned, examined, and sent through chutes to the mixing vessels on the floor below, whence they flowed through wide pipes to the kettles, and then to rattling lines of cans, which were filled, sealed, sterilized, labeled, and run down the belt to be boxed and put in the freight cars to start their passage to the stores. In the early 1970s, these plants were staffed mostly with black women who had come to work during World War II — at the employees' entrance there were honor rolls for the many workers who had passed their twenty-fifth anniversary with the company. For two weeks of every year, every worker in the plant donned candy stripes and became a quality-control inspector — and took the responsibility *very* seriously.

(One sidebar comment may be worth making before we move on. It's rather a pity Campbell never advertised the black work force in the big-city plants and the depth of their commitment to quality. Such advertising would have offered good vibes for race relations, for the inner city [the Campbell operation was absolutely all Camden had, but it was sound] — and, cleverly planned, for the product, too.)

So the basic task in advertising Campbell Soup is to maintain public certainty that the red-and-white can contains a good, safe product. Atop that, however, there are special missions. When ever-increasing fractions of women are in the labor force and not eating lunch at home, the advertising starts suggesting snacktime and/or dinnertime uses for good old soup. And, of course, there is the "male homemaker" market, which MediaMark Research (a supplier of much information to Campbell Soup) places at 18 percent of all households. Over 70 percent of male homemakers buy canned soup, more than buy canned tuna fish or frankfurters. Some of this market is gained by advertising, some by a directed product: "Soup for One," which also satisfies the mother's need for a product to give a picky child.

Competition among branded products is the expression of substitution at the margin — that is, giving people who are almost indifferent as to whether they buy this brand or that some reason to try that rather than this. In the case of the Campbell marketing problem, the effort has to be to position the heavier soups where they can be seen as potential substitutions for stews or chili or pizza. So we have "chunky" and "Manhandler" soups, and the advertising is asked to make sure the names resonate. Then there is the opportunity offered by the health crusaders, who have changed the climate of food marketing and in the process have raised a certain amount of anxiety about the heavy salting that consumer taste tests have led Campbell to use in its recipes. MediaMark says that compared to an average bunch of customers, women fifty and over are more than twice as likely to worry (probably correctly) about high salt intake. And that's a growing market that will start accelerating its growth in the later 1990s. The answer, of course, is a line of "Low Sodium" Campbell soups that must be advertised just right so as not to raise anxiety levels in consumers of the high-sodium soups.

Then there are products Campbell Soup makes under other brands. There's a line of spaghetti products — Prego and Franco-American and Spaghetti-O's. Swanson TV dinners are a Campbell Soup property and share with the soup factories the use of chicken processing plants, mushroom farms, and contracts with vegetable farmers who sell all their output to the Campbell company. (However, the maintenance of sanitary conditions is a very different problem for frozen foods: bacteria get boiled away in making soup, but may survive the freezing process; the visitor dons white coat and hair cover.) Swanson is downscale from Campbell, and one does not risk the Campbell name. Moving to an upscale frozen dinner, Campbell launched Le Menu, which does not make reference to either Swanson or Campbell. Nothing is hidden: the Campbell name is on all the packages, in very small letters after the list of ingredients. But you have to know to look for it.

In dealing with Pepperidge Farm, Campbell chooses to remain invisible for different reasons. The package for Pepperidge Farm cookies tells you about "Margaret Rudkin, the founder of Pepperidge Farm," but not about Campbell's ownership. People would see Campbell's as on a social level with Nabisco, and Pepperidge Farm cookies are supposed to be fancier than Nabisco's. Godiva Chocolates are even further upscale, and Campbell does not do anything at all to tell anyone but stockholders that this fancy "Belgian" chocolatier is a branch of the soup company. (For different reasons but by the same philosophy, Johnson & Johnson, owned by a family that until the present generation was devoutly Catholic, never wanted the corporate name attached to its highly profitable Ortho-Gynol division, which makes contraceptive products.) On simpler grounds that the brand is in direct competition with the company's own tomato juice, Campbell also does not wish to see the corporate logo on V-8, and indeed advertises V-8 in ways very different from the usual Campbell commercials.

What is the task entailed in advertising all these brands for the Campbell Soup company? How should the advertising manager or marketing manager or C.E.O. look at Campbell Soup as an advertiser? If there were one Campbell Soup account, covering the entire range of the company's products, how should an agency pitch it? Do any of these questions make sense? But before answering, remember that the company moved its Swanson frozen dinners line from Hal Riney to BBDO in early 1990, in no small part as a reward to BBDO for what management considered a bang-up job with the chunky soups.

1.

The world is full of such lists, and the one I happen to have (from Laurel Cutler of FCB Leber Katz) was drawn up by the Boston Consulting Group. Its title is "The Astonishing Defensibility of Being Number One," and it lists leading brands in 1923 and 1984, to wit:

Category	Leading Brand 1923	Current Position
Bacon	Swift	First
Cameras	Kodak	First
Canned Fruit	Del Monte	First
Canned Milk	Carnation	First
Chewing Gum	Wrigley	First
Chocolates	Hershey	Second
Flour	Gold Medal	First
Mint Candy	Life-Savers	First
Paint	Sherwin-Williams	First
Pipe Tobacco	Prince Albert	First
Razors	Gillette	First
Sewing Machines	Singer	First
Soap	Ivory	First
Soft Drinks	Coca-Cola	First
Soup	Campbell	First
Tea	Lipton	First
Tires	Goodyear	First
Toothpaste	Colgate	Second

One could also make a list of brands that were once number one and have now disappeared or very nearly: Lucky Strike, Schlitz, Western Union, Schwinn, Oxydol, and

Frigidaire, the last once so dominant in the refrigerator business that General Motors (which owned the brand) had to worry that the trademark would be lost because the word had become a generic description of a product. And there could be an even longer list of brands once ascendant that are somewhere in the process of losing their luster and their sales. While Coca-Cola probably continues to hold first place in the drinks sweepstakes, the company's astonishing stupidity in the aborted introduction of "New Coke" still haunts its future: New Coke and Classic Coke between them may hold a smaller share of the soft drink market than Coke alone had at the beginning of the 1980s. In some quarters, a loss of position over time is not necessarily considered a defeat. The dominant view in the business schools still sees a "product life cycle" in which brands that once proudly pawed the earth and dominated their part of the pasture descend to the status of "cash cows" that are to be fed as little as possible and milked for all that can be got out of them. This is why Larry Light said that M.B.A. stood for "Murderers of Brand Assets." Frank Stanton of Simmons says that Americans are handicapped these days in competition with Europeans, because Europeans have and Americans haven't internalized the knowledge that "products have life cycles, but brands don't."

In fact, the product life cycle approach is beginning to lose some of its appeal, as the bankers and corporate raiders who want to package consumer goods companies for resale propagandize the long-term value of brands even as they slash quality and reduce advertising to boost immediate profits. Some economists, moreover, have begun to recognize what the Nobel Prize–winner George Stigler once called a "survivorship principle" in the history of successful brands. Attempting to measure brand equity very indirectly (by examining the impact on the stock prices of their proprietors, following changes in the formulation and presentation of branded products), Mary W. Sullivan of the University of Chicago and Carol J. Simon of Chicago and U.C.L.A. "assume that the longer a brand has survived, the better the ability of the firm to produce a consistent quality product that meets consumer expectations. For this reason, our analysis includes the age of the brand as a determinant of brand equity."[1]

Advertising brands that dominate their markets is not like advertising anything else. Even firms that consider the maintenance of their brand franchise a prime consideration will wish to exploit a dominant position by letting momentum do some of the job. As John Philip Jones of Syracuse University likes to put it, number-one brands are more profitable because their "share of voice" (their proportion of advertising expenditures for this kind of product) is less than their share of market. They can save some of the money their less well known competitors must spend for advertising, and take it right down to the bottom line. And, virtually without exception, they do. Best of all, leadership is self-fulfilling, because the leader can devote much more of his marketing expenditure to advertising, while the followers are forever spending money on short-term price promotions in the hope of getting new customers to try their products. "They spend their dollars," says the researcher Larry Light, "not to tell people they're good but to say they're cheap. Market share costs money. Market rank makes money. Profit follows rank, not share." But the avoidance of promotion expense can work only to the extent that the new advertising for the brand carries forward the traditions of the old — usually in the claim made for the product, almost always in the logo, the color, the feel and focus of the ad, what Hal Riney calls "the tonality."

What makes a brand dominant is not its popularity over the universe of households, or even over the universe of purchasers of this product, but its command on the affections of the people who buy the product often. In virtually every category of packaged goods products, the 25 percent to 50 percent of the population that buys this sort of thing six times a year or more accounts for 80 percent or more of the total sales. As one wag put it about fifty years ago, it is not true that people, the general audience advertising reaches, buy products. The only people who buy the products are the people who already buy the products.

In his classic study *Repeat-Buying,* Andrew Ehrenberg noted, "Of the thousand and one variables which might affect buyer behavior, it is found that nine hundred and ninety-nine usually do not matter. Many aspects of buyer behavior can be predicted simply from the penetration and the average purchase frequency of the item, and even these two items are interrelated." In Ehrenberg's usage, *penetration* means simply the proportion of a population who buy the product at all in a given period, and *purchase frequency* is the average number of times they buy in that period. Great brands have high purchase frequency rather than high penetration. It is possible to have high penetration and low sales. Most housewives try Planters Peanut Oil once a year — but they buy more than ten times as much Mazola, or Wesson, or Crisco.

Thus, planning the strategy for a dominant brand is trickier than it looks, especially at a time when the M.B.A.'s search eagerly for the savings that can be achieved by using the familiar name to lead people to a new product. Secretaries and clerks buy more cosmetics than women executives and rich men's wives do, because there are more of the former, but if you broaden the distribution of your face powder to the discount stores, the full-priced store kicks it out and never, ever takes it back. William Weithas, chairman of Lintas: Worldwide, holding company for agencies billing more than $4 billion a year, looks back fondly on the growth of an account that has been under his ministrations one way or another since 1968: Lehn & Fink's Lysol. A million-dollar-a-year spender then, the product has gone to more than $30 million of advertising budget (from $400 million of wholesale sales) each year. As the name became more valuable, suggestions were forever arising to put it on cleansers, and Weithas participated in knocking them down. "The client understood," he says, "that anything under that name had to *both* disinfect and deodorize. If you lost either, you lost the franchise. This business was built on *understanding* the brand."

Al Reis and Jack Trout, "marketing strategists" in New York, give a splendid example of the dangers of line extension even where the activity seems natural: "For years, Procter & Gamble's Crisco was the leading shortening. Then the world turned to vegetable oil. Of course, Procter & Gamble turned to Crisco Oil.

"So who is the winner in the vegetable oil market? Wesson, of course.

"Time moves on and corn oil appears on the scene. Of course, Wesson keeps up with technology by introducing Wesson Oil.

"So who is the big winner in the corn oil melee? That's right, Mazola. . . ."[2]

Of the brands in the Boston Consulting Group list that lost primacy, Hershey has since for at least one year regained the number-one position, but Colgate is probably number two forever. The reason is instructive: Procter & Gamble in the early 1960s came up with a better product. Colgate had swept what had once been a crowded and narrowly grouped field with a pair of claims. One was that its "Dental Cream" cleaned your breath while it cleaned your teeth (a powerful argument in a country where Gerald B. Lambert, as the proprietor of a mouthwash, had taught people to worry about "halitosis"). The other was that people who brushed their teeth with Colgate *after every meal* had fewer cavities than people who didn't do that.

This latter information came out of a study solemnly conducted with money from the Ted Bates agency, under the supervision of Bates's own medical expert, Morris Rakieten, involving students at Northwestern University. It was classic Claude Hopkins: people brushing after every meal with *any* toothpaste would of course reduce their cavities, but only Colgate could back the claim with its brand name. This "unique selling proposition," however, had opened a door for Procter & Gamble, first for Gleem, with its reverberant claim as a toothpaste for people who couldn't brush their teeth after every meal, and then for Crest, with stannous fluoride in the mix and an endorsement by the American Dental Association. No amount of advertising cleverness can beat back the challenge of a better product. The man who was in charge of the copy for Colgate at the Bates agency had been at Benton & Bowles, Crest's agency, while the P&G product was being introduced, and had seen the evidence. He continued to insist that his kids use Crest after he went to Bates and took charge of the Colgate account.

Even the man who handled Colgate as a client, Bud McNelly, was less than sympathetic. "I watched a spectacular with nine commercials," he said, "about three generations, their teeth growing longer, no cavities. I told the Colgate people, the only way to handle a problem like this is to change the toothpaste." Because the agency essentially controlled these strategies in the 1960s, and because Dr. Rakieten thought the company had asked for its troubles ("Colgate had spent twenty years telling the ADA to kiss its ass, and finally got what was coming to it"), Colgate refrained from launching a negative campaign against Crest, though there was a serious argument available: as an acid, stannous fluoride raised the pH of the mouth, thereby increasing the likelihood of periodontal disease, which in older people is more serious than cavities. Instead, the company launched into an intensive product-improvement program, which many years later developed a *sodium*-fluoride base and a tartar-control agent — an interesting example of the value to consumers from this sort of oligopolistic competition — but by then the American Dental Association had become very careful about its position in the product endorsement business. "Colgate Tartar Control," its endorsement read, "has been shown to reduce the formation of tartar above the gumline, but has not been shown to have a therapeutic effect on periodontal disease." So Colgate's product improvement was not enough to restore its number-one position. Not that anyone need feel sorry for Colgate.

2.

What to do with lesser brands is a question that can be answered only with reference to the profitability of the marginal sale. In many product classes, as we shall see later in this chapter, the cost of producing another unit is so small that very large expenditures for advertising and promotion can still be profitable, and brands some distance down the share-of-market scale can keep their names before the public and their franchises strong without sacrificing profits. In other product classes, it may be possible to make a claim that segregates what would be the fifth- or sixth-ranking brand in a market into a different "niche" market where it enjoys the economies of being number one. The great example is still Lever's Wisk, a disaster as a detergent, which became a success as a prewash treatment agent that solved "ring around the collar." Still others — paper products are the industry's favorite example — are so dominated by pricing that the advertising has become pro forma for all brands. But it was in this category that one of the most disliked and most effective television commercials of the 1970s worked its magic: everybody thought "Please don't squeeze the Charmin" was stupid, and it ranked last in believability in all the commercials studied for a period of years, but it sold a lot of toilet paper.

In most categories, a second brand has an immensely valuable franchise — Schick for razor blades, Colgate for toothpaste, Miller for beer, Shearson Lehman Hutton (which briefly and very unprofitably passed Merrill Lynch) in the brokerage category, Avis (famously) for rental cars, Apple computers, American Airlines, MasterCard, Wells Fargo (as against Bank of America in California), and Chase (as against Citibank in New York). But the number two in packaged goods grocery-store situations is in some danger of falling back. The third brand is always threatened. And "number four brands," says Larry Light, "are not businesses, they're hobbies." Unless, of course, they can be moved up in rank. John Philip Jones in 1987 did a study of the costs and benefits of advertising to the clients of J. Walter Thompson, where he was research director before he became a professor. Surveying 1,096 brands, he found that those with less than 13 percent of the market for their category of product were typically "investment brands" (that is, their "share of voice," their fraction of the advertising for this sort of product, was considerably higher than their share of market). Conversely, brands with more than 13 percent of the market were "profit-taking brands," with a share of market considerably larger than their share of advertising expenditures.[3]

As noted, what makes brands dominant is not their universal popularity but their strength in the community of heavy users. And there are a few product categories where a customer does feel strong brand loyalties and will return to buy the same brand every time. Cigarettes is one. Frits Bodde, the tall, elegant, forcefully intelligent Dutchman who had been head of British-American Tobacco when its American subsidiary Brown & Williamson was riding high with Viceroy and Kool cigarettes, told of an argument he had with Rosser Reeves of Ted Bates about the need for a new campaign for Viceroy.

"We were going down to my house for the weekend," Bodde said. "He asked me if I had Kools in my house, because if I didn't he'd like to stop and buy some.

"I said, 'Now, look here. You come to my house, I offer you whisky or gin. You choose gin. I pour you some Gordon's. You don't say, 'I drink Beefeater's — it would be *damned rude*. You find Pears Soap in the bathroom. You don't say, 'I must have Colgate' — it would be *damned rude*. After dinner, I serve you a brandy. It's Courvoisier. You don't say, 'Hey, go out and buy some Hennessy' — it would be *damned rude*. But you will ask, and quite properly, whether I have your brand of cigarette.

"You won't go to a cocktail party with a hip flask in your pocket, so when a man is about to pour you Black and White you can reach into your pocket and say, 'Sorry, I always drink *this*.' But you'll do it with cigarettes."

What came out of this conversation was a once-famous campaign about "Thinking Man's Filter, Smoking Man's Taste," with men in white coats urging the television viewer to think for himself. Jerry Gury, who was creative director for the agency, fought to have the presenter be a working stiff or a fireman, an ordinary man telling another ordinary man to think for himself, but he was overruled: Bates in those days was big on white coats. For the better part of a year, this commercial for Viceroy was one of the best-known advertising campaigns in the world, the sort of thing that got parodied on the Johnny Carson show. Nobody knew whether or not it helped Viceroy, which went into a period of stagnant or declining sales (the cigarette had burst to prominence in the wake of a *Reader's Digest* recommendation of filters, and dominated its market only for the eighteen months in which British-American had a virtual monopoly on filter-making machinery). "But," said Bodde, "I'd hate to think of where Viceroy might have gone without it."

Except for a handful of products like cigarettes, however, advertisers cannot count on a monomaniacal group of brand loyalists. Normally, one-third to two-fifths of those who buy a brand today will buy another brand of the same product category the next time. Brand loyalties are "a leaky bucket." But in fact market shares are remarkably stable over periods of time. What brand loyalty means is that most of those who leak out on their next purchase will return for the purchase after that. A researcher, William Moran, speaks of the "share of need" that a brand satisfies. If a brand fulfills 80 percent of the "need" for this product among the 25 percent of its users who buy it most often, it has an unchallengeable franchise. But if it fulfills less than half of the "need" for this product among those who use this brand most often, *which is not an uncommon situation for brands that rank second or third in the market for this product,* it may be ripe for the plucking.

Meanwhile, as Moran points out, it is perilous indeed for companies to compete by giving their product values known to appeal to those who use rival brands. Some researchers measure the effectiveness of advertising by estimating the number of users of another brand who switch to this one as the result of a campaign. But a manufacturer who changes his product to appeal to those who *don't* use it risks a rapid bleeding off of the customers who *do* use it — especially in a situation where as many as half of those who bought it this week will buy something else next week in any event. It's easy to get this wrong: Seven-Up, in presenting itself as an alternative to the colas, lost more lemon-and-lime drinkers than it gained cola drinkers. What's safe for the proprietors of the second, third, and fourth brands in a product category is competition by means of price promotions, coupons, and payments for shelf placement. This may cost revenue as regular customers stock up to take advantage of the bargains, but it doesn't drive anyone away.

The compromise, again, is to seek a niche — to become number one in your own lesser market. Soaps have niches — Dial and Safeguard are not in competition with Neutrogena. Dove, with cold cream in the mix, was created by Lever Brothers in the 1960s and initially advertised by David Ogilvy as an upscale nonsoap that also did what soaps did. A generation later, it still commands the highest price on the toilet soap market. Oat cereals do not compete with sugared corn. Jaguars do not compete with Cadillacs. The task of the advertiser in a market where his product is not number one is usually to establish values that insulate his brand from the competition of brands that sell more. He necessarily dominates the market for his brand. By setting that brand aside from the rest of the market, he improves the monopoly rent he can charge even if he cannot expand his sales. Researchers and account people at agencies seeking to raise ad budgets are sometimes frustrated by clients who won't risk the loss of customers by raising the price.

3.

The most fun in the business — and the one time that the C.E.O. of even a large conglomerate company is likely to get involved with his agency — is the introduction of a "new product," usually but not always a euphemism for a new brand in an old product category. The key here is to find out both what the product has to offer and what the consumer will value in such a product. Market studies are often hopeless as guides. Sol Linowitz, who was chairman of the board of Xerox before he became ambassador to the Organization of American States and negotiator of the Panama Canal treaties, reports in his memoirs that IBM, after a study that took almost a year to complete, refused to go partners with what was then Haloid Xerox in the development of what became the Xerox 914, the first plain-paper copier. Market research done for IBM by Arthur D. Little had demonstrated pretty conclusively that there wasn't enough market for a plain-paper copier to justify the investment.[4]

The best stories are new-product stories, but for reasons that are good and sufficient for the proprietors, they rarely get into print. For example, take Smirnoff vodka, in effect a new product because its total sales nationwide were about 4,000 cases a year when Heublein bought it from its bankrupt proprietor in 1939. John Martin, an elegant but tough Oxford graduate who had married into the Heublein family and was running the company, reported later that he had known from 1941 what he had, though wartime exigencies delayed his exploitation of his knowledge. The former owners of the brand had cut back vodka and begun making what they called Smirnoff Whiskey, and that's what it said on the tops of the corks. Those being the only corks in the distillery, Martin used them for his first production of vodka. Cases of bottles with these mislabeled corks went to a distributor in North Carolina, where a salesman tried the product as a salesman should and prepared paper streamers reading, "Smirnoff's White Whiskey — No Taste, No Odor." Presently the wholesaler was ordering fifty, then five hundred cases of Smirnoff's. But without the Lawrence Gumbinner agency to supply "It Leaves You Breathless," with its Cole Porterish air of elegance — and without Martin's willingness to face down the Distilled Spirits Institute and become the first proprietor of a booze to break the taboo against pictures of women in a liquor ad — the product would not have acquired the luxury image that still allows Heublein (now part of Philip Morris) to charge a premium price for the product. Significantly, and sadly, foreign brands now command much greater premiums.

Cool Whip is a nice example of how serendipitous a success can be. Here the product was a by-blow of a major research project at General Foods, to find a synthetic milk that would provide the nourishment of cow's milk but could be kept a much longer time without deterioration — ideally, without refrigeration. This project succeeded, to the immense satisfaction of the team that had worked on it, who saw it as, among other things, a major contribution to good nutrition for infants in slum communities and in the Third

World. But when the resulting product was put into test marketing, it failed abysmally. Milk is a natural product in the minds of those who buy it, in slums and in Africa as well as on the Gold Coasts, and no amount of advertising could ever convince the American (or any other) public that a synthetic was "just as good." These results came back to the lab, where they provoked something not far short of a rebellion. Scientists who were now supposed to do other things kept playing around with their synthetic milk. One day some unsung hero put it under a mixer, and it whipped. An excited message came from the lab to the product group, about synthetic whipped cream. And a bored message came back: the whole whipping cream market in the United States amounted to less than $80 million a year, and General Foods simply had no interest in anything that did not sell in nine figures. But the lab was so unhappy that Cool Whip was put into tests, and it turned out that while the whipping cream market was tiny, the market for prepackaged stable whipped cream was huge.

Another nice story even more closely held by the proprietor is that of Gatorade, which I think (nobody who knows for sure will talk about this one, and the agency that introduced the product was never told whence it came) started off in the brain of someone at Stokely–Van Camp, the pork-and-beans people who had been the beneficiaries of Claude Hopkins's intuitions most of a century before. One of the significant uses of soft drinks was to replace the water lost in sweat after exercise. But clearly sweat contained many minerals and proteins besides water. Suppose one found out precisely what athletes lost through the pores of the skin during aggressive workouts. Then one could make a drink that would restore precisely that part of the body's chemical balance upset by exercise.

Arrangements were thereupon made with the University of Florida, which had a football team that entered into spring training in May, when it was hot as hell in Florida. The university agreed that the football players would wear sweatsuits in practice. Researchers took the sweatsuits off the players as they came into the locker room, wrung out the moisture, and analyzed the resulting fluid. And that's what they put into the Van Camp's product, which was named for the University of Florida Gators.

Carl Spielvogel of Backer & Spielvogel remembers that there was no budget for coaches or big-name players to endorse Gatorade, and very little money for advertising. So he went to the trainers of the athletic teams, who were delighted to be asked and wanted very little money for their endorsements. They also put the product in large labeled jugs on the bench for the game: "Soft drink companies that were paying fortunes for commercials," Spielvogel remembers with pleasure, "split a gut when they looked at the screen and saw the players drinking Gatorade. . . ." And soon the budget was big enough to pay for commercials.

This same agency, now Backer Spielvogel Bates and part of the Saatchi & Saatchi empire, scored one of the great triumphs of modern advertising with the first Miller Lite campaign. Philip Morris had acquired a brewery in Chicago which had a brand called "Lite." This was in the early 1970s, in the heyday of what John Martin of Heublein once called "the great American ice cream taste." Everything was "light." And the first low-calorie beer, Gablinger's, was being advertised (by Doyle Dane Bernbach) with two slices of bread beside the bottle to show how few calories went into your system when you drank a Gablinger's. The value added by such advertising meant most to yuppies, and yuppies weren't big beer drinkers, and Gablinger's did not do well.

Spielvogel's people went looking to find out who actually drank Lite beer, and it turned out the bars that really moved the stuff were around the steelworks in Gary, Indiana. And what the beerbellies said was "Good stuff. Doesn't fill you up — you can drink more of it."

John O'Toole of A.A.A.A. wrote of an "old master" of a beer salesman, "who stopped at the roadside inns of my youth to put this little sign at eye level above the urinal:

> Now you can enjoy
> another bottle
> of Stroh's Beer."

Philip Morris had stumbled on a product that generalized this approach. But the way to use it was not so easy. Advertising that stressed "light" would make the product seem insipid. Thus the stress on "taste" (the dullest of claims) to balance the "not filling." To which, of course, some genius added the idea of over-the-hill athletes to argue over which "value" advertising had added to the product seemed more compelling to them.

The new products that fail, as most of them do, provide much less good humor, but everybody in the creative end of advertising wants new product work, and the agencies that get it gain a reputation as hot shops. Though brand personalities can be changed around (the most famous example is Marlboro, which started out as a lipstick-tipped cigarette for women), most of the time the values attached to the brand by the first campaigns will stay with it, in one form or another, for life. Every research study plays back slogans that haven't been used in twenty and thirty years. The people who create the first ads leave a long-lasting imprint on their culture.

We shall have occasion later to look at the procedures —

which vary widely from agency to agency — by which these new campaigns for new products are generated and tested and deployed. For now it should be noted that they show both a love of the art for art's sake and a willingness to venture that are by no means natural for the bureaucrats and businessmen who run many of the larger agencies. A lot of new product advertising is and probably should be off the wall, like the commercial drawn from Orwell's *1984* by which Chiat/Day told the world that Apple Computer's new Macintosh could free people from the tyranny of Big Brother IBM. More usually, however, new products and their ads are tested in isolated markets before they are rolled out to the nation. The expenditure on advertising in the early phases is quite small, and the work tends to be a loss leader for the agency. Fortunately, what Wall Street wants to hear about from the agencies that have gone public is their growth for the year, and if you grow enough the bankers will probably be willing to forgive flat profitability. So even the most bureaucratic of the agency managers holds his nose and spends the money to compete for the chance to advertise a client's new brand.

4.

In 1967, in a paper entitled "What Do We Know about How Advertising Works?" written for a symposium in the Netherlands (but printed both by his employer, J. Walter Thompson of London, and by the American journal *Advertising Age*), the British researcher Timothy Joyce found it convenient and acceptable to restrict himself to "advertising for low unit-price, high frequency-of-purchase products."[5] That was advertising; everything else was something else. Even then, the simplification was heroic, because automobiles and tires for them, television sets and white goods (such as refrigerators and washing machines) were very significant categories, as was the public-relations advertising done for corporations (Better Things For Better Living Through Chemistry). But for schematic purposes the limitation was valid: the great advertising agencies lived on package goods. If indeed advertising agencies had to live by that definition a quarter of a century later, they would all be broke. Items sold in supermarkets, pharmacies, and drygoods stores are still very important, of course, but even more important these days are the airlines, hotels, and travel services, the banks and stockbrokers, movies, the computer manufacturers, real estate agents, and insurance companies.

What these advertisers have in common, mostly, is very low unit costs per additional unit sold. (Even in the case of computers, where a lot of integrated-circuit chips and relays, keyboards, and screens must be bought for each unit, the economies of scale from amortizing the development cost over more units and using the production line to full capacity can pay for a lot of advertising.) The airplane will burn about the same amount of fuel, and in most situations pay the same number of stewardesses, whether the plane has 75 or 115 passengers. The costs of selling another seat are a couple of bucks for paper processing and for a loathsome meal from the soup kitchens of the Marriott organization. The computers that handle the humongous reservations problem can work out how many seats are likely to be unsold without special advertising and price promotion, and can create budgets that show profits under a range of assumptions. Meanwhile, however, the advertising must maintain an image of safety and service without sacrificing the inherent adventure of flying and the lure of far places. Like everyone in the travel business, including the credit card issuers (for even the credit cards issued by banks for multifarious purposes are to a large extent "Travel and Entertainment" instruments), the airlines sell destinations. These advertising missions — what is the "task" of advertising? — are split up between television and magazines (for image) and newspapers and radio (for price promotions).

Airlines can lose their image quickly, by playing these mixes wrong, by cutting costs where passengers can see the damage, or by bringing bad publicity on themselves. Continental became a cheapjack airline under Frank Lorenzo because the sales pitch was nothing but price. Pan Am allowed an image of luxury to degenerate into an image of squalor after its purchase of National Airlines produced a string of losses. TWA is worth much less than when the Wall Street raider Carl Icahn bought it; Eastern went down in flames after a strike; and even United may have suffered long-term damage from its involvement with investment bankers and takeover lawyers. Advertising can do little about the values such publicized finaglings have subtracted from the public's perceptions of the services offered by these airlines. It's been much more fun for advertising people to work with Delta and American.

Generating another unit of products is even cheaper for a financial services company than providing another seat on an already scheduled flight is for an airline. The commissions paid to insurance salesmen and to customers' men in brokerage houses, after all, come out of the customer's pocket and are not costs to the financial services company. Both the companies and the advertising agencies were a long time recognizing the symbiosis they could achieve, but today most packaged goods brands spend less than Metropolitan Life, Prudential, Travelers, MONY, Kemper, Hartford,

State Farm, or Allstate, and even companies that do relatively little business with individuals, like Wausau, have become significant spenders. Some — Prudential especially — have sought to couple advertising for their insurance products with advertising for brokerage and other subsidiaries, but the public still sees insurance as apples, bank accounts as oranges, and brokerage accounts as lemons.

Much advertising for financial products is controlled by law, and until fairly recently stockbrokers, if they advertised at all, adopted an educational pose. Merrill Lynch ran full-page all-text newspaper ads in the 1950s to tell people what to expect if they began buying stocks. By the early 1980s, however, Merrill was showing a bull roaming about both rural and urban landscapes. This was a classic example of an in-joke moved out of doors, for the bull was the descendant of an illustration used in *Fortune* magazine almost half a century before to accompany the title of a piece about what was then far and away the largest brokerage house in the world: "The Thundering Herd of Wall Street." The herd became a single bull, linked to the long-running slogan "Merrill Lynch is bullish on America" (translated in at least one household into "Merrill Lynch leaves bullshit on America"). But the slogan and the logo were by no means without selling power.

Most of the other brokerage houses played variations on the theme that they gave the individual investor help in a world where, unless you had help, the institutional investors would eat you alive. E. F. Hutton showed how people listened when Hutton talked; John Houseman (an unreconstructed political radical to the day of his death) donned the character of a Harvard Law School professor to say Smith Barney earned its commissions the old-fashioned way;

Paine Webber had a tennis player losing a point to the assemblage of deskbound brokers and asking to have these guys on his side next time; Dean Witter and Charles Schwab showed all the helpful personal service they offered. Drexel Burnham mixed a dash of populist imagery with its retail advertising by showing giant basketball players who until recently had thought they were too small to be served by Drexel Burnham. The real purpose of most of this advertising in fact was to establish a climate of favorable opinion within which unsolicited telephone calls from neophyte brokers that were the industry's basic sales procedure could start a relationship. But nothing helped much when the market stopped going up.

Consumer loans are another financial services product where the high profit margins of the instrument justify enormous expenditures for advertising. Giants lock horns here: Citicorp, American Express, Sears (Discover), and AT&T, plus the Visa and MasterCard operations owned by the banks that issue the cards (but do not, however, have much to say about how the operations are run). Auto loans, once heavily promoted by banks and independent finance companies, have become part of the package of discounts offered by car manufacturers through the car dealer, who gets a piece of the consumer payments month by month (*not* a commission for making the loan: the lenders want auto dealers on the hook for their credit judgment), to compensate him for the fact that there's no longer any profit in actually selling cars. But changes in the tax laws have given the middle class reason to consolidate its borrowings in "home equity loans." Such loans are heavily advertised on a price basis, with some control over what can be said from a government that even in a deregulatory time feels responsibility for giving the borrowers information in easily comprehensible form about the terms of their loans. Well, somewhat comprehensible, anyway.

Loans from consumer finance companies have been with us longer, and advertising for such loans, while less salient than it once was, does persist. Such advertising probably does more harm than any other, more than cigarette advertising and more than booze advertising, for it gives a false value, a sense of ease, to what is for most people the hard business of paying back what they borrow. Many years ago, when I was writing a book about television, I had occasion to meet with Donald McGannon, who ran the Westinghouse Broadcasting Company, and was a pioneer of public service announcements on local television stations. His WINS in New York was the first all-news radio station. I suggested to him that he could do an outstanding public service by denying air time to what was then the Beneficial Finance singing commercial: "At Beneficial, you're good for more. . . ." But he said Beneficial was one of the top five advertisers on his station, and he couldn't do that to his stockholders.

5.

The most obvious of the tasks of advertising — when I first came visiting this industry thirty-five years ago there were still people around who thought it was the only task — is to make the sale for the manufacturer. For many of the old-timers, the wholesalers and retailers who intermediate sales in the normal procedures of a developed economy were excrescences who dirtied the potentially pure relationship of maker and user. The purpose of research was to strip away extraneous considerations introduced by retailers and wholesalers, permitting both the advertiser and his agent to see the results of the advertising.

The paradigm was what was then called "mail order" and is now, in a time of new technology, called "direct response." The definitive characteristic of this sort of advertising was that it had a coupon. By clipping and filling out and mailing in that coupon, the consumer got the product. "Clubs" — for books, records, fruit-by-mail — were the big users of this technique in the 1950s. So were educators selling correspondence courses, and magazines selling subscriptions, and proprietors of products that would be delivered in plain wrappers. There was, of course, the Sears, Roebuck catalogue and its imitators. These forms of advertising offered the immense advantage that the advertiser knew what he got for his money. Either the ad paid out, or it didn't. And you could test different campaigns by mailing different ads to comparable addresses or by "split runs" of a magazine, which sent one slogan to half the subscribers and the other slogan to the other half. The one that produced the most responses was better.

Variants of these techniques could be adapted to broadcasting. Horace Schwerin ran a theatre on New York's Sixth Avenue in which he tested television commercials. The audience was asked which brands of various products they would wish to be given if they won a raffle, then showed television programs with the commercials suitably embedded, and then asked again at the close. The whole system of test marketing was in a sense an extension of mail-order advertising, because the tests did not go on long enough to indicate whether brand franchises were or were not in process of creation. The testing measured only sales.

In the 1980s, "direct response" became more important than ever before. Once the punishing interest rates and deep recession of the first years of the decade had gone, cable television spread rapidly through the country, with increasingly sophisticated "head ends" from which the signals were generated. Cable audiences could be split as broadcast audiences could not be, and the techniques developed to measure different print ads in split-run publications were immediately adaptable to split cablecasting. Meanwhile, the telephone company had introduced, at reasonable prices, the "800" service, through which advertisers could take telephoned orders from customers who didn't have to pay for the telephone call. And the banks and finance companies had issued tens of millions of credit cards the customers could use to make their purchases (through coupons as well as on the telephone).

Makers of equipment that folded newspapers created machines that made it cheap to stuff inserts into large metropolitan papers and small suburban papers alike, which permitted a blending of all-inclusive mailings with the distribution of price-promotion coupons to newspaper circulations. Meanwhile, computerized mailing lists and envelope stuffing machinery allowed sellers to direct their advertising only to households where there was reason to believe this particular product might be of some interest. "Junk mail" was as unpopular as "clutter" in the television shows, and in fact the issuance of coupons rose more rapidly than their redemption, but coming into the 1990s this advertising unquestionably paid out. Cable television, indeed, lived off it. Reginald Brack, Jr., of Time Warner reports that in 1989, commercials aired on cable with an 800 number to be called generated more new subscriptions to *Time* magazine than any other kind of advertising.

A factor quite apart from sales, however, made this kind of advertising much more important to the agencies than it was a generation ago. The practitioners of direct response now not only knew things more conventional advertisers did not know about which slogans "worked" to sell merchandise. They also knew more about the consuming public. To the extent that the advertising and selling world of the next century would be built on giant data bases — and most people in the industry thought it would be — the "mail order" advertising experts were the people with the best and biggest immediately useful data bases. Their status in the agency business rose accordingly.

CHAPTER THREE

Agents

IN HIS MEMOIRS, Earnest Elmo Calkins complained, "The term 'agent' as applied to the profession I followed for forty years is inaccurate and misleading. Originally advertising agents were simply representatives of newspapers who secured advertising and were paid a commission — and that was about all they did. For the magazines they performed a similar service as soon as the early periodicals condescended, as old Fletcher Harper put it, 'to degrade literature with the announcements of trades people.' "[1]

Newspapers had always offered advertisers the service of writing their sales pitches for them, and the agents merely picked up the habit. They were paid not by the advertisers but by the papers. But it made much more sense for advertisers to deal with one supplier who would place their ads in many papers than with myriad representatives of myriad advertising media. So the advertiser rather than the newspaper or magazine became the agent's "client."

Once the agent began to work for the advertiser, it made no sense to have him paid by the paper or magazine, but the custom was hard to change. Calkins reports that he and his partner, Ralph Holden, tried to start their business on a basis of charging the advertiser for their time and output, letting the advertiser "place" the ad himself in the publication and haggle about the rebate. Indeed, the most important piece of business the new agency received came on that basis, from Cyrus W. Curtis, publisher of *Ladies' Home Journal,* who advertised his magazine in the nation's newspapers. The ads were placed by N. W. Ayer, far and away the largest agency at the turn of the century, and Curtis would not take that business away from them, for they had financed his purchases of advertising before he had the money to pay for them, and he was a man of principle who placed loyalty highest among the virtues. "No one in the Ayer agency," he told Calkins, "seems able to write the kind of copy I want. I shall expect you fellows to charge me enough to compensate yourselves for the fact that you do not place it." Calkins wrote an ad for Curtis ending with the claim, "All advertising in the *Ladies' Home Journal* and *The Saturday Evening Post* is directed to creating an eager market, to create a demand which will work back through the drummer, jobber, wholesaler, to the manufacturer."[2]

From the advertiser's point of view, because the mores of the time did not permit him to capture the commission for himself, his agent's work cost him nothing. From the publisher's point of view, the fact that he paid the agency gave him some control over what the agent did. The publishers of the most successful magazines insisted that commissions were only for legitimate agents and were not rebates to advertisers, and that they would pay such commissions only to agents who regularly placed ads for at least three clients. Calkins remembered that Frank Munsey told his partner that unless Calkins & Holden placed as much advertising in *Munsey's* as it did in *McClure's, Munsey's* would withdraw its "recognition" — to which Holden replied, "Mr. Munsey, you. run your business as you see fit, and we will continue to manage ours in our own way."[3] There was another danger, that market capitalism would intrude and agents would steal business from other agents by offering clients a kickback on the commission. This problem will remain (and, though the agencies don't like to hear it, should remain) with the business forever. If a man can deliver the same service at lower cost, he's entitled to the account, and if an advertiser is willing to accept lesser service there's no reason why he shouldn't pay less for it. But such attitudes were heresies for a long time, until the Supreme Court of the 1960s began to rule that the antitrust laws forbade the price-fixing of professional fees as well as other prices.

The music critic Virgil Thomson liked to relate musical styles to the sources of a composer's income: the more the fellow could count on government subvention or academic emolument, the more hermetic the approach. Certainly institutions grow according to the nourishment of their roots. The modern advertising agency arose in a time when revenues were a function of the "billings" incurred by the agency's clients in their use of "commissionable media." Large clients for which great quantities of repetitive advertising could be prepared and placed — automobile companies, cigarette manufacturers, cosmetics and shaving goods producers, coffee roasters, canners, soap companies — generated enormous profits for their agencies. Price competition being generally perceived as unethical in advertising, as in medicine and law, agencies took to competing for their business by providing additional services: consumer research, media research, even product research; packaging, public relations, point-of-sale promotion, political lobbying. The shape and size and self-image of the modern advertising agency came about because the commission structure produced earnings so large that agencies could become suppliers of marketing information and advice at a time when the C.E.O.'s of most client corporations were not sophisticated in these matters and did not employ much in-house expertise.

In addition to appropriating large roles for themselves in the client's business planning process, agencies got in the habit of doing personal favors for clients: box seats at the World Series and the Kentucky Derby; tickets to hit shows and dates with the chorus girls, etc. And none of this has changed. (Readers of *Barbarians at the Gates* will have noted the extent to which the advertising function was extended to include the activities of Team Nabisco, golfers and tennis players and racing car drivers whose duties as members of the team were to socialize with the RJR Nabisco C.E.O., Ross Johnson.) Because they don't pay the agencies' costs, advertisers have always been happy to add to them, often in very personal ways. Calkins told of an account offered to his agency on the understanding that part of the commission would be paid to "a lady to whom the president [of the advertiser] was indebted for many favors. . . . It is a loss to the gayer side of advertising," Calkins noted, "that we did not feel able to enter into such an eighteenth-century triangle. It would have put a lot of color into what is sometimes a prosaic business. The process of soliciting an increase of appropriation through the president's mistress must appeal to every resourceful agency representative.

"Scene: the lady's boudoir.

"'Do you love me as much as ever, George?'

"'Of course I do. Why?'

"'It's about time you made me a present.'

"'What is it this time?'

"'I want twelve pages in the *S.E.P.*'

"'Is that all? I'll add *Munsey's* and *McClure's.*'

"And the next day the agency gets the order for space.

"Newspaper flights and double-spreads instead of diamond sunbursts and pearls. There have been other ways of stepping up a client's appropriations no more legitimate than this."[4]

Kellogg's Corn Flakes was offered to Calkins & Holden if they would employ a friend of Mr. Kellogg's to handle the account. Aeolian Piano took an account away from Calkins because his agency wouldn't hire a relative of the company's president. Such personal relationship elements are common to all personal service industries: banks, brokerage houses, accounting firms, and law firms all have senior partners and executives who are there for no reason other than their access to profitable business. And these accommodations are not without redeeming social value. When the Milton Biow agency was collapsing in 1955, William LaPorte of American Home Products went to Dan Rodgers, who had been his account supervisor, and asked him to suggest a new agency that would take him with the account, for Rodgers was Jewish and LaPorte knew that many of the Madison Avenue agencies were hostile to Jews. Rodgers told him not to worry, that the account was big enough for these guys to swallow their prejudices.

The movement of business for reasons of friendship or even consanguinity has by no means disappeared. Chrysler had been a Young & Rubicam client for twenty-one years, but when Lee Iacocca came from Ford to take over, he almost immediately moved the account to what was then Kenyon & Eckhardt, which had worked for him at Ford. "We had a four-minute conversation," said Ed Ney, then C.E.O. at Y&R, "to end a twenty-one-year relationship." (On the other hand, this left Y&R free to take the Lincoln-Mercury business.) John Sculley went from PepsiCo to Apple Computer, and within three months Chiat/Day had lost the account: "The press will have its opinions why, and the man from Apple will have enough explanations to fill a small book," Stephen Kessler of Chiat/Day wrote in the agency's luxurious celebration of its own first twenty years, "but to the creative people who worked so long and hard to make Apple the most watched, most read, most talked about advertising in America, it will be a simple case of one man who did not like another man."[5] The bankruptcy court that decided to take Eastern Air Lines away from the stewardship of its owner, Frank Lorenzo, and place it in the hands of Martin Shugrue, who had run Pan Am, also inadvertently moved the Eastern account away from Lintas to Ogilvy, which had been Shugrue's agency when he ran Pan Am. The merger-and-acquisition movements of the 1980s kept roiling the agency business because new owners often wanted agencies with which they had worked before.

Even when the 15 percent commission was enforced as holy writ (or nearly so: Omnicom's Bruce Crawford says that American Tobacco always demanded and got rebates), agencies that worked for large advertisers like General Foods and Procter & Gamble complained bitterly that you couldn't make money on those accounts. Such clients knew

your costs better than you did, and in return for highly profitable billings demanded extra services or immense efforts
on new products that would bill paltry sums through their
test period and then, often enough, expire without ever
generating revenue for the advertising agent. At P&G, the
rule was that the agency paid for all copy-testing; at General
Foods, the agency was supposed to allocate one-half of one
percent of all billings (a little more than 3 percent of its
commissions) to pay for research on GF products. In the
1960s, clients as large as Lever and American Home
Products, Quaker Oats, and Gillette opened "in-house"
agencies to capture the commission revenues for themselves. William Claggett, C.E.O. of Ralston Purina, chaired a
meeting in 1971 on "advertiser self-sufficiency." Eventually,
they all returned to more traditional arrangements (Lever
spun off its international house agency as Lintas, which
acquired many other clients and became one of the two
largest jewels in the Interpublic crown). "They got a lot of
inbred advertising," Bill Bernbach explained in 1982.
"Once you bring this work in-house, you don't have the
scope." But they didn't necessarily give back to the agencies
all the work the agencies had once performed.

The successfully transplanted Englishman David Ogilvy
made the first publicized break with the commission compensation structure, announcing that the 15 percent commission paid the laborer less than the value of his hire, and
that his agency would in the future negotiate fees for service. Shell Oil (which in fact cut its commission to Ogilvy
from 15 percent to 10 percent) and General Foods went
along. Quietly, at about the same time, Marion Harper, Jr.'s,
McCann-Erickson and Edward Ney's Young & Rubicam
began unbundling into separate, wholly owned subsidiaries
the group of services previously presented to the client as

part of what the commission paid for. "If the agency has never come to you to talk about your account," said Herb Ahlgren of the Association of National Advertisers, "you know it's profitable. If they call to talk about compensation, you know it's unprofitable."

But clients didn't want to pay extra for the services that were spun off, and except for the public-relations companies (which the agencies acquired, buying already successful firms), the little subsidiaries shriveled. Top designers feel hemmed in rather than supported by client lists and historic relationships. And many of these subsidiaries were research firms. If there was one thing the clients definitely were not going to do, it was to pay the agencies to do research on whether the advertising was working.

BBDO instituted a system of time sheets kept by everybody who worked on an account, with the agency's non-allocatable costs shared out according to a formula embedded in each contract with a client. Commissions paid were then compared with the agency's costs. If the agency showed a profit margin of 1½ to 2½ percent on billings, well and good. If the margin was less, the client had to pay the difference; if it was more, the client was entitled to a refund. A clever fellow at BBDO pointed out that the system gave the client an incentive to help push the agency's profits toward the top of the range, because once they went over that top, he got what it is now fashionable to call cash back.

"Well," said Sam Vitt, who owns and operates a service that does nothing but buy television time, thinking back to the mid-1960s, when he was working at an agency and the fee issue was heating up, "I remember a lot of meetings to talk about fees. The clients would listen patiently, then say, 'Thank you very much, but it's your problem. There's another agency down the street that would love our business at fifteen percent.'" Alvin Achenbaum and his friend Stanley Cantor ran a service for advertisers to help them pick agencies, and in 1976, after they had chosen Dancer-Fitzgerald-Sample for Toyota, the Japanese car company asked them to develop a compensation system, too. They came up with a mixture of fee and commission that is still proprietary (though Achenbaum has gone off to be executive v.p. of Backer Spielvogel Bates). "Len Matthews [then president of the American Association of Advertising Agencies] attacked us unmercifully," Achenbaum recalls, "but Dancer-Fitzgerald-Sample made more money on Toyota than you could shake a stick at." Actually, most agencies made a good deal of money in the late 1970s, when media prices rose more rapidly than agency costs. For a while, profits soared, and the agencies once again began designing packages for new products without charge. Then the early 1980s recession cut advertising expenditures, and when business turned up emphasis remained on quick sales, which meant price cutting and promotion, not advertising.

From the *client*'s perspective, as Alvin Achenbaum put it when he and Cantor were proselytizing, straight commission meant that the big brands subsidized the small brands. Cigarettes were incredibly profitable, accounting in some years for as much as two-thirds of the profits of the firms that had tobacco accounts. In the 1970s, most large agencies became publicly owned companies, with shares traded on the exchanges. Among the handful that didn't "go public" was Chicago's Leo Burnett, creator of the Marlboro campaign for Philip Morris; and the line in the industry was that Burnett couldn't go public because the prospectus for the shares would have to reveal how much money the agency was making. In 1990, the experts estimated that Philip Morris spent $600 million a year through the Leo Burnett agency.

The problem with negotiating fees is that it takes a lot of time, and puts the client and the agency — and this is, after all, an *agency* relationship — into an adversarial mode. On both sides, there is inevitably a sneaking feeling that the rewards are not worth the winning. Charles D. Peebler, Jr., of Bozell, a $1.5 billion agency that does Chrysler corporate and American Airlines, among others, argues that the question is simple: "We have to put a certain number of people against the problem; we have to pay them; and we're entitled to a profit. And I would hope there are some incentives in it." But in practice the situation quickly becomes very complicated. "If you'd asked to see the standard agreement between agency and client in the old days," Don Johnston said a few years ago when he was C.E.O. of J. Walter Thompson, "it would have been at the most one-and-a-half pages. Now it's a fifteen-, twenty-page document, with twenty, thirty, forty pages of appendices. Most of them dealing with liability." Procter & Gamble carries its pattern of cost control through the production process for their commercials. "They have a book," says a filmmaker. "You sign a cost-plus contract, and that's the way it's done."

In spring 1990, DDB Needham, sister agency to BBDO in the publicly traded Omnicom group, announced a new payment-by-results policy, which the press presented as a way of hooking compensation to sales results. There was some scorn expressed at this announcement, because the agency said that of course it couldn't make such deals unless DDB Needham was given complete control of "orchestrating" the client's marketing effort for this brand. (Campbell Soup, a client, said immediately that this control couldn't be given the agency because there were 22 separate control centers within the company that worked on the company's marketing strategy, and no one agency could possibly coordinate their efforts.) John Bernbach, Bill's son, shrank from the word *orchestrating*. Bernbach, a gray-haired administrator in a dark suit and bright white shirt and severe tie (but still with some of his father's Brooklyn in his voice), runs account servicing for DDB Needham. The new compensation plan was simply an extension of management by objectives. The objective might be a shift of consumer attitudes, or the growth of showroom traffic in automobile dealerships. The negotiations with the client would be over defining these objectives, and how to measure whether or not they had been attained by the end of some separately agreed-upon time period.

What goes wrong with these plans is that they are narcissistic: the agent asks the advertiser to study the quality of his own image. Too many of the results that are to generate the compensation cannot be measured, either because the baseline is unknown or the end line is subjective. The real world is one where the results of what an advertiser does are a function of the uncontrollable actions of his real rivals. As Ahlgren of the Association of National Advertisers said in the early 1980s, expressing an eternal truth, "Incentive compensation schemes are put in on a two- or three-year basis, and then they fall apart. There are so many factors involved besides your own advertising."

And relations between large client and large agency are further complicated by the fact that the large agency is now likely to be a publicly held corporation itself. The agency as promoter of the price of its stock wants to tell the security analysts that it's cutting costs while the agency as seller of its services wants to tell clients and potential clients that it's improving quality. The advertiser says, "In our business, we find it hard to cut costs and improve quality at the same time." Eventually, even the British-owned agencies (which don't have to make quarterly reports to their stockholders, as American companies do) get tangled in the inconsistencies. One of the top men at Procter & Gamble said sourly that "the only reason for an ad agency to go public is to make a lot of old avertising men rich." Philip Geier of Interpublic makes the point that "the trade itself having LBO'ed, agencies have a lot of debt."

James Burke, formerly of Johnson & Johnson, thinks both agency and advertiser gave up their best incentive compensation scheme when they abandoned the commission system. When Burke made Tylenol a proprietary medication in the early 1970s (previously, it had been for sale only with a prescription), he suggested to Compton Advertising that they handle it on a straight 15 percent commission basis. Advertising appropriations track sales: if the brand did well, the agency's income would rise proportionately. But Compton preferred to work on a fee basis. "I felt that commissions gave the agency a stake in the product," Burke said recently. "When we moved to a fee basis, we eroded the incentive system."

1.

In their recent textbook *Advertising: Principles and Practice,* William Wells, John Burnett, and Sandra Moriarty note, "The original title for [the client liaison] function, 'account service,' has been changed in most agencies because it suggests that the agency should be subservient to the client, rather than providing an independent professional viewpoint. 'Account management' suggests initiative and responsibility by the agency.'"[6] This function, they add, is broken into four levels — management supervisor (who "reports to the upper management of the agency"), account supervisor ("the key working executive on the client's business and the primary liaison between the client and the agency"), account executive ("responsible for day-to-day activities that include keeping the agency team on schedule and delivering the services as promised to the client"), and assistant account executive ("normally the entry-level position").[7] One notes that the management supervisor is an intermediary between the account group and the top dogs at the agency, not with anyone at the client company, and the top level of the agency relates to the client essentially through its own management information system.

In point of fact, agencies had more influence on their clients' strategies and, indeed, advertising when the account function was called "service." Clients know they need "service" from outside suppliers; they think they can provide the management themselves. The only "management" that can really be done at an advertising agency is the management of the agency itself.

At most of the companies that advertised heavily, the C.E.O. himself used to meet once or twice a year with the head of the agency and discuss what "my man and your man" should work out between themselves over the next months. To Howard Heinz, Earnest Elmo Calkins wrote, Ralph Holden was an equal. . . . Calkins could not hold the Heinz account after Holden died because he was deaf and nobody else in the agency was Heinz's equal. When the agency had prepared its story boards and layouts for a major campaign, the C.E.O. came to the meeting and had to be sold. "I always dominated the advertising department," said Edward H. Little of Colgate, a lean man with bushy eyebrows and an unblinking stare. "We had to sell goods and I had to make our money go." Preparatory sessions for such conferences were the source of the best cynicism in the business, for the question was always the salability rather than the intrinsic quality of the idea; the archetypical gag line was "Let's run it up the flagpole and see who salutes." Frequently, the market strategy for the brand grew out of the advertising. And this is not as dumb as it sounds. "How can we start thinking about the strategy," says an old-timer in a creative department, "until we know what we want to say?"

But as the clients and the agencies got bigger — as corporations began to market more and more brands that competed with each other and therefore used the services of different agencies — relations between advertiser and agent sank down the table of organization. If "positioning the brand" is the great objective of advertising strategy, and a company has three competing and six related brands to position, the advertising agency that handles one or two of them cannot have very much influence on strategy. When a company decides on "line extensions" to use the same name on products advertised by other agencies, or emits what the veteran direct-response expert Lester Wunderman calls "flanker brands," the agency will be held to narrow channels in directing the work of its creative staff. What the agency considers the best approach for Brand X may have already been adopted for Brand Y, and the internal politics of the corporation cannot stand much of that. "There are more Procters around these days," says Frank Stanton, "and that controls what the agencies can do." (It should be noted, however, that a corporation that produces competing brands does not absolutely have to allocate them to different agencies: Jack Hewitt, who sold Anahist to Warner-Lambert and ran that conglomerate's family products division for some years thereafter, sent all his cold medicines to Ted Bates: "Here are these people who know more about the cold remedy business than anybody else in America. We'd be fools not to go along with them." Hewitt never had an advertising department: he let Bates do the work. That was then, and this is now.)

Such power positions reflect themselves organizationally. William Pitts of Lois Pitts Gershon, a midsize agency, said in the early 1980s, "Big corporations are hierarchical. They need people with whom to interface, so you have to have a lot of bodies for them to interface with." As early as the 1960s, now seen in retrospect as the golden age of creativity in advertising, Henry Schachte at J. Walter Thompson warned that the result of spreading bureaucratization was an extravagant increase in the number of people who could say no. "You keep yielding," said George Lois, "to the client's desire for mediocrity." Even when the C.E.O. does give the new campaign a final review, all he sees is what his brand managers have approved. At both the agency and the client, midlevel executives spend their lives processing information and relating almost entirely to each other. "One of the funny things at Ogilvy," says Hal Riney, "is that they recognized that clients had staffs capable of doing what account management used to do. There were meetings about 'what shall we do?' I said, 'Fire them — we'll make more money.' They said, 'No, we'll use 'em to sell more services,' which was probably a good idea for the bottom line."

Once upon a time, the "account service" people were indeed salesmen: their job was to sell the agency's work to the client. "I grew up with the old system," says William Weithas, C.E.O. of Lintas Worldwide. "The account man was the generalist. I thought I knew everything about the account, and I was the dominant strategic planner. Then creative took that away at the agency, and at the client you got the brand manager system, all decisions moving up an approval process." When Weithas started, the heads of the agencies came mostly out of account service, not because they were more sober and presentable (though that was true, too), but because they concentrated most directly on selling. Their authority with their own creative departments grew out of their skill in getting that work accepted by the client; their authority with the client grew out of their skill as salesmen and everyone's understanding that the point of this business was to sell. "Yes," said Burt Manning, a bearded man in zippered boots, when he was creative director of J. Walter Thompson a few years ago. "Clients no longer look for the guru who comes down from the mountain and is always right. He's still there, but the environment is no longer receptive."

Some companies still are organized to put decision-makers more closely in touch with advertising agencies. Apple Computer, headed by the former soft-drink marketer John Sculley, is a notable example; so is Wrigley. August Busch stays close to Budweiser advertising; Ray Kroc, while he lived, vetted everything for McDonald's, and the advertising showed in interesting ways his passion for cleanliness. At PepsiCo, the product managers have nothing to do with advertising, which is the direct responsibility of the division presidents. Roger Enrico, president of PepsiUSA through the goriest days of the cola wars, reports that he not only met personally with the people creating the advertising for all the Pepsis and for Slice (two different agencies), but set up the Michael Jackson deal and wrote some of the key sections of the ads himself.[8] "We believe as a matter of agency philosophy," says Allen Rosenshine of

BBDO, who worked with Enrico, "that the more involvement we can get from the C.E.O., the better the advertising." More often than the odds would predict, small companies get better advertising than big companies, because relations are less structured. "The people at Dreyer's [a West Coast ice cream] were very good," Hal Riney said, "until they hired brand managers and began to develop contemporary marketing systems. Then they lost direction."

Agencies never had much influence on budgets, because, except in connection with the introduction of new products, budgets for advertising invariably tracked sales. Later the business schools would sell corporate managements on the idea of designating their product lines as "stars," "cash cows," or "dogs," with higher-than-average advertising as a percentage of sales for the first category, to build the brand; lower-than-average advertising for the middle group to milk the profits; and none at all (or very little) for the declining product. Nevertheless, within each category, expenditure tracked sales. What happened to the agencies in the 1980s, as I noted in Chapter 1, was the drive at the corporations to replace advertising expenditure with promotion expenditure, which promised more measurable results. When the agencies tried to cultivate the promotion people in the client corporations, they found those chairs occupied either by number-crunchers from the business schools or by former truck drivers (after all, who could know more about how you got store managers to play along with your promotions?). Neither group was much interested in what the advertising agency thought was happening. The account executives — the "suits," as the creative people called them — became less effective where it counts year after year.

2.

The next most populous group in an agency is usually the media buyers, once divided between politicians and show-business types. The world of print buying was clubby and largely Irish Catholic, with its own pubs and hangouts; the world of broadcast was a mix of vaudeville and Ivy League until the Hollywood studios accepted the existence of television in the mid-1950s. Until then, agencies themselves produced many programs for broadcast, on prime-time network as well as daytime and local syndication markets; at a conference in the Museum of Broadcasting in the spring of 1990, Sylvester (always "Pat") Weaver, who was head of Young & Rubicam's broadcast production unit before he became president of NBC in the 1950s, commented sourly that he and his people made better television shows at the agency than he was ever able to make at NBC, because NBC was a distribution system and understood only the wire, while Y&R was always close to the consumer.

Here again, the upper echelons of the client were once involved in decision-making, because their company "sponsored" a program and would be identified with it in the public mind. "Niles Trammel [president of NBC] came to me right after the war," Edward Little of Colgate remembered twenty years later, "and said, 'Ed, I want to develop the biggest show in the country,' and we committed five or six million dollars" to what became *The Colgate Comedy Hour,* NBC's major entertainment venture in the days of little screens with black-and-white pictures. The star of the first episode was Eddie Cantor, whose blackface routine was much admired in the next morning's *New York Times* (Sept. 11, 1950). John Keezer of ABC remembered that when that network was pushing *Ben Casey,* the first of the hospital shows, an agency recommended it to a cosmetics company. "The head of that company was on his way to a vacation, and he stopped by at 7 West Sixty-Sixth Street to look at the pilot. He had his twelve-year-old son with him. This was a show where Casey was slugging a guy in the heart in a resuscitation technique. The son fainted, and the guy said he couldn't buy. A year later, *Ben Casey* was at the top of the ratings, he was back looking at something else, without his son, and he told me, 'I could kill that kid.'"

In those days, the networks sold access to the audience of their stations. The advertiser bought the stations he wanted, with a minimum purchase and a discount from the rate cards that grew as he took more stations, and usually he supplied the program. The network paid the stations substantially less than their time rates, and the stations got the programming for nothing. The stations also retained "adjacencies" to the network-supplied programs that they could sell themselves as "spots," normally through representatives not unlike the newspaper representatives of Calkins's time. Other spots were available in the time periods when the networks did not program and the local station presented movies or kinescopes of old programs, or their own news shows.

Phil Richardson, who ran the nation's first corporate "media department" for Procter & Gamble in the 1930s, liked to say that "media is a question of how many seats and how many arses." The Ted Bates agency was from its inception in 1940 the great promoter of buying spots directly from local stations rather than through networks. In the unending war between the believers in reach (how many arses) and the believers in frequency (how many kicks at each arse), Bates held firmly for reach, and thus denigrated the network show that was seen mostly by the same people every week. Colgate's E. H. Little said he suspected that the agency's situation rather than its philosophy had dictated the preference, for its two original clients were Continental Baking (Wonder Bread) and Colgate. Continental was a chain of local bakeries that had been put together as a 1920s Wall Street ploy, and had a relatively uneven national distribution with much to gain from concentrating its advertising efforts in those markets where its bread was most easy to find. And Colgate in the radio days had been handicapped in getting its message out by the "protection" Procter & Gamble had gained by getting to the networks "fustest with the mostest" and checkerboarding its shows through the schedule. Local stations were not bound by the network's protection rules, and by purchasing spots Bates could at least lessen Colgate's disadvantage.

Bates's research director, Clifford Parsells, argued that radio and television — particularly television — had reversed the old rules of advertising media. Sunday magazines distributed with the newspapers had always charged less for their pages than an advertiser would have had to spend to buy pages individually in all the papers. But it was possible to buy spots on all the stations covered by a network program, at a comparable time period, for less than the network rates. Volume discounts were substantial, and once you bought 8:59 P.M. to 9:00 P.M. from a station, you owned it, year after year. The comparative cost position was not as simple as Parsells liked to make it, because he was comparing the costs of sponsorship or half-sponsorship against the costs of single minutes, but what Bates cared about was reach rather than frequency. Bates, as the leading purchaser of station spots, built up a huge inventory of high-audience local minutes in which the agency could put its clients' commercials — and was invariably given first crack at any such minutes that came loose from others. Rival agencies felt that Bates's central strength was not its touted Unique Selling Proposition approach to copy or even the personal force of its executive cadre, but the low cost-per-thousand at which the agency could deliver commercials for its clients.

Building media plans out of little blocks in individual stations was and is a pain in the neck. "If I buy a thousand shares of stock," said E. A. Grey, Bates's media director in the days of its heaviest involvement with the spot market, "I get a full report the next day, on one sheet of paper. To buy a twenty-five-dollar spot takes fifteen sheets of paper." Money also had to be spent to find out what ran, and to calculate the size of the audience, which was clearly something less than the audience for the adjacent programs. (Bates was partners with J. Walter Thompson in a service that performed those chores.) An Arthur Young study in the mid-1960s identified media buying as the most expensive activity in the average advertising agency.

Coupled with growing respect for the skills of his network buyer (Richard Pinkham, graduate of Choate and Yale but a free spirit for all that, who had come to the agency from NBC), the costs of buying spot eventually moved Bates to much lesser reliance on that procedure. The people in the agency's media department saw handwriting on the wall, and in 1969 a number of them left, following Sam Vitt into his Vitt Media International, a spot-buying service that can be used by agencies or advertisers. The aim was to place at the disposal of many smaller clients the sort of clout Bates had accumulated.

Vitt's clients are roughly divided between agencies and advertisers, and they have a choice of fee arrangements: 15 percent of 15 percent (2.25 percent) on the billings, or hourly "like lawyers and accountants," or entrepreneurial. In the last, the client brings in his media objectives and the budget he has been told he will need to buy them; Vitt does the buying, and keeps half of the difference between the budget and what the client actually pays. Arrangements of this nature are very common in Europe, where one agency, Gilbert Gross's Carat Espace, controls a third of the French advertising market, 15 percent of all the space and time sold in England, and 10 percent of the market in West Germany and Spain. "The Gross brothers," writes Alice Rawsthorn of *The Financial Times,* "are renowned for their negotiating skills. Gilbert Gross is a world poker champion."[9] American agencies have been buying into such arrangements: Lintas owns Belgium-based Initiative Media; Omnicom (BBDO and DDB Needham) and the American WPP agencies (basically J. Walter Thompson and The Ogilvy Group) jointly own what they call The Media Partnership.[10]

For such operations, of course, there is no distinction between "spot" and "network." Indeed, the distinction has been essentially artificial for thirty years, since the costs of producing television shows drove advertisers out of sponsorship and agencies out of show business. The networks themselves became the producers of the programs, selling first part-sponsorships, then individual minutes, finally individual thirty-second pieces of time within the program. Among the changes wrought by the new selling regime was the virtual disappearance of client senior management from the process of placing the advertising. The only exceptions are extraordinary situations like Texaco's commitment to opera or Hallmark's identification with more or less serious drama — and the sports events, where all bets are off because the C.E.O.'s of companies advertising in these programs get the best seats and the best entertainment. A few advertisers let their agencies know that there are shows they simply do not wish to see as the ambiance for their commercials. (Procter & Gamble, in straitlaced Cincinnati, is especially severe in this area.) But as a normal matter, advertisers on television now buy guaranteed audiences of a certain age and sex, as measured by the Nielsen ratings, and they pay so much per thousand viewers. The minutes are placed by agreement on certain shows, and if you bought time on this show last year you probably get first refusal this year, but the show itself is not necessarily the crucial component in the deal. (A lot of television shows really are pretty interchangeable.) Client media departments supervise the process to assure effectiveness and improve efficiency, but the C.E.O. has better things to do. And the people at the agencies who prepare the "media plans" are media specialists and nothing else.

The executives in the media departments make the decisions allocating money among the different ways to advertise — television, newspapers, magazines, Sunday supplements of various kinds, inserts, radio, "outdoor," cable. The grunts in the trenches mostly buy in only one medium, because each has its own customs and bargaining procedures. There is nothing new in most of this: Calkins wrote of the early twentieth century, "Space buying was a matter of barter. The most valuable employee of the old-line agency was the man who knew from experience, not the card rate, but the very lowest the publisher would accept. The tricks employed to hammer down that rate were as dark and devious as the subterfuges of the publishers, to overplay their circulation. It was diamond cut diamond."[11] Broadcast minutes, for all the publicity given to rate cards, were even more inevitably a commodity: their price is never anything but the price quoted by the fellow at the other end of the telephone at the moment of the call. But the level of complexity is now infinitely greater. John Bernbach of DDB Needham says that the media plans that come to his desk are nine inches thick.

One school of thought holds that the most important service an agency gives an advertiser, day in and day out, is the correct choice of media at the best price. Keith Reinhard of DDB Needham calls media "the second creative department." But the rival school has been dominant. Just as banking theorists insist that the law of large numbers averages out the credit judgment of banks that make a lot of loans, advertising theorists argue that great advertising that really sells the product is a random event, while only "pressure" can be planned and purchased and delivered.

Finding out what you actually get for what you buy is one of the more abstruse tasks of advertising. The idea of audited circulation for publications goes back to the nineteenth century, and was acceptable data for comparison purposes until the era of broadcasting, but it always concealed almost as much as it illuminated. Subscriptions could be sold cheap or linked to promotions more valuable than the paper: when I was a boy, we had a set of Dickens's novels and an album of Caruso recordings, courtesy of (I think) the New York *Post,* not yet a tabloid. Presumably, people paid less attention to what they were bribed to buy.

How should the media buyer judge the relative values of newsstand sale versus subscription? Even people who bought the magazine or newspaper at list price might not read much of it, and if they did, they might not notice the ads. Various services to determine who saw what (and who remembered what) were launched as early as the 1910s, to be supplemented in the 1950s by surveys of how many people saw each copy of a magazine. Knowing the audience of a publication was the art of the media buyer: supermarkets didn't advertise in *The New York Times,* because readers of the *Times* sent their help out to buy at the greengrocer's and the butcher's; department stores and fashion boutiques did advertise in the *Times,* not only because the lady of the house read it, but also because it specialized in news of the clothing industry. All cities had more or less specialized daily newspapers that sold to different communities, and sophisticated buyers knew which of them matched their agencies' "stereotypes" for which products.

Broadcast was much more difficult to measure, starting with the problem that there was no tearsheet to be submitted as proof that what the advertiser bought, he got. F. Kent Mitchel, marketing director of General Foods, said mildly in the 1970s, "One of the weak links in spot [that is, the purchase of time from local stations rather than from networks] is that there's no sure way to know it gets run." I once spent an astonished morning in a large brick one-story taxpayer in Philadelphia where seventy women worked at little tape decks, wearing earplugs, listening and noting on a printed data sheet every commercial broadcast on 265 television stations monitored for Broadcast Advertising Reports. One of the continuing weaknesses of cable TV as an advertising medium is that the local "head ends" are often careless about inserting the commercials, and there is no service to monitor them. Not until 1990 was BAR (now owned by the ratings service Arbitron, itself owned by Control Data) able to eliminate such handwork with a computer program that recognized the "pixels," the illuminated dots on the screen, that characterized each of the commercials being tracked. Eventually, as stations learned not to make up their logs to fit the affadavits they had to submit, BAR became more a source of information on what competitors were doing, but the verification facility remains important. Some of the old problems persist on cable.

Even if you knew the commercials had run, of course, you didn't know who had heard or seen them. At best, the act of turning a dial left no audit trail. Beginning with Archibald Crossley and his Cooperative Analysis of Broadcasting in 1930, various systems to measure the audience for programs grew up. Crossley's was based on "telephone recall" — someone called the household and asked whoever answered what was watched yesterday. Claude Hooper then offered Hooperatings based on "telephone coincidental" research — someone called the household and asked what was being watched right now. Other services involved diaries that people were paid to keep, others employed door-to-door interviewers who asked people what they had listened to the night before.

In 1952, the Advertising Research Foundation did a study on the reliability of such measurements, and came down on the side of A. C. Nielsen's machine-based system. Nielsen was already important to advertisers and agencies as the proprietor of a grocery-and-drugstore survey that measured retail sales by comparing the invoices the stores had received from suppliers with the inventory actually on the shelves. For the Nielsen ratings, households were paid to let the research firm install an "Audimeter" on their radio (later — same system — on their television set). The Audimeter automatically made a record of the time the set was in use and the station or channel to which it was tuned. Every two weeks Nielsen would send each member of the sample a new film cartridge, and he or she would take the old cartridge out of the Audimeter and mail it back. The Nielsen disadvantages (the small size of the thousand-home sample and its relative permanence and possible bias) were judged something advertisers could live with, while the disadvantages of the other systems (chiefly the doubtful accuracy of the data) were considered crippling. Art Nielsen, as I can testify, was extremely convincing: a lean, athletic older man (he and his son for a number of years were U.S. amateur doubles tennis champions), he had started life as a chemical engineer and was full of scorn for the social scientists who were his rivals.

In point of fact, however, Nielsen's system was not as strong as everyone thought. The sampling design went back to 1947, and the households that accepted the meters were not nearly so random as the sample said they would be. And there were some inaccuracies inherent in the data collection service. "My radio," an older lady who was part of a radio panel told a congressional committee investigating Nielsen, "plays almost all day every day as I like to wake up to it and hear it as I come in the door at night. And my dog enjoys it as much as a dog can."[12] But Nielsen beefed up his procedures (increasing his prices in the process), new ARF studies approved his data, and since the early 1970s advertisers have learned what they bought chiefly by studying the Nielsen reports. For local data, Nielsen has a rival in Arbitron, with machine-measured panels in the 14 largest markets reporting results overnight, and diary panels in another 196 markets to cover the thrice-yearly "sweeps weeks." In the early 1980s, the networks tried to stimulate national competition, too, bringing over a British firm called AGB, which employed a German technique called the "people meter." This did not work well as a source of competition (Nielsen drove the interlopers off rather quickly), but it did persuade Nielsen to switch to its own people-meter technique, which we shall look at in Chapter 5.

Exposures to newspapers are still measured by audited circulation figures, reasonably enough, as not many papers pass from hand to hand. MediaMark Research asks 20,000 households a year which papers were read or "looked at" in those households during the preceding week, and does similar measurements on magazines. Simmons Research, a subsidiary of Britain's WPP holding company (and reputedly more profitable than any of the advertising agencies in the holding company, which also owns J. Walter Thompson and Ogilvy & Mather), publishes a syndicated service describing, among other things, the readership (as distinct from the circulation) of magazines, delivering ratings-type data as to the age, sex, family status, and income group of the people who see the advertising.

But what all of this amounts to is the purchasing of numbers, an activity of necessity carried forward in large part by machine. The machine does not have to be in an agency, which is a threat to both jobs and revenues in the industry. On the other hand, these big numbers mean less and less: all the markets are fragmenting. Where once most Americans had a choice of four or five television stations, they now have as many dozens of cable channels. And everybody has a VCR, with about as many videotape rental shops in the big cities now as there are drugstores. The United States in 1990 had 1,100 television stations and 9,000 radio stations (up from 4,000 in 1960). There are fewer big-city newspapers, but many more suburban weeklies and indeed dailies. At the beginning of the 1980s, there were 1,100 magazines; at the end, after what was not generally regarded as a golden era for magazines, there were 1,760. And the development of selectronic addressing has made it possible to send different magazines under the same name to different subscribers.

For reasons we shall be exploring in the next two chapters, these developments are potentially an opening of opportunity for agencies. The 1990s could well become a decade of apotheosis for the media departments. "Mass marketing," says Laurel Cutler of FCB Leber Katz, "has been dead for ten years. Technology now makes it possible to market to one person at a time — or to a small number of people motivated by the same hot button." The direct-response specialist Lester Wunderman notes that "if it's a mass medium, it can't be an efficient way to reach a discrete group." Every agency has its own sometimes proprietary pitch for how the media plans it develops will multiply the value of the advertising. Don Pepper, while at Lintas, made a brilliant new-business presentation called "The Miniaturization of Communications," about all the ways the new targeting of messages "will increase the opportunity to profit from brand loyalty." Keith Reinhard speaks of DDB Needham's "personal media network. I want," he says, "to get to an individual, map his media path, find the aperture of receptivity." When the C.E.O. risen from the creative department begins talking about finding the aperture of receptivity through choice of media, the status chart is in process of revision.

3.

I first met William LaPorte of American Home Products when I was writing a history of the Ted Bates agency on commission from its then chairman, Rosser Reeves. Bates was picking up my expenses, so I ate well, and I invited LaPorte to lunch with me at Brussels, the now defunct 1960s equivalent of Le Cygne, if not Lutèce, in the pantheon of New York restaurants. I had teased Reeves about eating every day at Baroque and had urged him to try Brussels, and while I was lunching with LaPorte, Reeves suddenly walked in. He shook hands with us and went over to his table, where his guest was already seated. Reeves was perhaps the only man who ever lived who looked belligerent walking away from you. LaPorte, knowing I would carry the word back to Reeves, watched him cross the room, and said to me, "You know, that's really a very good agency. All they need is a few more lucky commercials." The aluminum exterior walls of 666 Fifth Avenue shook from the force of Reeves's reaction later that afternoon.

Asked for the names of people who really had to be seen to understand the state of the advertising business in 1990, President John O'Toole of A.A.A.A., himself a former C.E.O. with Foote, Cone & Belding, spoke first of the creators: Jay Chiat, Hal Riney, Keith Reinhard, Phil Dusenberry. The machine, after all, exists to power the messages. Everyone who works in this business knows, as Y&R's John Rindlaub puts it, that "advertising doesn't work, but ads do." The power of a great campaign is beyond the measuring capabilities of the research tools. All the other skills become important when the ad itself is mediocre. And it's a pretty dull business when the advertising is mediocre. There was for years, then, a willing suspension of disbelief. "When I started at Leo Burnett," said Len Matthews, then head of A.A.A.A., "there was a lot of the copywriter holding his hand over his heart and saying, 'Trust me.' Then you'd build the strategy around the ad campaign." Now the advertiser is more likely to trust the numbers being supplied to him at the same time. This disheartens the people who make the advertising. No small part of the feeling of malaise in the advertising industry grows from a sense that, to quote Bernice Kanner of *New York* magazine, "Much of today's advertising is flat and forgettable, commoditylike."[13]

The top leadership of an agency is more likely to come from the creative department today than it was a generation ago, but the ad-makers as a group have been descending the totem pole. Crawford Greenwalt, when C.E.O. of DuPont, once cheered on a gathering of teachers of literature by announcing that he felt the chairman of a major corporation should be a liberal arts graduate. A faculty dean who was not cheered said, "Sure: it means he wants to hire *one*." It is no longer fashionable in the account service departments to say, as F. Wallis Armstrong once did, that "a copywriter is a necessary evil, but an art director is just a damned nuisance." But it is true that the creative types do not feel in their gut the overriding importance of ROI (Return On Investment). They do care about selling, because it's sales that legitimize the work. But they rarely have a deep commitment to efficiency, and in today's competitive world it's efficiency the clients can measure, and it's efficiency the clients, mostly, want.

Jim Burke, ex-C.E.O. of Johnson & Johnson, remembers from his days at Procter & Gamble, fresh out of the Harvard Business School, a woman named Ruth Farquhar, part of the Milton Biow agency, which had been hired to sell Lilt, the first home permanent to take on Gillette's Toni (with its great campaign, "Which twin has the Toni?"). "For the first six months after she came on the account, we never saw her. She was out talking to women. She came to understand that what sold our product was that you got a more natural curl. We took apart a brand that had an enormous lead; I watched that business come out of her head, all done by copy. My premise was that the added value of advertising was extraordinary, you couldn't measure it."

George Lois, art director turned entrepreneur, started with Bill Bernbach. "You'd show something to a client, he'd say, 'Wow! That's great! That's what I came to this agency for. Let's use it.' Now, he wants to research it." One of the great American ads came from Lois's ability to convince a client he had a great idea. This was the early days of Xerox, in 1959, and Lois had sold its chairman, Joe Wilson, on the idea of buying minutes on *CBS Reports,* a documentary show that had a lot of minutes to sell cheap. The commercial showed a little girl visiting her father at the office and making copies with the Xerox machine. A. B. Dick, the nation's largest maker of mimeograph machines, complained to the FTC that a Xerox was much too complicated a device for a child. The FTC relayed the complaint to Lois, who called Wilson and said, "The next ad, let's show them a chimpanzee operating the machine." Wilson said, "Hell, let's do it"; and they did.

William Thompson, head of advertising strategy for Kodak at J. Walter Thompson, noted in the early 1980s, "People make judgments today on the basis of a lot more information. The smoke and mirrors business can't survive today — this is a much more disciplined business. But you lose something. You may be losing the real innovative spark. People are hard pressed today to separate the agencies from each other." Copywriters once created new products for clients. Clint Ferris, who headed the copy group for Continental Baking, suggested "Profile" bread, a product designed to be toasted, not as a way for people to lose weight, but as a way for them to keep it off after they'd finished their diet. Today, says BBDO's Allen Rosenshine, "agencies' involvement in new products is zero. It's unprofitable, and ninety-nine per cent of new product ideas don't go anywhere."

Alex Kroll, now chairman of Y&R (the largest of the agencies), is a broad-shouldered man in his early fifties who came to the agency three-and-a-half days after he left Rutgers, worked half a year in the research department, and quit to play professional football. "I suffered enough in that year," he remembers, "to realize advertising was better." On his return, he became a copywriter. "You were trained hand-to-hand in those days, it was a cottage industry. There was this loving attention to the kids. We were like Indian braves, we would gather around the campfire and tell tales, say, about Tang, which came down from White Plains as a white powder and we made it orange and it went to the moon. In those days you used to be able to trial-and-error your way into an ad. You'd jump on a train or a plane and visit the factory, see how the thing was made, and then you'd hang around the stores and see how people bought it, and then you'd write the advertising.

Kroll sighed and squared the broad shoulders, facing an undesired truth. "But the whole tempo of the creative business is so much faster now than it used to be — you don't have time to do that. In 1970 we had as many ways of writing advertising strategy as we had clients. Now we have one. Real strategic discipline makes work sharper. Without that, you have no common language. We can move people around, and know they'll do good work wherever they go."

The great operational change from a generation ago is the arrival of the art director as an equal partner. "Art directors today don't draw," says Allen Rosenshine. "It's not even a requirement that he can draw; he's supposed to think, how can we communicate a strategy. We've come a long way from what we used to call 'wrists.'" This began with Bernbach, whose shop spawned both George Lois and Carl Ally, who became agency chiefs in their own right. Even where the idea rests on verbal cleverness ("the new generation of Olds"), visual execution is now understood to be the heart of image generation. International brands want a logo they can use everywhere, and an advertising look that moves across borders. Mike Koelker's commercials for Levi's 501, the original blue jeans, didn't require him to write a word: "If I try to write it, I'm going to wind up imitating movies. We called the campaign Sweet Nothings because there was nothing behind it, just kids we recruited to come into the studio, pick out a pair of jeans to wear, and talk with each other." And though sound is almost as important in television as in radio and the faster the cutting the more important the sound (which supplies continuity), the ability of great directors to suffuse a picture frame with suitable emotion may count for as much as the idea. In the trade, the fantastic success of Oil of Olay was credited more to filmmaker Gennaro (Jerry) Andreozzi than to anyone else.

"We've been put into beauty," said Andreozzi some years ago, explaining his ambivalence toward the business that was his living. He was in his studio on the top floor of a reconditioned factory loft in the East twenties, wearing a Cliffside Park, New Jersey, basketball cardigan. "You have to do things as ordered. There are unbelievable meetings. Decisions on whether her dress should be red or blue, whether her hair should be up or down. Decisions I could make like *that* . . . there has to be a meeting. So much of my work is instinctual, but you have to explain, give marketing reasons or research reasons. My father was a mural painter for the WPA. He got into advertising through being an elevator operator in a building where there was an agency.

Now the schools produce everybody. You don't get a mix of people. And they teach the kids in school by showing them what's been done in advertising, not in art or literature or communications. Then the people from the agencies migrate to the client side. You no longer have the naive client who came out of the cheese factory in Wisconsin. He has two hot-shot kids from the agency telling him what to do. On the set, everybody sits around talking Hollywood, Academy Awards. But you're not in the movie business; you're in the advertising business."

Ed McCabe, who came out of the Carl Ally agency and was the hottest copywriter of the 1970s, organized his own agency on the principle that people moved from brand to brand, to keep them from getting bored. "The creative wave is over," he said, "because the people who made it got *used.*" But it is by no means clear that the average quality of creative work in 1990 is any worse than it was thirty or forty years ago. The problems it faces are simply harder. "Advertising in the 1950s and 1960s had far more leverage than it has now," said Alvin Achenbaum. "It had not pene-trated the markets for traditional products as completely as it has today. And there were so many new products to sell. There were many places where advertising built the busi-ness. The fabric softener guys built the business. The deo-dorant guys built the business. Dog food was hardly used in 1957, people fed their dogs on scraps from the table. The guy with that product went into television and it was a golden medium, he really began to sell. [And sell, and sell. In 1978, a young woman came out of Dartmouth to work in the Gaines division of General Foods, and was given the problem of proving that cheese-flavored Gainesburgers tasted like cheese to a dog.] There were industries where the advertiser's advantage was still latent — fast food, hotel chains, the financial services, banks, insurance, brokers, H&R Block."

An internal memo at Y&R notes that these days most of the agency's brands "are established brands, for which we usually have two main tasks:

"a) Maintain Perceptual Presence, i.e., saliency;

"b) Augment Perceived Quality.

"The former is mainly (say, 70%?) the responsibility of Media Selection and Tonnage . . . vehicles and volume carried, so to speak. The latter is mainly (say, 70%?) the responsibility of Communications Content, i.e., the value per ton of the cargo."

The maintenance of perceptual presence is what the advertiser can measure, and tends to be what he buys.

Quite a lot of the best advertising, like new products themselves, doesn't measure up at the start. Roger Enrico tells the story of the consumer tests for Slice:

"In every comparative test against 7-Up, we got slaughtered.

"And each time consumers preferred 7-Up, we played around with the formula. Was it crisp? Was it juicy? Not for long. Pretty soon it was a Xerox copy of 7-Up.

"Finally we decided to go back to the formula we all liked and examine our testing methods.

"It was the hardest thing to figure out.

"If people see a clear soft drink, they assume it's 7-Up. Then they taste it. It's different. 'No,' they say, 'I like the other one.' Meaning the one they're familiar with: 7-Up.

"At long last we came up with a radical idea. We told people what they were drinking. . . . And we learned a very simple truth about marketing. . . .

"When you are working on a product that has a real point of difference, it's pretty damn tough to beat the product that people are used to. . . . You've got to say, 'I have a concept. How many people are interested in it? Of the people who are, how many think this product delivers on the concept?'"[14]

When it's advertising, you don't have the backstop of the actual product, and you can be killed by the innate conservatism of the consumer, especially when dealing with the "badge" products that help people identify themselves. Robert Goldfarb, then director of program development for CBS Television, explained the year-to-year sameness of network television with a story "about the African tribe who saw their first movie. It was *King Kong,* and after it was over there were big cheers. The next week they were shown a movie again, and they tore down the tent and the screen and trashed the projector — because it wasn't *King Kong.* I think people want to see the same thing week in and week out."[15]

The art of the creator of advertising is to know when the opening exists for something new that can enter the culture and the marketplace in roughly the same time frame. If advertisers are not prepared to bet on the creator's art — if the decisions must be supported at every turn by research or planning or the insight of the M.B.A. — there's a limit to how much value advertising can add to the brand. Which means there is a limit to how much the work of an advertising agency is worth.

4.

The division of the agency that was truly decimated in the 1980s was research. At major agencies — DDB Needham

New York, for example, and FCB Leber Katz — the research department was eliminated entirely. Until the 1980s, research had been one of an agency's greatest sources of strength, not only for the suggestions it could give the creative department and the demonstrations of "how we know we're right" that could be presented to the client, but also because in commercial relationships information is power. Controlling much of the most important information about the interaction of products, brands, and consumers, the agency spoke to its clients with an authority they could deny only at their peril.

But as the 15 percent commission structure wound down, the agency had no revenues to pay for research. Testing of the agency's creative output, both print ads and broadcast commercials, had always been honestly done within the limits of an enterprise that inevitably — remember *King Kong* — tended to rank imitative work above original work. Agency-controlled labs and test kitchens had never been widespread phenomena, and larger-scale research about trends in the society, the markets for products, and the movement of brand shares simply became too expensive. The N.Y.U. statistics professor Ben Lipstein, who helped put together the computer programs for processing bar code data from the stores, notes that during the past decade research in the advertising business has moved from being a labor-intensive activity to being a capital-intensive activity.

Research involving test markets became too expensive in the 1970s, and was rapidly replaced by computer simulations and programs that "roll out" new products on a staggered and interruptible schedule. What's left, and is done everywhere, is "nonprojectable research," the focus-group interviews and small flights of questionnaires that generate ideas for advertising strategies and tactics. Hanno Fuchs of Y&R cites a neat example of what such groups can do to guide advertising. General Foods has a line of international coffees, canned with dried milk and various flavors, which were sold rather like candy. "One day, some research person said, 'We don't know who is buying this and why.' And we found out that this had nothing to do with dessert: it had to do with a sense of entitlement. Women consumed it alone a lot: it was 'my private reward.' Having a cup of this coffee had more in common with soaking in a bubble bath for an hour than it did with drinking coffee. So we stopped advertising amaretto flavors and began advertising role." At small expense, focus-group research permits the agency to make the claim it absolutely must make: that it lives closer to the consumer than the client can. To validate that claim, the agency must have ideas the client doesn't have on how this brand is bought, used, talked about, and regarded by people who buy this sort of product.

Even here, however, it is often the manufacturer and not the advertising agency that contracts with some outside research source to find the tactics as well as the strategy for a campaign. The British journalist Eric Clark reports on a piece of research done for a painkiller by Planmetrics, Inc., a company founded and operated by a cultural anthropologist, Steve Barnett: "Sufferers from a 'certain type of disease' were taped as they discussed the pain which they suffered. Barnett says he later found forty-five facial and body expressions that the people had used when they talked of the pain and its relief. Those gestures were then studied by actors and incorporated into commercials for the painkiller."[16] The channel of communication is from research firm to advertiser to agency to filmmaker.

Where the research department survives, as at Y&R, it often operates now under another name. Satish Korde, a young Indian whose father is chief of police of Bombay, heads what Y&R calls "Consumer Insight," worldwide. Following the lead of its president, Peter Georgescu, Y&R accepts Abraham Maslow's view of the hierarchy of human needs, with self-actualization at the top. "Understanding people is critical," Korde says. "As products become more commoditized, understanding people has incremental value. If I knew how each consumer makes decisions, I would know what I want to say to him." But the data that discriminate among individuals are, as we shall see, expensive to store and retrieve in useful fashion, and the agencies will certainly not have priority in their acquisition or use.

In many agencies — starting at J. Walter Thompson, but especially at the very democratic Chiat/Day, where all the walls are five-foot-high partitions and nobody has a really private office — what happened to the research department was that its members got reclassified as "planners." The notion of a "planner" who saw an account in the round came from England, where agencies had always had to deal with relations between manufacturers and store chains. British advertising people had never thought highly of sociological or psychological research, and found planners more credible because they factored in the trade elements of the selling effort. Unlike the account supervisor, the planner could claim an information edge over the brand manager at the client company, because his range was broader and his professional background was deeper. And because he was not the client contact person, he could lay out problems and possible solutions for the creative group without stimulating suspicions that he was really a shill for the

client's brand manager. All research — demographic, economic, psychosexual, copy-oriented, evaluative — would
come through him, to be given the most useful spin.

What the planner doesn't plan, mostly, is research projects other than the low-cost focus-group work. But at Interpublic, where the Marion Harper tradition of social research
still lives, the C.E.O., Philip Geier, speaks of "Quest, a one-
man operation that taps universities." A project at U.C.L.A. —
"eight or nine key clients participate" — has developed a
research technique called "emotional bonding, determining what emotions come out of this kind of product. You
match the brand personality with the emotions. It helps creative people do better creative advertising." Another project
explores the possibilities of interactive cable, aimed for the
1992 Olympics, permitting people to choose from a menu
of the events they would like to see — and a menu of the
products they would like to see advertised. A third, at the
University of Pennsylvania, involves a video simulation of a
trip to a store, a game people play after they have seen the
advertising that is being tested, choosing the brands they
would like to buy. Price and display can be varied as the test
operator wishes. "Unilever has verified the accuracy of the
simulation in test markets," Geier says; "the figures from the
simulation were within three or four per cent of the result
in the test markets. And you can do it in three weeks cheap
instead of six months at huge expense."

But if an advertiser wants simulations, he can buy them
in greater variety from research firms, notably Steven Rose
Research, a spinoff from the former Daniel Yankelovich
Group, which had once been a subsidiary of a life insurance
company. Looking toward the horizon, the perceptive
observer can see onrushing data that will largely supplant
life-style and psychosocial research material because they

describe the universe rather than just a sample. Those data are being found and saved and massaged by the likes of Citicorp, AT&T, a Sears-IBM consortium, and Dun & Bradstreet. It is not clear how effectively even a giant advertising agency, with maybe a billion dollars of gross revenue, can keep up with such competition, and the publicly held agencies can't even try. "Ask me whether I think we should have gone public," said John Bernbach bitterly. "The answer is, we shouldn't have gone public. There are investments we should make that we don't make because they would cut too deeply into the next quarter's profits and kill the price of the stock."

But the problem of the allocation of agency resources is larger than the question of expenditures on research. Young & Rubicam and Leo Burnett, the two largest agencies that have remained in private hands, have put more money into data-base marketing than the stockholder-owned agencies. Burnett has a fourteen-member group working on scanner data, and Y&R has a hush-hush development program with American Express, designed to give shape to that company's mounds of consumer purchase data. And both agencies are in general more confident of their role in the economy and the society. But even here, one finds some degree of malaise, some sense that the world is passing by the advertising agencies. It is an insecurity that feeds on itself: the more the agencies exist to do the clients' bidding, the less sure they can be of their function. Too much money, time, and effort goes into pleasing executives in the client company who make no bones about the fact that they expect (and expect to pay for) only a rather narrow set of services.

To add sustainable value to a brand, agencies have to know a lot about a product and its consumers. Much of this information comes of necessity from the client, but unless the agency people can contribute from a different perspective they are not likely to be much (if at all) better than the client in giving the information structure and utility. Spending less on keeping the clients happy and more on determining what it is they ought to know — whether they want such services or not — would help in every aspect of agency life, except perhaps the immediate, short-term profits that determine the value of the stock options. That's what Bernbach means when he denounces the decision to sell stock to outsiders. Most people at most of the publicly held agencies would agree with him.

CHAPTER FOUR

Media

ONCE THE TELEVISION NETWORKS were completely wired across the country, a process interrupted by the Korean War but pretty much finished by the end of the 1950s, the pundits declared that local or regional brands of beer were necessarily doomed. For a product so widely consumed as beer and so susceptible to branding, the economies of buying time on sporting events telecast from coast to coast would simply swamp competitors who had to advertise locally because they had only local distribution. Among the regional brewers who decided to see whether perhaps they could take their brands national was the Blitz-Weinhard Company of Portland, Oregon, proprietors of Henry Weinhard's Private Reserve. This was a family operation run by two brothers and their father. The father was more or less retired but didn't like to think so and came in to the office every morning to keep an eye on the business by opening the mail, as he always had. In midmorning, an already retired crony would call from one of the Portland clubs and invite the old man for a game of billiards, and he'd excuse himself happily for the day.

The brothers had been reading of the danger to local breweries posed by the national brands. And of course they consulted their advertising agent, Howard Gossage, a witty and ultimately tragic iconoclast full of ideas other people didn't have and might or might not understand, founder of the San Francisco school of "advertising that people enjoy" and remember enjoying. (Hal Riney, who took over the Blitz-Weinhard business after Gossage's death, is the current exemplar.) "We were looking," said Frederic Wessinger, one of the brothers, "at the possibility of putting a dark beer into the New York market. It was, in retrospect, a dumb idea."

Gossage came up with a remarkable way to test the waters: a one-insertion full-page ad in *The New Yorker* praising the wonders of the Oregon countryside and water that made the local beer so delightful. "It was a low-expense ad," Wessinger recalled, "and it was going to keep Howard happy, and Howard was a super guy." To attract attention, the ad carried the headline KEEP TIMES SQUARE GREEN! To retain attention, it offered a premium: clip the coupon and send it in with a quarter, and Blitz-Weinhard would send you two Oregon fir seedlings to plant in the big city. This was the most successful coupon promotion since one-quarter of New York's households in the 1900s returned the coupon from Claude Hopkins's newspaper ads for Van Camp's evaporated milk: from *The New Yorker*'s 430,000 circulation, 140,000 coupons were sent to Portland.

"The mail came in avalanches," Wessinger remembered. This was very hard on his father, who for several days tried to get through all of it, stacking quarters and smoothing coupons, missing his billiard game and going home at eight exceedingly weary, until his sons persuaded him that in these emergency conditions they should be allowed to hire a couple of new people to go through just the heavy mail with quarters in it. In the story as I first heard it, the demand was so heavy that purchases by Blitz-Weinhard pushed up the price of fir seedlings, but Wessinger said that wasn't so: "We've got these things by the millions out here." The cost of handling the mail, however, was quite heavy both in terms of out-of-pocket expenditures and psychic disability.

A few months after this ad ran, somebody (Wessinger said it wasn't Blitz-Weinhard) commissioned a horseback survey in New York to see if it had, indeed, established an identity for the brand or the company in the big town. None of those queried had ever heard of Blitz-Weinhard or Henry Weinhard's Private Reserve. For the hell of it, a second cut was taken to see how many people had heard of the campaign to KEEP TIMES SQUARE GREEN! Though *The New Yorker* is not a mass-circulation magazine (and not an especially New York magazine in its readership), 15 or so percent of the people queried had heard of the campaign. They just didn't associate it with beer.

"Howard loved it," Wessinger said. "But of course he never really connected with the beer business; he was always talking about the advertising business." There seemed to be some branding values for Henry Weinhard in the companion campaign that ran in the Oregon papers, urging people to send fir seedlings to friends in New York for the greening of Times Square. Gossage's agency sent around the country the message of the ad he had written that drew more than 30 percent response from *The New Yorker*. The magazine was if anything even more excited, and printed up a promotion piece about this demonstration of its pulling power. The brand never did jump the mountains and prairies to New York, though Pabst, an East Coast company that bought Blitz-Weinhard, gave some thought to trying; but Private Reserve did move down the Pacific rim, replaced Coors in student circles in California, and became one of the most popular brands in Los Angeles — without the economies of national advertising.

Consider now the case of the 1981 cablecasting of the Westminster Kennel Club show, which was purchased in its entirety by Quaker Oats as an exclusive sponsorship for its brand Ken-L-Ration. This was the second year the dog show had been put on cable coast to coast, by a cable program service in which Madison Square Garden had a considerable stake. Young & Rubicam, which recommended and made the buy for Quaker Oats, had commissioned a special study of the audience drawn by the show in San Diego, the nation's most heavily cabled city. (You needed cable in San Diego to get the Los Angeles stations — and, in the city's many hidden valleys, to get the San Diego stations, which had been allocated inferior UHF channels by the FCC.) In prime time, the dog show had pulled 6 percent of the San Diego audience. There were then about 18 million cable households in the United States (in 1990 there were almost three times that many), and about 10 million could receive the USA Channel. If the San Diego experience proved typical of the nation, Ken-L-Ration would be buying exposure to its messages at a cost of about $1 per thousand homes per commercial, at a time when network thirty-second spots cost four and five times that much. And the audience for a network show would contain a number of people who had no pets, not to mention people who kept cats, while virtually everybody watching the Westminster Kennel Club show would be interested in dog food.

"Narrowcasting" of that kind was already in the forefront of advertising people's minds in the early 1980s. J. Walter

Thompson made a two-minute film about riding motorcycles, for its client Kawasaki, to be slotted into the Music Channel, watched almost exclusively by a community that was also interested in motorcycles. *Family Circle* magazine then had a daytime cable show called *It's a Great Idea,* aimed at the full-time housewife. Reynolds Aluminum bought long stretches of commercial time on it to teach viewers how to make their own Christmas ornaments with aluminum foil.

Also in 1981, Jay Chiat of Chiat/Day acquired Apple Computer as an account by purchasing the advertising division of a small Palo Alto public relations firm. The personal computer was still a novelty, and the agency did ads to tell people why they needed one. There was a spectacular magazine double spread of one hundred paragraphs with willfully spotted pictures of a dog, an outfielder catching a fly ball, a litter of pigs, a space shuttle, a medieval devil, and an Apple, under the headline "Will someone please tell me exactly what a personal computer will do?" At best, personal computers were not going to be as big a market as business computers, and the Apple engineers had IBM in their sights. Their first product, the Lisa, was too expensive and too complicated to operate, but on the drawing boards was a remarkable design based on a new systems architecture, which the Apple people called the Macintosh. "They think it is more than just another product," the Chiat/Day history recalls; "they think it will change the world. They want to do a big introduction, maybe throw simultaneous parties across America with the most famous rock bands in the world, people dancing in the street, the heralding of a new age. After a brief cost analysis, they realize that they can either throw the parties or make the computer. They tell Chiat/Day, 'Well, do us a TV commercial or something.'"[1]

The Macintosh was going to be introduced in January 1984. The Apple president, Steve Jobs, who was all of twenty-eight, believed it would cause a revolution, democratize the world by giving ordinary people access to information once available to very few. George Orwell had written a novel entitled *1984,* projecting the apotheosis of totalitarianism. What Chiat/Day decided to say for Apple was that this company had made the real 1984 marvelously different from what the numbers had come to stand for. There would be a hollow voice-over Big Brother, thousands of marching clones obeying without any need for explicit orders, and a girl in red shorts who would smash the screen to announce the introduction of this new computer for home or office. To make the film, Chiat/Day engaged the director of the movies *Alien* and *Blade Runner.* To get the commercial to the largest possible audience for its one and only appearance, Chiat/Day took a spot in the 1984 Super Bowl. To reinforce the impression of the TV spot and say a little more about the product, the agency bought no fewer than 24 pages in a single issue of *Newsweek.* One worries about waste audience when selling a brand, but not when launching an idea.

Then there's radio, promoted by a Radio Advertising Bureau that has been wonderfully and successfully aggressive since the medium was declared dead and gone in the aftermath of universal television viewing in the 1950s. Radio, says the RAB senior vice president, Laurence W. Norjean, gives the advertiser an opportunity to speak to the consumer near the "Time of Purchase." He says, "Fifty-five percent of all people listen to radio within an hour of making a purchase. McDonald's has learned that people decide to go out to eat on the average only an hour before they go, and decide *where* they're going to eat only five minutes before they stop there. So you don't advertise breakfast the night before; you advertise breakfast in the morning. Only radio can do value-added merchandising in a local market; radio has the personalities who can do live remotes from the stores. Folger's [this is salesman's hype] does eighty-five, ninety percent of its advertising on early morning radio. People are drinking their breakfast coffee. If it's Folger's, the commercial reinforces them. If the coffee is lousy, they hear the Folger's commercial, they decide to switch.

"Seventy-nine percent of the shopping for automobiles is done Saturday and Sunday," Norjean continues, warming to his task. "What good does it do you to be on television Monday or Tuesday? And people are loyal to radio stations. You ask people which is their favorite television station, you get blank stares, eventually somebody mentions *Cosby* or some other show, not a station. But you ask them their favorite radio station, they answer like *that.*"

The choice of a medium through which to present advertising messages is by no means a simple one.

1.

In his book *The House of Morgan,* Ron Chernow argues that the creation of national industrial enterprises at the turn of the twentieth century was not the doing of the great merchant banks; instead, the merchant banks became so important because the spread of communications and transportation channels meant that industrial enterprise would need financial services on a very large scale. Similarly, neither national magazines nor advertising agencies caused the growth of the national market for branded products; the agencies and the national media were called into existence by manufacturers' needs for such services. National media and advertising agencies grew together symbiotically for most of the twentieth century, as network radio followed magazines, and then television's coaxial cable tied in the entire country.

For all the shabbiness of the black-and-white picture tubes and the deficiencies of the tele-cine chains that converted film to electronic signal, television's selling power in its early years was something quite new in the world. "I sincerely believe," says Jim Burke, formerly C.E.O. of Johnson & Johnson, "that television saved us after the second world war. Without television, we'd have gone back into the Depression." In city after city, fire departments reported reduced water pressure in their hoses when prime-time TV shows ended and people left their chairs to go to the bathroom. Advertisers that "sponsored" TV shows, which was the norm until the 1960s, reported that if their program was preempted for any reason, they felt the loss of the advertising pressure in their next week's sales. As the handmaidens of this radiant force, the advertising agencies shone brightly in reflected glory. That fire, inevitably, has cooled, and advertising has paled in turn. And now the data processing revolution has begun to cast doubt on the future of all mass media as efficient selling instruments.

What media sell to advertisers is, of course, access to their audience or readership. It is a sad commentary on the quality of American social criticism that this tautology is taken as discreditable to the nation's newspapers, magazines, and broadcasting stations. This said, it must also be admitted that there is a difference between serving and whoring. Until the second half of this century, good magazines would not have dreamed of selling pages in the central "text sandwich," where all the main articles and stories started and the illustrations were most prominent. David Sarnoff, founding father and maximum leader of RCA and NBC, felt that manufacturers of radio sets should own and operate stations. They had the greatest stake in offering the public the best programs, and their profits from producing the sets that the programs made people want to buy would easily pay the costs, without the sale of time to advertisers. That wasn't true. The costs got much too great. Academics, politicians, and journalists had to face the fact that people *liked* advertising, and would certainly rather put up with "commercial messages" than pay a fee or a tax for broadcast services.

As late as 1928, the Federal Radio Commission — whose members had been appointed by Calvin Coolidge to license stations and award them exclusive use of a piece of the frequency spectrum — insisted, "Such benefit as is derived by advertisers must be incidental and entirely secondary to the interest of the public."[2] A year later, the National Association of Broadcasters published a code insisting that "commercial announcements, as the term is generally understood, shall not be broadcast between seven and eleven P.M."[3] Sponsorship was a chaste activity. Gilbert Seldes noted "the total advertising, direct or indirect, [spoken on] a very popular and successful program" in 1925: " 'Tuesday evening means The Ever-Ready Hour, for it is on this day and at this time each week that the National Carbon Company, makers of Ever-Ready flashlights and radio batteries, engages the facilities of these fourteen radio stations to present its artists in original radio creations.' "[4] Ever-Ready had put together its own network. Later in the decade, companies were formed for the purpose of linking together local stations in different cities. These networks, which were not and are not licensed in any way themselves, assumed throughout the radio era and into the early years of television that they had an obligation to the public to put some air time aside for community service. "There was a feeling," said CBS's Jack Cowden, "that you *shouldn't* be more than 80 per cent sold. If you were, your prices were too low, and you should raise prices until sales fell back to 80 per cent. Then you had the other 20 per cent for your own 'sustaining' shows."[5]

Oddly, considering the extent to which advertisers automatically wrapped themselves in the mantle of a medium's reputation, neither newspapers nor magazines ever concerned themselves much with the probity or suitability of an advertisement. "All mediums," Calkins wrote of his early days, "carried patent medicines. Customers bought space and said what they wished. No Better Business Bureau or Food and Drug Act censored their claims. Thus we find Scott's Emulsion (with a testimonial from Henry Irving), Doctor Pierce's Golden Medical Discovery, Lydia Pinkham's Vegetable Compound (whose patients continued to testify from their graves), Mrs. Winslow's Soothing Syrup, Horsford's Acid Phosphates (Horsford invented baking powder), Hall's Hair Renewer, Antipyrene (precursor of aspirin), Beecham's Pills (their profits financed grand opera), Grove's Chill Tonic (which built Grove Park Inn at Asheville), and Doctor Scott's Electric Belt, which, if you believed Doctor Scott, would cure male and female neuralgia, sciatica, asthma, consumption, catarrh, erysipelas, piles, and epilepsy. The only reason the good doctor did not include diabetes, pernicious anemia and cirrhosis of the liver was that he had not heard of them."[6]

Broadcasting was a little more careful, with "continuity"

departments in all the networks to make sure commercials stayed within the bounds of what would be acceptable to the government, because the licenses of the affiliated stations ran for three years only and had to be renewed. But the stations were not permitted (by law) to censor what a politician might say as part of an election campaign. (They also could not be held liable for any resulting damages from the abuse of their frequency by a politician.) The issue is in fact a complicated one. Freedom of the press, A. J. Liebling once said, "belongs to the man who owns one."[7] And a unanimous Supreme Court in the *Red Lion* case stressed "the right of every individual to speak, write or publish. . . . The licensee . . . has no constitutional right to monopolize a radio frequency to the exclusion of his fellow citizens."[8] This argument, of course, does not apply to print promotion or advertising, for constitutional reasons. *Good Housekeeping* flaunts a banner proclaiming that it permits advertising only for those products that have earned its "seal of approval." In practice, despite *Red Lion,* advertisers do not have any right to put their message on a licensee's frequency, and the networks, of course, worry less about the Supreme Court than about Congress.

Worries about suitability, indeed, run almost entirely the other way: the advertiser is concerned about whether this medium provides a healthy ambiance for his message. One of the great stories of recent years tells of Rupert Murdoch's monstrous efforts to build the circulation of the New York *Post* up to and beyond the numbers of *The New York Times.* Having reached his goal, he sent his director of advertising sales off to Bloomingdale's, which had no interest in his numbers. "Their readers," the Bloomingdale's man said, "are our customers. Your readers are our shoplifters."

Back in the 1950s, I was on the staff of *Esquire* magazine, then regarded as a dirty book. It had once been denied a second-class mailing permit by Roosevelt's Postmaster General, Frank Walker. Much of the reputation was political in origin: *Esquire*'s owner, David Smart, had launched a newsmagazine called *Ken* in the 1930s, featuring reports by Ernest Hemingway and Dorothy Thompson from the Loyalist side of the Spanish Civil War; Patrick Joseph Cardinal Hayes had used the Catholic Church's influence to get all *Ken*'s publisher's magazines banned from New York City newsstands and punished in Washington.

In my time, management was in a state about the arrival of competition in the men's market in the form of *Playboy,* and I argued we should be grateful. As a dirty book, we had been denied much advertising we should normally get — travel advertising, for example: we couldn't sell Cunard, though we had the best travel writer in the country in Dick Joseph, and the shipping company was using his line about "getting there is half the fun" as the centerpiece of all their advertising. Once *Playboy* cut under us in the morality rankings, we would get travel and automobile advertising that had been denied us. This turned out to be true, and the burst of advertising that came to the magazine in the late 1950s made possible *Esquire*'s efflorescence as the prototypical book of the 1960s under the leadership of the infinitely curious Harold Hayes. (George Lois, art director turned agency boss, made his reputation designing the *Esquire* covers, many of which were memorably provocative: for example, the supposed portrait of Nikita Khrushchev being debriefed in a CIA office.)

Much of what has been most pernicious about advertiser influence on communications media grows out of this endless search for suitability, the avoidance of anything that might upset the reader or listener or viewer, or give rise to

uncomfortable thoughts about the product being advertised. The classic case was a *Playhouse 90* episode in the
golden age of television, a drama dealing with the
Nuremberg Trials, sponsored in part by the natural gas
industry. "In going through the script," an agency man told
a House committee, "we noticed gas referred to in half a
dozen places that had to do with the death chambers. This
was just an oversight on somebody's part."[9] In February
1991, the networks complained bitterly that advertisers
wouldn't buy minutes in reports on the Gulf War, and CBS
threatened to stop covering the war to protect the network's
profits. Pressure groups lean on advertisers all the time to
prevent both serious and frivolous presentations of subjects
relating to sexual behavior, detrimental to "family values,"
and so on.

Self-interested pressure is by no means unknown. Mobil
Oil pulled its advertising from the *Wall Street Journal* after
the paper's unfavorable coverage of a lawsuit involving the
chairman of the company. In spring 1990, the U.S. Treasury
Department proposed to Congress that some arcane rules
be changed to impose some of the risks of its own activities
on the Federal National Mortgage Association, a "government sponsored enterprise" that puts its profits in the
pockets of its stockholders while relying on government
guarantees to absorb possible losses. FNMA was in the midst
of a giant advertising campaign in all media to show the
public how much nice affordable housing resulted from its
activities. *The Economist* magazine ran a favorable story
about the Treasury's proposals, and FNMA pulled its ads
from the magazine. The magazine was read by all the foreign money men who bought Fannie Mae's paper, but it had
become no longer suitable.

For many years, well into the television era, advertisers

insured the suitability of the programs in which their commercials appeared, by paying their agencies to produce the
shows as well as the ads. As late as 1951, Neil Borden, professor of advertising at the Harvard Business School, could
write in his best-selling textbook, "In constructing radio or
television programs, the advertiser is, in a sense, his own
editor, building his own audience appeal."[10] They wanted
more than just suitability: they wanted gratitude. Shows
bore the sponsor's name: *The Colgate Comedy Hour, The
Bell Telephone Hour, The Voice of Firestone, Armstrong
Circle Theater, The Texaco Star Theater.* Gillette sponsored
the World Series all by itself. *Brands,* not companies, sponsored shows — *The Jack Benny Program* was sponsored by
Jell-O, not by General Foods. The network operated
through options to buy time on their member stations, and
required all advertisers to buy a basic list of stations if they
wanted to put the show on the network. Stations not on the
basic list might or might not receive the show, depending
on whether they wished to pick up the line charges, and
they wouldn't be paid. The network made money by a
markup on the member stations' time, and also by the rent
of the facilities in which the shows were produced.

The advertiser paid a fixed price for time from a rate
card, gained from the hits, and lost from the bombs. Hits
could be astonishingly effective in moving a product that
benefited by their halo. Revlon was just another cosmetics
company before *The $64,000 Question* hit emotionally
involved viewers with emotionally oriented advertising.
Other hits might not suit their sponsors' purpose: Philip
Morris withdrew from the sponsorship of *I Love Lucy* when
research indicated most of its viewers didn't smoke. (This
may be why the show has done so well in reruns: the people who watched it tended to live longer.) The network

always had an interest in how well a show did in terms of audience size, because the value of the time before and after would be a function of its ratings (*The Voice of Firestone,* the last of the middlebrow "good music" shows, lost its time slot even though Firestone was prepared to keep paying the freight, because the network said it couldn't afford the drop-off in audience). And the affiliates cared deeply, because the prices they could charge for the "adjacencies," the minutes the network left them to sell for themselves, were a function of the popularity of the programs. But until the late 1950s, it was the advertisers who owned the air. If a time slot didn't sell to an advertiser, the network would produce a show itself, and seek to recoup the cost by selling individual minutes within it.

Color and production values and Hollywood came to television, and the prices got too high for advertisers to pay. The first stop was joint sponsorship — two brands per program, one of them receiving two of the three commercial minutes in the half-hour one week, the other receiving the two minutes the next week. If the agency couldn't sell a half, the network sold it. The networks guaranteed advertisers "protection" — no commercial for a competing product would be permitted within fifteen minutes before or after a sponsor's show. Soon everyone began to see the virtues of Pat Weaver's "magazine concept" — minutes sold in network shows like pages in magazines, with the network responsible for the program. In 1959, heightening the networks' understanding that in the end they had to be responsible for what went out over their channels, the quiz show scandal put NBC and CBS, not Revlon or the producers, in the congressional doghouse.

By the mid-1960s, the networks had taken control of the time and the programming. Advertisers bought minutes in the shows the network decided it wished to put in this time slot, and the advertiser had a continuing right neither to the show nor to the placement of the minute. In the early years, the networks announced the schedule for the next fall at ceremonials in February (CBS, with pride of leadership, opened the game on Lincoln's Birthday). Advertisers and the television experts at the agencies — a shrinking cadre, now that the agencies were no longer producing the shows — went to the screenings of the pilots for the new programs. For more years than now seems plausible, the advertisers continued to take the risks: the price they paid for this minute on that show in this time slot was fixed per insertion per year, just like the price for a schedule of magazine pages. Not having control over the shows, the advertisers and agencies soon demanded that they be freed of such risk, and the networks began selling their time not by the minute but by the ratings, the number of homes exposed to the message because the set was tuned to this show. Rather than refund the money, however, the network would give the advertiser a "make-good," another spot with a similar audience large enough to compensate for what the first spot failed to deliver. These "make-goods" in many cases would simply be added to the number of commercial minutes broadcast, "cluttering" the airwaves, and probably reducing the value of all television commercials.

The move to a guaranteed audience for the commercial was a sea change, neither felt nor understood by either party to the transaction. Ultimately in a market economy, it's the party who takes the risks of a decision, gains when he's right, and loses when he's wrong, who will and should control the decision. The advertising agency that merely chose among the minutes embedded in the offerings of the networks had a far less influential position in the world than the agency that had once supplied the programs.

From the public point of view, the bottom line almost certainly showed a loss. Different advertisers had different objectives when they purchased TV time: Bell Telephone, General Electric, DuPont, U.S. Steel were using broadcasting to affirm their own images rather than to sell cigarettes or soap or soft drinks. Advertiser control, for all its problems, offered more diversity. At the networks themselves, the old belief that some part of the schedule should be given to "sustaining" programs of educational, artistic, or informational value was shattered by the new reality that all minutes were equal and that the failure to sell any of them would reduce corporate profits. Though ambition outran (and recollection outruns) reality, there was a golden age. "I suppose the mistake we made," Bill Paley once said in the presence of his then news director Fred Friendly, "was in ever going public."[11]

Pat Weaver, then out of both businesses, under contract to a new company called Subscription Television (STV) to develop a pay-per-use cable system in California with the Los Angeles Dodgers and the San Francisco Giants among his partners, made great claims for his era and great criticisms of what was happening when he testified before the House Committee on Interstate and Foreign Commerce in 1963. "[A] professional group of managers who knew show business, who knew advertising, and who knew communications, were able to solve the problems of getting more and more revenue to put on better and better shows for larger and larger audiences. In the process they were able to reach out to get and hold the attention of even the light viewers, while introducing the vast audiences to experiences beyond their previous experiences and expectations. The whole thrust of this grand design was not to give the public what it wanted, in the trite, limited sense, but to use television as a porthole through which to see the real world including the world of entertainment and make believe, but also the world of problems and real people.

"We said that it was our responsibility to introduce our audience of all Americans in all homes to those adventures of the mind and soul that come from the kinds of entertainment and activity that have been considered more civilized, more literate, more cultural, more worthwhile than the more popular arts. [The public] wants to be sold on the better, not the worse. ... The change in television has come about because in the interaction of the elements in the business, there is not enough fighting for better things with intelligence based on experience and knowledge. ... The belief that the advertiser is the heavy in what we see on the screen is wrong. Naturally no advertiser wants to present programs to make enemies instead of friends, but advertisers supported a sold-out schedule of great programming for many years. ... The talent agents and the program companies do what the buyer wants, and the buyer is the network."[12]

2.

The 1950s and early 1960s were the great years of peacetime nationalism in the United States. The whole country watched the same entertainments — some 93 percent of Homes Using Television, which meant more than half the nation's households, were tuned to the networks in the evening. The advertising culture was still print-oriented, and the largest fraction of print advertising for brands (as distinguished from retail advertising) went into "general-circulation" magazines. In 1958, *Life* alone had revenues from the sale of pages to advertisers that totaled 70 percent of all the money spent on the CBS network. An advertiser could get his message into two-thirds of all the homes in the United States with a buy of *Life, Look,* and the *Saturday Evening Post.* Network willingness to let advertisers buy only a "basic network" had given the magazines an advantage in reaching middle America. When the networks started selling minutes, however, and denominating the price of those minutes in terms of cost per thousand homes delivered, all the affiliated stations were automatically included in the buy.

The shift to the sale of "participations" rather than sponsorship also gave television a significant systemic advantage that was not well understood in either the television or the magazine industry. Purchasing space in a magazine, advertisers received a guarantee that nobody else would be able to buy similar space for less, except as specified by the scale of volume discounts on the rate card. But broadcast time was perishable. Minutes that were not purchased in the grand buying spree before the beginning of the season were up for sale until the instant of their broadcast. Jerry Jordan, remembering his years as advertising manager of American Airlines, said, "I bought lots of minutes this morning for tonight." By the conventions of the business, such minutes could be sold for whatever they might bring. "The sales proposals department," said Jim Shaw, who headed it for ABC in the early 1970s, "makes the shoe to fit on Cinderella's foot before midnight." At the margin, which is (as economists know) where things happen, business moved from print to broadcast.

Television network time sold in two ways — in an "up-front" market, with advertisers buying a package containing a season's worth of minutes, and in a "scatter" market, where the minutes still available were sold off closer to their arrival on the clock. The price was expressed, always, as a cost per thousand viewers as measured by a ratings service. Up-front minutes were sold in programs, not as a collection of points in time; they could be preempted at ninety days' notice without penalty if the network wished to put a different "special" show into this program's time slot. Minutes in the "special" were usually part of the scatter market.

Supply and demand factors are very different in the two markets. Advertisers come to the up-front buying period with "media plans" that call for a certain minimum of pressure for each brand, and their agencies have orders to guarantee that pressure. If the market is soft, the buyer can wait; if the market is tight, the network can hold back a few spots and make it seem tighter. But these people do business with each other every year, and on both sides there are relationships to be cultivated. The man who buys at auction buys once; the man who buys at negotiated prices may get first grab at the best stuff — next year if not this year. Up-front is a highly concentrated market: more than half the up-front minutes are sold to a roster of less than twenty corporations.

For the cost-per-thousand number is by no means the whole story. It is understood that a thousand women aged eighteen to forty-nine watching a hit show are more valuable to an advertiser than a thousand women eighteen to forty-nine watching late at night. The show that is talked about at the beauty parlor sells more soap. A hit gives the network salesmen sweeteners for their packages; you don't get into the hits if you buy in the scatter market, or if you try to chisel around the package that's offered. "It's always been true in this business," says Dan Burke, C.E.O. of ABC–Cap Cities, "that you make money when the profits from the successful top third of the schedule more than pay off what you lose from the rest of the schedule." Minutes in the great events — the Super Bowl, the Academy Awards, the World Series — are presumably sold separately from the rest of the schedule, and their price reflects a higher cost-per-thousand. "Campaigns," says BBDO's Rosenshine with some distaste, "have been built around the fact that you had a commercial in the Super Bowl." But even here a top salesman well placed in the politics of his network may be able to add such a goody to a package. Advertisers in its normal schedule of televised pro football games get priority from the network that has the Super Bowl this year.

Part of the up-front market has always been seasonal rather than year-round: the florists want time before Mother's Day; the soft-drink makers hit hardest in the summertime; Weight Watchers wants the weeks right after New Year's Day when people are thinking about their resolutions; the makers of toys and fake champagne and the miners of diamonds push for the weeks before Christmas. Much of this can be accommodated by alterations in other people's packages (the Weight Watchers buys are especially easy, because most advertisers regard the first couple of weeks of the year as a dead time). The rest becomes part of the scatter market, to be acquired usually a month or two before broadcast, as sales move from projected to actual, competitors execute unexpected strategies, and budgets are refined. In a normal season, something between a third and a half of all network minutes are sold on the scatter basis. If an advertiser decides he doesn't need all the spots he acquired up-front, the network will often try to accommodate him and sell some portion of his schedule together with its own inventory in the scatter market; but if nobody else buys, the original purchaser is stuck with the inventory. The 1960s were the glory time for the television networks: the videotape machine, a tremendous technological accomplishment, relieved the medium of the need to process film; the satellites flew, making possible worldwide instantaneous news coverage; audiences grew. And in the inflationary prosperity of the years 1962–1969, advertisers were willing to pay more for time. Agencies were delighted: "It was awfully easy," said Ed Ney while chairman of Young & Rubicam, "to walk up to that supermarket counter — and there are only three counters — and say, I need eighty million people the third Tuesday in February." But clouds were visible on the horizon. Seeking to preserve some local presence in programming, the Federal Communications Commission limited the number of hours in each "daypart" that could be optioned by networks for national shows. With access to Hollywood film libraries and syndicated shows the networks had already run — and with growing local news telecasts — the stations were becoming more serious rivals for the national advertiser's dollar. When the economy turned in 1970, it was the networks that took it on the chin. And then the government struck a body blow at the economics of the medium, prohibiting broadcast advertising of cigarettes after January 1, 1971. That spring, prices in the up-front market dropped by 25 percent. But the government also took away from the networks the 7:30-to-8:00 P.M. half-hour, which meant that each network had 21 fewer minutes to sell, and the prices recovered.

In the 1970s, moreover, the sales departments of the networks did a brilliant job of bringing in new advertisers. Some of this was made possible by a reduction in prices that came with the move from sixty-second to thirty-second commercials, but most of it was consciously planned and superbly executed hard selling. Food, clothing, travel, cameras, all the brands and services that had spent their money on magazines because coated paper and color printing gave the feel of the product; financial services that advertised (if at all) on radio and in newspapers; corporations looking for reputation now that gratitude had been taken away — all were worked over, all were sold. William Firman, ABC's vice president in charge of marketing in 1971, described what he was doing and what he was going to do: "I started in 1969 from scratch, from ground zero. The idea was to create new dollars for the medium. Television had been delinquent here, because people didn't have the time to devote to it; these were difficult dollars to come by. When you talk to one of these companies that have never been on television, they'll say, 'I only want to reach one hundred people in the whole country — that's all, just one hundred people.' 'Well,' I'll say, 'are you interested in recruitment? in morale? in Congress? in stockholder relations?' — and by the time I get through it makes a hell of a lot more than one hundred people. But they know the names of the trade publications, and they don't know us from Adam's off ox.

"I make a presentation at lunch in sixteen major advertising cities across the country. Subject: 'Televised sports as a way to reach the nation's influentials.' That starts the dialogue. Sports is only one thing we do — we have talk shows, news, documentaries. Then I show them a reel we've stolen, of corporate commercials — Clark Equipment, 3M, North American Rockwell, GE for recruitment — and a slide presentation, *Fortune's 500,* with success stories.

"But the whole game with these cats is *extensional thrust.* If you can make it work for him off the air, you keep him stimulated. Say a guy buys a documentary. We can arrange to have key people preview it at nine-thirty in the morning at studios all across the country. Elmer Lower [then ABC News president] gets on camera just before it rolls, and says how pleased we are to have this company associated with it. Or he buys *Issues and Answers* and he can come to the studio for the show, have a cocktail or lunch with the guest. Then he gets home the next day and he says, 'Hey! Do you know who I had a drink with in Washington? . . . *Melvin Laird* [then Richard Nixon's Secretary of Defense]!

"Maybe he buys NCAA Football. We can get him tickets; he can take his key people. Ditto National Football League. Golf. We have a hospitality tent at the big tournament. He can play a round with Byron Nelson, meet Jack Nicklaus. When it's done, he can have special film, news clips, audio tapes, fliers. . . . "[13] This worked. In the 1960s, the NCAA telecasts had four sponsors, one for each quarter of each game, for the entire season. By 1980, the sponsor list ran four single-spaced pages. Interestingly, the networks had to do this by themselves: the agencies didn't have the access.

3.

All sales, says the old cliché, are local sales, and an even older cliché says there is no accounting for tastes. At the height of the mania for national advertising, there were pockets of resistance where agencies and research firms stressed the variations in market shares of even the most national products when the market was broken down by geographic or socioeconomic categories. National mass media audiences paid for according to a cost-per-thousand calculation inevitably waste most of the money, because most of the people reached are not going to be customers for the advertised brand. The magazine market began to fragment as early as the 1950s, and over the next twenty years the general-circulation dominoes fell one by one — *Collier's, Saturday Evening Post, Look, Life.* In their place came many more magazines with much smaller, more narrowly directed circulation. Advertisers would pay more per page because a much higher proportion of the readership was interested in the brands they were advertising. Radio, once the general-circulation medium par excellence, became intensely specialized: hard rock, soft rock, jazz, easy listening, good music, classical, religious, talk, news. The trick was to match the Values and Life Styles (VALS) of the users of this product and the consumers of these media.

Even on television, of course, the nature of the programs determined which advertisers wanted which commercial breaks. News was for health and geriatric products, the average age of the news audience being high (and the average education level low, by the way: people who read easily are still more likely to rely on newspapers for news). Soap operas were for housewifely products, mothers of the young being home (mostly); sports was for beer, automobiles, travel, business machinery, and corporate image, plus cigars while they were legal and chewing tobacco for a while after that. For the prime-time schedule as a whole, the measurement that counted was the coarse mesh of women eighteen to forty-nine: the samples used by the rating firms were large enough to give a reasonably good idea of how many people in that category were watching each show.

The larger question was how to handle geographical variations in the era of the nationwide mass medium. If an advertiser's brand had a 16 percent share of market in one city and 11 percent in the other, and the ratings for the television shows in which he bought minutes were 11 percent for the first and 16 percent in the second, rational planning would call for supplementing the pressure in the city where the ratings were too low. And, slowly but surely, all the national media began to offer some kind of local option. The first was the *Wall Street Journal*. As early as the 1950s, the *Journal* scattered its printing plants around the country, setting type by electronic message in many cities simultaneously, to guarantee tomorrow morning's delivery of tomorrow morning's paper; and as part of this process developed the capacity for selling ad space separately to run in different parts of the country. Somewhat grudgingly, the networks from the early 1960s began offering some regional breakdowns (the manufacturer of antifreeze really did not want the southern stations that were carrying the football game), and magazines did the same from the latter part of that decade.

Newspapers, interestingly, having consolidated to one per city in the confines of most old cities, moved both toward greater differentiation of their product — separate sections for different neighborhoods and suburbs — and toward greater hospitality to national advertising designed to reach all households. The number of big-city papers nosedived while the number of suburban papers soared as the shopping centers denuded the downtowns. Improved folding machinery and computerized distribution lists permitted papers like the Miami *Herald* to offer a Spanish section only to those homes where Spanish was spoken. Meanwhile, national advertisers, especially retail chains, used newspapers as carriers of preprinted advertising supplements inserted in weekend papers. The "manager of field media services" for Sears told a conference of newspaper financial executives in 1986 that for Sears the per-page costs of printing and distributing these preprints *through* the papers were one-eighth what the papers charged them for a page the papers would print themselves.[14] To the extent to which these preprints were prepared in-house by advertisers that had previously used advertising agencies to produce and distribute stereotypes for newspaper use, the agencies were losers.

For some in the industry, the proliferation of media, especially targeted media, is the agencies' great opportunity. Y&R's Georgescu likes to point out that in 1989 there were 800 different magazines in West Germany — and 500 *new* magazines, less than one year old, in the United States. Keeping up with the rapidity of media change was a costly activity that would not be worth the price to the individual advertisers. But agencies can spread that cost over their entire range of clients, adding significant value to their services. The case is attractive, with the usual caveat: the provision of such services has become increasingly capital-intensive, requiring large computers and investment in their programming. For clients, such investments are routine; for agencies, they are still extraordinary. Keith Reinhard's "second creative department" — for this is what Georgescu means, too — requires a research base of a kind the agencies have become increasingly reluctant to finance.

Advertising in 1990 stood at an intersection of geography and interest group, with a general assumption at the agencies that the road to mass media was petering out. That spring, in a rerun week, the networks' share of Homes Using Television fell to 56 percent. Then ABC-Cap Cities launched a drive to reduce its risks of not delivering audiences of the size assumed when the up-front contract was signed. "Make-good," the network announced, would be given, not on the basis of Nielsen audience numbers but according to ratios relating the show to historic audience trend lines. We shall look at the arguments, which are research-based, in the next chapter. For now, we consider only the politics. After an initial statement that advertisers and agencies could not accept the loss of so vital a security blanket, the commentators pulled back and began arguing that large advertisers that needed the pressure would have to go along because they had no other place to put so much money. And until the recession caught up with them, the networks had a good up-front season.

Still, the influence of the networks seems sure to diminish through the decade. The satellite has freed the local stations from dependence on the networks for national and international news; many local stations have become part of consortia that send each other their coverage of what happens in their bailiwick, coverage they often consider better than what the networks offer. In the big cities, two-and-a-half and even three hours of local news programs a day have become routine, and national advertisers buy those minutes not only as supplements to but sometimes as substitutes for network minutes. Game shows, films, syndicated reruns of network shows — many affiliated stations now carry less than eight hours a day of network feed.

Even more important is the continuing growth of cable, now in more than half the nation's homes and still spreading. From the point of view of station *owners,* this is deadly competition. "The founding fathers of the local stations are gone," says James Joyella of the Television Bureau of Advertising. "They sold to the greater fool people, who assumed the franchise had to keep growing in value, because there was a government restriction on entry. That string has run out. There's a cable channel in Rochester, WGRC, looks just like a TV station, has call letters to prove it, and they do everything a station does."

More frightening than this doppelgänger, however, is the specialized channel. Like special-interest magazines and format radio, cable fragments audience. "If the advertising industry had to invent the perfect segmentation tool, it would be called cable," said Eugene Secunda, a fast-talking little man with a cigar and a New York accent, when he was developing program ideas for N. W. Ayer in 1982; he identified himself as "a Broadway guy, a movie guy now in the advertising end of the entertainment and leisure business." At one point, agencies expected to be active in producing programs for cable, and Procter & Gamble, which had never stopped producing daytime shows, put several toes in the water. But the networks, with their much greater resources, moved in on the program-supplying end of the medium. Between sports, movies, and network reruns, there wasn't much time left. And the costs of producing for cable were more than an advertiser wished to undertake, especially for the rather small and geographically accidental audiences the cable channel could offer.

The pay channels did some of their own production, having perforce recognized that the cable medium is hospitable to repeats at short intervals. The free channels ran increasingly like the networks of old, as the exclusive suppliers of programs to the local head ends. What was different was that the broadcast network had always paid the station for the time it used, while in cable the owners of the channel had to pay the program supplier.

Ahead lies the adventure of "interactive cable," with the control box empowered to send messages to the head end.

Interpublic (McCann-Erickson and Lintas) in particular has concentrated on developing the potential of interactive. The ideal time for its introduction is the 1992 Olympics, when millions of viewers will be deeply grateful for the opportunity to escape the garbage interludes and jingoistic choices of network coverage and make their own choice among, say, four events in progress. In addition to choosing the sport they wished to follow, fortunate possessors of the new cable feedback box would choose from a menu of possible advertisers — or perhaps, at a higher price (this one is highly controversial within the agency), no commercials at all. People who choose to see commercials for automobiles or air conditioners or cruises will find themselves not only watching such advertising on their screens but opening mail with further suggestions about how to buy such goods and services.

Interactive cable not merely multiplies the efficiency of advertising, it closes the information loop now being woven by the Norns of the research firms, the credit card companies, and the supermarkets. As optical memories come on line, it will be possible for the supercomputers to merge their records of who sees what advertising (data from newspaper and magazine subscription records, interactive cable, direct-mail companies) with their records of who (credit or debit or check-cashing cards with mag stripes) buys what merchandise (checkout counters and department store cash-register stations that read the Universal Product Code labels and stickers affixed to every product). Don Pepper, who left Lintas for Chiat/Day/Mojo, suggests that before the twenty-first century arrives, everyone with disposable income will be a cable subscriber, and all cable subscribers will have a choice of at least 100 basic-service channels. For, say, $15 a month, the subscriber chooses not only his programs but also products for which he wishes to see the commercials; the computers will keep a record of his choices and make the information available at a price to the marketing community. For $50 a month, he gets the same programs and choice of commercials, but he buys privacy in the form of a guarantee that no record will be kept of his preferences in products being advertised. For $75 a month, he can get all the programs without any commercials at all.

That would change a lot more than the advertising business.

CHAPTER FIVE

Research

MOST ADVERTISING is planned, created, and put before the public in the hope of selling goods and services. But from very early on, it was generally agreed that you couldn't tell how many sales your advertising had in fact produced. Stores know better than manufacturers. James Joyella, president of the Television Bureau of Advertising, says that when he ran CBS sales, he never hired anyone who hadn't been through the mill selling broadcast time to local retailers, because only the retail salesmen really know in their gut that advertising works. But even the stores have always had to admit uncertainty. The department-store owner John Wanamaker said (probably knowing that Lord Leverhulme had made the same comment in England), "I know half the money I spend on advertising is wasted, but I can never find out which half."

There were a few exceptions. Bakeries and newspaper publishers made daily deliveries of bread and papers. Nabisco, as the extension of a bakery, always knew how many biscuits and cookies it sold, because its own drivers went directly to the stores (not to anybody's warehouse) and stocked the shelves. The various milk marketing boards that bought the raw milk from the farmers of a government-specified milkshed knew how much beverage milk was being bought because the farmer was paid according to how much of his milk was used for just plain milk drinking (top price) and how much for milk products like butter, ice cream, cheese (lower prices). But the only large category of advertisers who knew precisely what they got for their money were those who sold by mail. In its simplest form, mail-order advertising put a coupon in the ad (the bottom right-hand corner was all but invariable after 1900, an interesting example of the self-reinforcing custom). The customer clipped the coupon and sent it in with his payment, and the advertiser shipped him the merchandise.

Comparing the total payments the ad drew against the cost of the goods actually sold, the advertising, and the "handling and mailing," the advertiser knew beyond peradventure of a doubt whether this ad for this product paid off. He could compare the relative value of different advertising media simply by counting the orders that came in to different addresses or box numbers from the same ads in different newspapers and magazines. And he could compare the relative quality of advertising slogans and ads themselves by arranging "split runs" of newspapers or magazines, in which one ad would run in half a particular issue, and the other ad would run in the other half. Again, just counting the orders to the different addresses or box numbers would give you all the information you wanted.

One of the three strains of advertising research derived from the methods of the mail-order practitioners. John Caples was an Annapolis graduate who came out of the Bell System's engineering department in 1925 and almost immediately gave a mail-order music instruction program the great headline: "They Laughed When I Sat Down at the Piano but When I Started to Play . . . !" He became director of copy testing at BBDO, where he remained active into the 1970s, and relied almost entirely on split runs to test ads that were designed to sell goods in stores, not by mail order. He thought coupon returns a measurement equally valuable for either purpose: "Suppose I have to write an ad to sell a book by mail order. And then suppose I were writing an ad to get someone to go to Brentano's and buy the book. I'd use the same headline for both. With a few exceptions the same rules hold for both mail-order advertising and general advertising."[1]

But there are, obviously, combinations and permutations. Book clubs and magazines have been among the most persistent users of mail-order. By rule of thumb, a book club makes little or no money out of a single year's membership, and a magazine is a loser if the new subscriber takes the publication for no longer than the term of the specially priced introductory deal offered by the ad. Mutual funds solicit requests for their "offering statements," and brokers use ads with coupons to provide lists of names for salesmen. Here the effectiveness of the advertising cannot be measured entirely by the number of coupons returned (KEEP TIMES SQUARE GREEN!), and must be correlated with the number of returned coupons that actually generate a sale. And profitability is hard to measure here, too, because only the active customer makes money for the broker, and only the inactive customer makes money for the mutual fund company with varied products.

Moreover, both the mail-order medium and the advertising approach may be subject to laws of diminishing returns, which apply at different rates in different situations. An ad that yields 500 new orders month after month after month may be more profitable than an ad that yields a thousand orders the first month, then 650, then 300, then 175, still spiraling down. Obviously, there is much to be said for an ad that rapidly milks a high fraction of the potential customers for this product who read this magazine and are drawn by this ad — but you have to know enough to pull it quickly, or perhaps find another selling proposition that can start the cycle again.

Right now is the heyday of what it has become fashionable to call "direct response" advertising. Technological developments have greatly cut the costs of such advertising, extended the reach, heightened the yield. The introduction of the "800" telephone number reduced exponentially the get-up-and-go a customer had to display to order the product. The spread of credit cards eliminated the nuisance of both C.O.D. payment and check handling. The arrival of cable television with its narrowly directed programming lowered the costs of reaching likely customers. And the installation of computer memories meant that far more elaborate and detailed "lists" of customers could be kept (and sold, and swapped, and bought).

Most of the big agencies have become involved in direct response, usually through the purchase of an existing mail-order house, though Ogilvy and Leo Burnett have essentially grown their own. Perhaps the most interesting story is that of Burnett, which waited until the late 1980s, and took the plunge only after its biggest client, Philip Morris, asked for mailings. "Our feeling was that junk mail wasn't advertising," says Rick Fizdale, the agency's creative director, a man in his early fifties with a splendid Gene Shalit mustache. "Aw shit, we don't want to do that." But Philip Morris said they wanted to have some direct-mail work done by people who really understood the brand, and among all its tobacco brands, General Foods, Miller Beer, and Kraft, Philip Morris spent more money than any other client. Fizdale decided that there should be no difference in pay or status or duties between the general advertising team and their direct-response compères. "Direct isn't a separate profit center," Fizdale says. "It doesn't have its own books. It won't have its own clients; it will do our clients. Why can't our creative group write a decent letter? They design an ad. Why can't they design an envelope?"

Mostly, the direct-response divisions of the big agencies run as separate enterprises inside the shell of the corporation. The first major transaction, in the 1970s, brought Young & Rubicam Lester Wunderman and what is now called Wunderman Worldwide, with Wunderman himself still in the saddle at age seventy. Y&R usually retires people at sixty, but neither the chairman, Ed Ney, nor his successor, Alex Kroll, could see why the rules should apply to Wunderman, and so long as Lester gets his three months a year in the south of France (where the computer and the fax machine keep him as close to the office as he cares to be), he's happy to stay in the business.

"People in direct marketing talk about aiming their message directly at the customer, but I don't believe it," Wunderman, a small, exuberant man with a long face and not much hair, says, waxing enthusiastic in the windowless little conference room off his office in the most unfashionable part of New York's Chelsea. "We still do mailings only to people who are *suspects* — an old sales manager's word. What we should want is *prospects,* people who are not only eligible to buy but actually in the market." Wunderman's most breathtaking claim is that direct-response technology has made his sort of advertising the best way to build not individual sales but repeat sales and brand loyalty. He can illustrate his point with General Foods' Gevalia Coffee, fancy Swedish coffee sold exclusively by mail. The customer puts in an order that produces a new can delivered every month or two months. It arrives in the mail without further ado. "General advertising," Wunderman says, "is Cyrano. He comes under your window and sings; people get used to it and ignore it. But if Roxane responds, there's a relationship. We move the brand relationship up a notch. Advertising becomes a dialogue that becomes an invitation to a relationship."

Wunderman does the Book-of-the-Month Club advertising, and has done it for roughly forty years. "The thing about Book-of-the Month Club," he says, "is that people feel a moral commitment, and they will fulfill their moral commitments. Advertisers should build these moral commitments. They should say, 'If you make a commitment to buy Pampers, we'll give you a crib.' Or, 'If you commit to buy Maxwell House, we'll give you a coffeepot.' Or just a badge saying, 'You're a nice person.' We should pay off for loyalty, not for trying the brand, which is what price promotion does. For me, the main component of a brand is its potential for relationship and dialogue. Retailing is a business of discontinuities. We have to be a business of continuities, binding manufacturers and consumers to each other in a moral contract."

People are prepared to respond to messages on television more than anyone realizes, Wunderman argues. "French TV had a documentary on Louis XVI with a crawl down the bottom," he says, remembering where he was on Bastille Day in 1989, "and the crawl said, 'What shall we do with Louis?' The choice was send him to jail, kill him, set him free. More than a million people with Mintels responded — and, after all, everybody knows what they did with Louis."

Nevertheless, when push comes to shove, what Wunderman is talking about is data-based marketing, and the interactive communication aspect is merely part of the data frame. Because we know the customer's previous purchases, we can have great confidence that what we are aiming at him is what he wants. For direct-mail purposes, because every recipient can become a customer without leaving home, the data base can be pretty small. For selling through stores, which may not be conveniently located for many of those who get the mailing, it must be much larger. But now, as we shall see in the last part of this chapter, it *can* be much larger. This thread in the research fabric will color all thinking about selling in the 1990s, but first let us look at conventional old threads that remain the warp and the woof of *advertising,* as distinct from marketing, research.

1.

Research on Audience

In 1912, at the age of twenty-nine, Daniel Starch at the University of Iowa made a study of teacher grading of adolescents' papers. He gave copies of two student papers in English to 142 English teachers, copies of a geometry paper to 118 math teachers. The range of grades on one English paper ran from 50 to 98; on the other, it was 64 to 98. The math grades showed a "probable error" of 7.5 points — that is, if the "true mark" (the average of all the marks given by the teachers) was 85, half the teachers would give the paper less than 77.5 or more than 92.5.[2] Six years later, having moved on from educational research, Starch applied the same commonsense cleverness to advertising. He published a paper arguing that the only advertising that worked was advertising consumers noticed and remembered. Later, in 1923, he wrote, "An advertisement, to be successful:

"a. Must be seen.

"b. Must be read.

"c. Must be believed.

"d. Must be remembered.

"e. Must be acted upon."[3]

As Timothy Joyce pointed out while still research director of J. Walter Thompson in England in the 1960s, this "is probably an unsatisfactory model, if only because it implies that the effects of each individual opportunity to see an advertisement are independent, and does not allow for 'build-up' . . . [or for] increasing returns or diminishing returns."[4] But it was for some years the only game in town. In 1931, Starch put his argument to commercial use, launching a service to tell agents and advertisers how many people could "recognize" their ad in magazines they claimed to have read.

This was perhaps the most labor-intensive activity in the history of social science research. Interviewers were sent out into the streets with packets of recent issues of some 24 magazines. They would ask passersby which of these magazines they had read, and then painstakingly, page by page, go through the magazines noting down whether or not the respondent "recognized" the ad. Interviewers started flipping pages at a different place in the magazine for each respondent, to make sure that burnout did not occur in the same section. A respondent might be asked to "recognize" or not recognize as many as 100 ads. For each magazine,

300 respondents would be polled for each issue. The proportions recognizing each ad were then extrapolated out to the circulation of the magazine, giving advertisers a measurement of readership per dollar spent. Starch ran a syndicated service available to all, but saved his subscribers time and energy by tailoring his reports to them to show the comparisons they would want among the readership of ads for different brands in the same product category.

These numbers were taken very seriously indeed: in the 1950s, Marion Harper, Jr., and Herta Herzog, building McCann-Erickson into a challenger for the title of World's Largest Agency, worked up a list of 178 factors that seemed to influence how high a Starch score an ad could receive. George Gallup thought up a rival system. Gallup was a less austere figure, definitely hearty and outgoing, another Iowan (this time by birth: Starch had been born in Wisconsin, in a town so completely settled by Germans that as an old man he still had a faint German accent). In the Gallup studies, a respondent was shown the cover of a magazine, asked if he had read it, and then shown a deck of cards on which were printed the names of brands advertised in this issue. If he remembered an ad for that brand, he was asked what the ad said, and what thoughts had gone through his mind when he saw it. Because this "aided recall" technique did not involve showing actual copies of the publication, it could easily be extended to broadcast, which Gallup did when research director for Young & Rubicam in the 1940s. In those days agencies paid for such work out of the commissions clients paid them, and Raymond Rubicam's successor thought Gallup too costly, pushing him out to full time work on the American Institute of Public Opinion, which he had founded while still with Y&R. The new firm of Gallup

& Robinson continued the Institute's political polling, but made their money mostly by rating media.

But the fact that people did or did not recall an ad might be quite irrelevant to its selling power. Alfred Politz, a German refugee physicist turned sociologist, liked to tell the parable of the three mirrors: one was cracked, the second was perfect and in a beautiful gilt frame, and the third was perfect but unframed. All faced an open window, and a visitor was asked to look at the wall and to say what he could see. Of the first mirror he said, "I see an old, cracked mirror." Of the second: "I see a mirror in a beautiful frame." Of the third: "I see a beautiful view out of an open window." A good ad, in other words, reflects the product favorably without attracting attention to itself.[5] Politz was an immensely clever man who loved to tear apart other people's questionnaires. He had another favorite story about the man who proved that soda made you drunk: he had changed all the other variables — used rye, Scotch, bourbon, brandy, and others — but he got drunk every time. The soda was the only constant, and therefore it was the soda that made you drunk.

The size of the audience an advertiser bought in competing media was by no means a cut-and-dried proposition. Broadcast ratings measured the number of homes tuned to a station, magazine circulation figures measured the number of magazines sold. But some of those magazines went to doctors' offices, where dozens of people might see them, and others were passed around at workplaces or among friends. So the magazines commissioned Politz, the most aggressively "scientific" of the researchers, to create a system for measuring the total readership, as against the mere circulation, of magazines. In 1952, measuring the readership of four magazines against the audiences of four radio shows and five television shows, Politz drew a sample of 8,060 households, of which 7,141 actually participated. Each household was visited every other month for a full year, by one of over 200 employees, armed with a long questionnaire.

When *Reader's Digest* began to accept advertising a couple of years later, it commissioned a separate study from Politz, measuring "reading days," arguing that the *Digest* was an especially good buy because its subscribers picked it up more often than they did other magazines. "The superficiality or the intensity of contact with the medium, the respect, the indifference, all play important roles," Politz wrote in his introduction to the final report. This study attempted a sample of more than 19,000 households, and proved the commonsense proposition that people picked up a monthly magazine more often than they picked up a weekly magazine. . . . [6] Eventually, these procedures were standardized, and one firm became a dominant factor in measuring magazine readership: Simmons Research, with a rotating panel of 40,000 homes, quizzed twice a year.

Meanwhile, broadcast ratings firms began tackling the question of who was watching. Here again, a single technique was eventually adopted: the diary, kept by households chosen by random sampling techniques and paid a little for their trouble. The two firms that maintained such panels were Chicago-based Nielsen (later to be taken over by Dun & Bradstreet) and New York–based Arbitron (acquired by Control Data Corporation). Diary reports were to be used to establish levels of viewing by locality and by demographic characteristics (such as housewives aged eighteen to forty-nine), and thus the samples had to be fairly large. Black working-class families were much less likely to keep diaries than white professional families, so interviewers made telephone calls in black neighborhoods and surveyed television viewing as it happened. (Black and Hispanic families are also paid more than white families for completing their diaries.) Various clevernesses were created to give the researchers confidence that they were not being victimized by diary-keepers who filled out the whole week on Saturday, and checked off certain shows not because they had seen them this week but because they "always" watched that show. With the passage of time, simple meters were developed to give a rudimentary check on whether the diary was being kept correctly or not.

I wrote in the 1960s, in a pamphlet for the Advertising Research Foundation called *The Intelligent Man's Guide to Broadcast Ratings,* that what we needed to get accurate ratings of what people watched was an army of ghosts, who could drift in through the walls, note down who was looking at what in each household, and drift out again. In the 1980s, the Germans created, a British firm introduced to the United States, and Nielsen rather reluctantly adopted a "people meter" that promised to be a cost-effective substitute for ghosts. Each person in the family was to log in on entering the room where the TV was playing (or on turning it on), and then log out when leaving. Getting people to accept people meters in their homes was not easy: only about 60 percent of those who turned up in the random sample Nielsen drew from the computer were willing to sign up for the two years the company required. Therefore Nielsen couldn't use the obvious enforcer of a meter that wouldn't allow the set to turn on until someone punched in as present, and was reluctant to interfere with people's viewing by placing on the screen the prompt to the viewer who hadn't told the meter he was there. Arbitron's rather different people meter did remind viewers, on the screen, that they hadn't yet punched in, and repeated the message three times in fifteen minutes. If nobody proclaimed himself present within the fifteen minutes, Arbitron assumed that nobody was watching and scratched the entry for this household.

In its lab facility in the Chicago exurb of Bannockburn in the summer of 1990, Nielsen showed off to visitors experimental systems that would completely pass the ghost test. Atop each TV set was a rectangular box about the size of a large art book, with a reddish dark glass plate running about four-fifths its length. Behind that glass plate was an infrared light and camera. The lab director Daozheng Lu explained that the earliest of these systems, called "Scan-count," simply used the reflections from the infrared beam "to count the warm body; but," he said, "the system is too complicated." Instead, Lu and his colleagues designed an infrared camera backed by a computer with a memory trained to recognize facial characteristics. Turning on the set also turns on the "infra-red face-recognition system. Works in very dark rooms," said Lu, "and household people don't see infra-red light. But we worry people will resent having face memorized by infra-red camera. We are testing reaction."

2.

Research on Products

In the 1950s and 1960s especially, agencies did product research. The test kitchens at agencies like BBDO and J. Walter Thompson were facilities as elaborate as anything the client had. Bates, with its specialty of "white-coat" advertising (lessons to the viewer from actors dressed as doctors), maintained a "technical department" to find characteristics of a product that could be advertised and also, on occasion, to develop new products for a client to make. The first director of that department, Frank Kimball, who came aboard in 1945, was the idea generator behind the much more famous Rosser Reeves, and one of the most remarkable figures in the advertising world of the glory years after World War II.

Self-educated, overweight, strong, and aggressive, with a black belt in judo, Kimball lived a bachelor life (but not without visiting ladies) in a world of weight-lifting apparatus and medical journals. He almost never came into the office, conducting his business instead at the Chemist's Club opposite the New York Public Library, where he met the university scientists and directors of research labs whose work he commissioned. He was coarse-minded to a degree shocking even to men who were not normally fastidious. "His sense of humor," Reeves recalled, "all came out of the Journal of the American Medical Association. He'd come in and say, 'I just heard a great story,' and after you heard it you'd feel sick all day." He wrote pornographic poetry and had it printed privately, and one year he sent copies of it to all the agency's clients, as a Christmas card.

Among the major products that grew out of his work was the first combination of an antihistamine with the standard APC headache remedy, to make "Super Anahist" for an ethical drug company run by a man named William Lasdon. This was not even a Bates client at the time — Kimball developed the product, commissioning Hoffmann-La Roche to work on a coating that separated the antihistamine ingredient and the other acids in the tablet, as part of a new business pitch by the agency. Lasdon's professional people were far from happy about working with an advertising agency.

"Our medical director," said Jack Hewitt, a venturer and promoter who was Lasdon's partner, "wouldn't go to meetings with the agency people. He'd say, 'That's advertising, it's dishonest, it's not professional. Then we put him on profit-sharing, and he became a businessman. He'd say, 'Well, perhaps you *could* say that....'" Kimball's best remembered contribution to a copy conference was the comment that "A good cough would help a laxative much more than vice versa."

Kimball's successor, Morris Rakieten, was perhaps an even more remarkable person to find around an advertising agency: a research biochemist with his own lab, Yale Ph.D. and M.D. While Kimball had concentrated on finding advertising slogans in the product, Rakieten would take the claims the copy department wished to make and see if the product could be changed so that the ads would be "FTC-able," solid enough in their documentation to gain approval of the government agency charged with keeping advertising honest. He even developed for Viceroy the technical demonstration of a claim that cigarette smoke in the mouth killed bacteria, but wiser heads at British-American Tobacco decided not to try that. At the height of Rakieten's influence in the agency, the copy director, Jeremy Gury, said, "Molecule manipulation is no great shakes these days — if you know what you want to say, they can change the product so you can say it."

Product-based research by an agency is a hunt for what both experts and consumers would consider the best product, and for ways to convey that perception of quality to purchasers. The attitude that the product should live up to the advertising is one of the more wholesome aspects of the business. Keith Reinhard points out that the "good neighbor" campaign has made the State Farm agent a better insurance agent; and there can be no question that when it was new, Bill Bernbach's "We Try Harder" made the Avis counter people more pleasant to the customers. All this goes far back to before the use of researchers. Calkins offered a charming example from his early days as a copywriter, when his boss brought in a photograph of a resort hotel owned by a man whose cigar company was already a client of the agency. " 'I want you,' " the boss said, " 'to write three thousand words about the kind of hotel you would like to spend your vacation at.'

"I did just that. I described a hotel where the service anticipated the wants of the guests, where the clerk was human and approachable, and the manager a sort of good angel hovering in the background. . . .

"My employer submitted my copy to his customer friend, along with a dummy of the proposed booklet. The hotel man read it with chuckles of approval.

" 'This is bully!' he exclaimed, 'but — you see — well, that isn't quite the kind of hotel I keep!'

" 'Maybe not,' retorted [my] imperturbable [boss], 'but it is the kind of hotel you should keep.' "[7]

What the agencies of the 1950s and the 1960s did was to find for their clients, in part through product research, the kind of hotel they should keep. The economics of the industry — the 15 percent commission structure and the very low level of capital investment necessary to do business — left money on the table in those days to pay for such work. And the strength of the agency relationship as then understood — the visible truth of the proposition that "we grow when the client grows" — gave agencies incentive to help advertisers find new products.

Leo Bogart reports that these fiduciary feelings began to erode as early as the 1950s. "In 1958," he told an audience at the University of Illinois in his James Webb Young address thirty years thereafter, "I was working at McCann-Erickson, which had, among others, the Chrysler account. Chrysler was known as a difficult and demanding client, resistant to research and sluggish in its marketing posture. That year the automobile business was in a deep recession and Chrysler was hurting very badly. Along with many of the other executives of the agency, I was sent out on a special project to interview automobile dealers around the country and to find out how they felt about the state of the market and about automotive advertising in general. We thought we were working on a project for Chrysler. But that's not what our boss, Marion Harper, Jr., had in mind. He used the results of that crash study to build a presentation to General Motors in a pitch for the Buick account."[8] Harper's assertion of the independence of the agency, its self-interest as separate and possibly different from the client's interest, was formalized in the first ad agency holding company, Interpublic: a holding company, clearly, had interests that might be different from those of its agency's clients.

But even the largest agencies soon could not play in the same leagues as the research departments of their growing corporate clients, who took over the research functions, one by one. Bill Phillips, C.E.O. emeritus at Ogilvy (he has caused to be placed in the corridor leading to his and Ogilvy's office in the agency's new headquarters a sign with an arrow to the "Elephants' Graveyard"), reports that as a young account executive on the Maxwell House account he sold General Foods the idea of an Elektro-Pak grind of coffee. "Not part of our job," he says, "just one of the services an agency *did*." Today, says Allen Rosenshine of the BBDO he heads, "our involvement in new product development is zero; they're not interested in our ideas."

Once they had expanded and formalized their own technical research operations, clients were no longer very interested in the free-lance activities of scientists working with advertising agencies. Meanwhile, agencies became much less interested in helping clients develop new products, in part because the sale of shares to the public, having created a market price for the stock and a chance for anybody to second-guess decisions, had made agency managements reluctant to undertake investments that would have to come out of quarterly earnings.

"We still do get heavily involved with new products from our larger clients," says Ed Meyer, C.E.O. of Grey Advertising, a multinational $3 billion-plus operation that he grew from roots in the New York fashion district, in large part through the imprimatur and satisfaction of Procter & Gamble. "After product development has come up with a product that wins consumer blind tests and is feasible to make, we will be co-venturers to some degree. Most clients have developed ways to give you some level of compensation for new products. But the compensation structure doesn't make it possible for us to do work that doesn't generate income. The fee structure doesn't let agencies make profits on new products. I need help with cash flow during the gestation period." A few agencies that are *not* publicly traded companies maintain closer relations with the experimental departments at the clients. Burnett's Fizdale claims that his people still come up with new products for Kellogg, because they are so close to the company that they know which plants have excess capacity — but that's not based on the sort of research the larger agencies did with their surplus revenues a generation ago.

3.

Research on Brands

One other set of facts touching on brands and advertising could be unearthed through research: people's evaluations of brands. Perhaps the most ingenious system for measuring these opinions was developed by Cornelius DuBois of Foote, Cone & Belding, who designed a game board with slots for "one of the best," "good," and so on. Interviewers would come around to the front door and ask householders to play the game. Another Foote, Cone test took two identical products, packaged each with one of two slogans, sampled a neighborhood with both, and then came around to ask housewives which they had liked best. There being no difference other than the slogan, the test presumably measured the relative effectiveness of the two advertising approaches.

Of course, much more than "better" or "worse" is involved in attitudes toward brands. Timothy Joyce of MRI, the U.S. subsidiary of the British MediaMark, suggested twenty-odd years ago while still a young researcher in London that human psychology created "a drive toward integration of the set of attitudes held by an individual towards a brand, with the consequence that a change in one attitude (brought about, let us suppose, by advertising) may cause changes in other attitudes, so that contradictory beliefs are not obtained. Experienced advertising people certainly know that success in registering a given point may have consequences which extend far beyond that particular point . . . for example:

"a. A bottled beer advertised with a 'manliness' platform was as a result regarded as stronger.

"b. A washing powder advertised on an 'efficiency' platform was thought less gentle to hands. . . .

"d. A hard toilet paper advertised as 'what the men in your house want' was thought of as even less comfortable than it had been before this particular campaign."[9]

Such discoveries could be made through "copy testing," in which any aspect of a marketing/advertising campaign could be tried out by interviewing people cold, or by visiting them after their exposure to the new advertising or packaging or product, by coupon returns from split runs, or even by sales in test markets, or (later) simulated test markets in computer models first designed by the sociologist Daniel Yankelovich and his associates in Yankelovich Clancy Shulman. Jack Andrews, then research director for General Foods, said in 1981, "Few advertisers can afford to invest millions and risk important consumer franchises on copy which has only the author's stamp of approval."[10]

Copy testing was the first of the activities once performed by agencies to move to the clients. "Clients," said BBDO's Rosenshine, "feel they need a third party, a disinterested party. In the old days, the agencies did it and bitched about it, probably with good reason, and the client found it hard to accept an agency's doing the research and then saying it's irrelevant." Keith Reinhard's objection to copy testing is that creative people who know it's lying in wait will write to the test. His research director, Bill Wells, remembers that when he first met Reinhard in 1974, "He said, 'If you come to Needham, what sort of copy testing would you do?' I said, 'I wouldn't do any copy testing.' He said, 'When can you start?'" John Ward of England's B&B Dorland writes, "Advertising is a craft executed by people who aspire to be artists, but assessed by those who aspire to be scientists. I cannot imagine any human relationship more perfectly designed to produce total mayhem."[11]

Testing for attitudes fails because attitudes do not necessarily control buying behavior. Just about everybody thinks Rolls-Royce is the best car, but not many people buy one. In 1954, DuPont, one of the pioneers in marketing research, ran a study in which interviewers stopped no fewer than 5,200 women on their way into a supermarket, and asked them what they expected to buy. Then the DuPont interviewers checked the subjects' purchases on their way out, and found that only three out of ten who had bought the product category they had expected to buy had bought the brands they had expected to buy; seven out of ten had bought other brands. Charles Ramond, who was market research director for DuPont before he became technical director of the Advertising Research Foundation, reported, "[M]uch of the time, we cannot find that we 'communicate' before we 'sell.'. . . An advertiser who regularly obtains both attitude and sales measures will, if his advertising is communicating, see the effects in sales increases *before* they show up as communication changes."[12] Indeed, Bill Wells and his colleagues suggest in their textbook that a major function of advertising is to "reduce postpurchase dissonance by restating the features and confirming the popularity of the brand or product."[13]

A number of agencies, most notably McCann-Erickson and Ted Bates, claimed that their versions of the Starch system enabled them to judge the effectiveness of advertising, and one service any agency or advertiser could buy claimed to measure precisely the effectiveness of television commercials. This was run by Horace Schwerin, an energetic transplanted Canadian who eventually moved on to be an in-house consultant for Campbell Soup. His system involved a theatre (on New York's Sixth Avenue, before all the large office buildings were built there). A sample selected from census data would be invited to see new television shows at that theatre. The sample actually achieved was of course only a fraction of the sample invited, and variously skewed, but in these matters the validity of the sample was not considered important. (CBS judged television shows in its Stanton-Lazarsfeld Program Analyzer on the basis of responses from a group solicited on streetcorners near the company's headquarters.)

As Schwerin's invitees settled in their seats, they would fill out a questionnaire asking them which brand of a given product category they would like to receive as their prize if they won a lottery to be conducted at the end of the show. Then they would be shown the show, with commercials embedded in it, and asked the same question again. Winners would get a carload of the brand they chose, to discourage them from simply trying something new. (The questionnaire specified a dollar value rather than a quantity as the prize, to eliminate price considerations.) Shifts from one brand before viewing the commercial to another brand after viewing it were supposedly measures of the effectiveness of the commercial.

In the end, belief in predictions like Schwerin's was a matter of faith, because the advertiser couldn't measure his sales. He knew what he shipped, but he didn't know how much of that was piling up as inventory in the wholesalers' warehouses or in the stores. In response to the advertiser's need for this information, A. C. Nielsen started the service that generated most of the company's revenues: a Food-Drug Index. In this incredibly painstaking process, Nielsen auditors visited about 5,000 drugstores, grocery stores, and supermarkets. They came at regular intervals, and did a thorough inventory, noting how many of each of thousands of "stock keeping units" were on the shelves at each visit, and, by examining the store's records, reporting how many units had been delivered for sale between visits. This was a "syndicated service" — that is, every subscriber got all the data, and could thus see how well his competitors were doing. Subscribers paid according to the number and volume of the brands they owned. Reports were routinely broken down into geographical areas and types of store, and the data were submitted to the subscribers in large part in the form of charts. Over and above the published reports, Nielsen offered supplementary analyses that told an advertiser about featured displays for his own and other brands, about the allocation of shelf space to this category and to the brands in the category, about price reductions, and so on. It took a lot of time to prepare this material. Reports were issued only every other month, and the data in them were on average close to three months old. Nevertheless, David Ogilvy, on his first visit to America (in 1938), pronounced that "Nielsen has been to advertising in America what Galileo was to astronomy."

From the point of view of advertising agencies, the Nielsen reports were an area of vulnerability. They were expensive, and priced in a way that essentially made it impossible for an agency to subscribe. So they were bought mostly by advertisers (and to some extent by store chains, which got reports at low prices in return for cooperating in the studies). As the Nielsen service grew in importance, agencies that were supposed to know what consumers were doing found themselves at the mercy of their clients for information about how products were moving, and how the brands they advertised were doing in relation to the other brands in the category. The best that even the biggest agencies could offer as a counterweight was a "panel" of consumers that reported (to the agency research departments) on their purchases — and even here the advertiser could buy a superior service (larger panels, and daily rather than weekly or even monthly diaries) from Market Research Corporation of America. Nielsen's competition in the 1970s and early 1980s was from a company called SAMI (for Sales Area Marketing Information), which counted units not in the stores but at the warehouses and transshipment points of the wholesalers and chain stores. This was a less expensive activity than Nielsen's store-based report, and as a monthly report SAMI scooped Nielsen with some regularity, but even so the agencies didn't buy.

The agencies could also argue, and did, that while sales measures were certainly of prime importance to the advertiser, they couldn't be related to advertising. "You can run a bad advertising campaign," Rosser Reeves said in the 1950s, "and sales go up. You can run a brilliant campaign, and sales go down. Why?

"A) your product may not be right.

"B) your price may not be right.

"C) your distribution may not be right.

"D) your sales force may be bad.

"E) your competitor may be outspending you five to one.

"F) your competitor may be dealing you to death with one-cent sales and premiums and contests and special discounts to retailers."[14]

It is, perhaps, a measure of what great salesmen the advertising men of the 1950s were that this argument carried weight. Arguments gain weight, after all, not because they are true (which this one clearly was), but because they are useful (which this one clearly wasn't). Still, by the late 1960s, after Anheuser-Busch released the details of an experiment in which it reduced advertising expenditure on Budweiser from $1.79 to 79¢ a barrel while increasing the brand's market share, advertisers began to want more reason to believe that money spent on advertising increased the numbers on the bottom line.[15] The agencies couldn't give it, or dissuade the clients from wanting it.

4.

Social and Psychological Research

From 1965 into the late 1980s, advertising research was dominated by the social psychologists, who explored the demographic and psychographic characteristics of the consumers of various product categories and brands and then gave guidance on the advertising appeal and media choices most likely to make contact with people who had those characteristics. William Wells's textbook *Advertising: Principles and Practices* offers a set of concentric circles from a center called "Individual" to explain what is going on. Above the line that runs through the individual are

> Family influences
> Social influence:
> 1. Class
> 2. Reference group
> Cultural influences.

Below the line are

> Personal influences:
> 1. Age
> 2. Gender
> 3. Family Situation
> 4. Education
> 5. Occupation

6. Income
7. Race and Ethnicity

Psychological influences:

1. Perception
2. Learning
3. Motivation
4. Attitudes
5. Personality.[16]

Among them, these elements give the individual what the sociologists call "life-style." It is remarkable how much of the work on life-style goes back to a single book, *The Lonely Crowd*, published soon after World War II by David Riesman, Reuel Denney, and Nathan Glazer. To Riesman's typology of "inner-directed" and "outer-directed," S.R.I. (Stanford Research Institute) in its "VALS" (Values and Life Styles) taxonomy added only two categories. One was "need-driven," or poor people, by definition not of great interest to the advertiser. The other was "integrateds," a very small group who can handle their problems rationally and presumably take a well-armored utilitarian view of consumption. (A later refinement, "VALS 2," gave eight categories — "Strugglers, Believers, Strivers, Makers, Fulfilleds, Achievers, Experiencers, and Actualizers.")

In Wells's book, products are divided into "low-involvement" and "high-involvement." Oddly enough, the discussion of "high-involvement" products tends to neglect the values added by advertising, speaking instead of "information search" ("Advertising helps the search process by providing information in the advertisement itself") and "evaluation and comparison" ("Advertising is important in this evaluation process because it helps sort out products on the basis of features").[17]

But where a consumer is looking at what Keith Reinhard

of DDB Needham calls "badge products" — the things you own that people notice, that in some sense define you to yourself as well as to others — the badge is to a large degree the creation of the advertising. Indeed, the genius of the standard Procter & Gamble advertising approach — described in the trade as "two c's in a k," a phrase bowdlerized by *The Economist* as "two consumers in a kitchen" — has always been that it tied a housewife's self-esteem to the laundry soap she used. The advertising that seems most foolish is that which tries and fails to hook a badge onto a utilitarian object.

The stability of such images is the brand franchise, and one would expect that a good fraction of advertising research money would be spent to measure whether changes in the campaign or the marketing strategy were endangering that stability. Instead, the money has always been spent to look at whether there have been changes in the community at large. "Understanding people is critical," says Y&R's Satish Korde.... Wells does the advertising world's largest and best-regarded study of "activities, interests and opinions" in the American community. "We have data on trends going back fifteen years," he says. "About half the trends you read about are real trends, and about half are phony. It's very valuable to know which are real." Keith Reinhard says admiringly, "Bill can sift through a mountain of work, see the strategic insight, and put it into English."

Peter Georgescu, president of Young & Rubicam, has abstracted the advertising process into "ladderings." Every product, he says, has "Attributes (grease cutter), Benefits (cleans the floor) and Values (makes you a better housewife). The Procter & Gamble formula was developed when products were different, and their effort was mostly in attributes; they wanted advertising that said, 'Better product.' As competition comes in, you get product parities. P&G first tried to get minuscule differences that were not meaningful to the consumer, and they failed, because under conditions of product parity you have to start with values. And now it's tricky because of segmentation. The differences between people are widening, and you can't talk across groups. You have to find a crisper niche."

William T. Moran, ex-Lever and ex-Y&R ("he trained all of us," says the Y&R C.E.O., Alex Kroll), now runs a service called Longman-Moran Analytics, Inc., analyzing sales and social data provided by others. He has his doubts about the willingness of American manufacturers to seek crisper niches, even when they understand intellectually that a given amount of sales will be more profitable when it expresses a larger share of a smaller market. "American businessmen," he writes, "never have been really willing to buy into the economic premise of market segmentation. Every time a segmented-appeal product or positioning concept is tested — no matter how intensely it is preferred by some segment — someone sets about to modify it so that it will appeal to a larger group in order to increase its potential market share. Pretty soon, every brand is trying to appeal to every other brand's customers.

"The market research community has aided and abetted this constant dilution of market segmenting positioning through its devotion to multi-variate analytical techniques — which identify confusing, overlapping and totally ambiguous clusters of people or product attributes which, more often than not, are not even related to any common market behavior. These clusters quickly become the subject of a parlor game mentality as the research challenge is to assign meaningful names to them.

"The very fuzziness of these multi-variate segments

encourages marketers to trade off sharp positioning for greater *potential* market share. Of course, these marketers never achieve those potential market shares because they then find themselves head-to-head with more competitors — all trying to expand into the same middle ground. They just end up spending more money in price promotions for no more market share than they could have had with a more focussed positioning.

"Successful market segmentation begins with *mono*-variate attribute positionings."[18]

Combining the known characteristics of the customers for a category of product with the known characteristics of consumers of a given medium can lead researchers down a garden path to a thorny dead end. Stephan Buck of AGB, the largest British research firm, gives an example:

a) heavy savers are old;
b) old people view a lot of television;
c) therefore, heavy savers view a lot of television — which is not the case!"[19]

What survives at most of the agencies is "nonprojectable" research, where the purpose of asking the questions is not to prove any point but to get ideas for the advertising, for the fact is that the people who work in the creative departments of the advertising agencies are as remote as the executives of the client corporation from the consumers of the products they advertise. "We gave our lifestyle questionnaire [the heart of the trends survey] to people in the agency," Wells says, "and compared their answers with the real answers. They were very different. These people are very isolated. They don't know what the heavy user of cake flour thinks like, or the woman who buys all her clothes at

Sears." So someone from the research department conducts an interview with four to ten people in a conference room with a one-way mirror, and the creative people watch from behind the mirror. Then the copywriters and the researchers discuss what went on in the session. Not everyone agrees that this is the best way for an advertising person to learn about the relations between the product he is advertising and the people who consume it. "The copywriters," says Joel Raphaelson, who was until recently head of Ogilvy's Chicago office, "go to the focus groups and take two weeks at it. You can visit a lot of bars in two weeks."

5.

Scanners and Data Bases

"There have been two critical events in the history of market research," says Ben Lipstein, a retired N.Y.U. professor of statistics and one-time research director for Benton & Bowles. "The first was in the first decade of this century, when we discovered we could ask questions. The second was in the eighth decade, when scanner data taught us that we didn't have to ask questions."

The Universal Product Code and the infrared scanner that reads it arrived in American supermarkets in the 1970s. Instead of reading a price from a sticker on the product, the clerk at the checkout counter would wipe the package over the glowing scanner. The scanner would read the assemblage of thicker and thinner black bars printed as part of the package. A computer in the rear would tell the cash register what the price for this package was today, and the cash register would print it out. The value for the consumer was that her register tape told her what she had bought and what she had paid for it. The value for the store was a saving of clerk time and an ease of repricing, because stock boys would not have to be sent around the store to put new stickers on packages. In the inflationary atmosphere of the late 1970s, this was a considerable recommendation.

In the event, the cost savings were slight. Even when prices were attached to the shelves on which the packages were displayed, consumers would not tolerate the loss of the information on the stickers. And the early scanners were picky about how the label had to be set on a round bottle or can with relation to the flat plane of the reader. But there were other values to having a record of what was being bought, for the computer could be taught to tell the store manager — and the distribution warehouse, and the corporate center — what the customers were buying at what price. Again, there were hitches and snags. Communication among scanner, computer, and cash register was not always what it should have been. The programs for the computers originally installed were often unsuitable for mass storage and retrieval. But once this engine began to roar, the sound would be heard everywhere. Nielsen's Index had presented sales data every other month, and SAMI's measurement of withdrawals from warehouses had given slightly less convincing monthly figures. Now, at least in theory, there could be accurate sales figures every week, or even every day.

The first man to see the future was Leo Bogart, the scholarly, lean, tall sociologist who ran the Newspaper Advertising Bureau. NAB's purpose was to promote the sale of space in newspapers. Among those performing that mission for Bogart was Richard Neal, who had come to the bureau from *This Week,* where he had done studies of grocery retailing. "Neal was an authority on that," Bogart said not long after his retirement to the status of Fellow at the Gannett Center of the Columbia School of Journalism. "He had good contacts with the manufacturers. He saw scanner data as a source of real evidence for the sales power of newspaper advertising. He started collecting case histories, information on sales before a newspaper ad ran, sales the week the ad ran, and sales in succeeding weeks. I was sure it was the wave of the future, applicable to shelf-position and pricing and all the elements of the marketing mix. I wanted to develop a facility that created a nationally projectable sample, plus mechanisms for controlled testing. We started a commercial service, NABSCAN, for 'Nationally Advertised Brand Scanning System,' just happened to have the same initials as the Newspaper Advertising Bureau."

From its first days, scanner data convincingly demonstrated that advertisers and their agencies had been operating on false premises. Nielsen's Food-Drug Index had always shown only glacial changes of brand shares as sales passed in stately review every two months. "Thus," Bogart wrote in 1987, "marketing management has tended to assume that changes in market size and brand position usually occur slowly over time and that competitive strategy is best planned on a national or broad regional scale."[20] N.Y.U.'s Ben Lipstein, who had no love for old Art Nielsen and deep distrust for his insistence that what he did was science, says cynically that Nielsen had jiggered his system to produce such results, "having surmised that executives don't like dramatic changes." But the truth was, to quote Bill Moran, one of the earliest converts to scanner data, that "sales bounce around like a ping-pong ball in a storm."

Bogart printed a few examples. In a group of Chicago stores with scanners, Palmolive dishwashing detergent varied on different days between a 60.6 percent and a 5.8 percent share of market. One week, Scott towels had 47.7

percent of the Chicago market; another week, it had 4.7 percent. The week Scott's share was 47.7 percent in Chicago, it had a 2.5 percent share in Los Angeles. And this is, of course, a nationally advertised product, for which shares on the every-other-month cumulative basis do not vary anything like that much between Chicago and Los Angeles. "Advertisers always think," Bogart says, "'What is the effect of what I'm doing?' They have a narcissistic preoccupation. But what's happening in the market relates to what *their competitors* are doing." One company's image-building television or magazine advertising campaign can be stomped in this weeks' war for market share by another company's newspaper ads and price cuts or store displays.

In those days, the stores with scanners were not representative of the universe of American stores, and the data were, in Bogart's words, "grungy," arriving on reels of tape that often made no sense. (The first time the Advertising Research Foundation looked at scanner data, in the mid-1980s, half the tapes submitted were deemed useless.) Bogart brought in a statistician named Jerome Green to help manage the data, and Neal bought the services of a mathematician, Al Kuehn, who had a computer in Pittsburgh. Kuehn in turn brought in Lipstein from N.Y.U. All of this got a little overscale for the Newspaper Advertising Bureau, and Lipstein made arrangements through Leon Levy, a Wall Street friend who ran Oppenheimer Fund and had a venture capital firm called Odyssey Partners, to capitalize NABSCAN as a commercial service. The resources available through Levy proved insufficient for NABSCAN's needs, and Lipstein sold it to MRI, a British-owned U.S. research firm based, as noted, on an old-fashioned but very efficient consumer panel of 20,000 homes visited twice a year by interviewers with questionnaires.

Meanwhile, out in Chicago, a new company called Information Resources, Inc. (IRI), was finding its own ways to use scanner data. IRI's founder, John Malec, had seen that by providing customers with an ID card and a reward for using it, the scanners could keep track of who bought as well as what was sold. The IRI service was called BehaviorScan, and it was a superior system for conducting test markets. The data came from stores in a handful of suburbs and small towns. Through BehaviorScan, advertisers could get numbers that seemed to tell them *immediately* how new products or new campaigns did and whether their sales would change if they "heavied up" or cut back their advertising expenditures. They could compare the costs and effectiveness of various advertising approaches, using "split cable" techniques (half the households whose purchasing habits were being measured got one commercial, and half got the other one). IRI offered BehaviorScan for the first time in 1979, and sales took off like a rocket. In ten years, the company conducted more than 600 studies, which satisfied or at least intrigued a majority of the nation's major packaged-goods advertisers.

In 1986, IRI took the plunge into direct rivalry with Nielsen, offering an InfoScan service designed to be an accurate statement of sales and market shares in the food business across the country. Another Englishman, Gian Fulgoni, who would become IRI's C.E.O., was hired to run this service. BehaviorScan, because of its test market orientation, had been sold to advertisers, though agencies of course saw most of the data through their clients. InfoScan's fact book, however, was offered to one and all, "and the agencies wouldn't buy it," says Fulgoni with a shrug, "for fifty grand [a year]." InfoScan put IRI into a different relationship with the stores, because the information IRI pulled from the scanner data told stores the profitability of each foot of shelf space. With the announcement of InfoScan, Nielsen rolled over in its sleep, realized that the days of the paper-and-pencil store audit were numbered, and started its own long march toward the creation of a scanner-based service. Thereupon, SAMI also awakened, though very reluctantly, and too late.

"The SAMI position," said David Lipson, who ran scanner services for what became Arbitron/SAMI, "was that scanner data are inherently noisy. SAMI sat on their hands and said, people will realize scanner data are noisy and not very good. If you want accurate samples, the scanner services won't give them. Stick with warehouse withdrawals. We can give you reports on fifty-four markets, so accurate that manufacturers use them as the basis for paying their salesmen. But people who go to an Advertising Research Foundation conference feel they will be left in the dust if they don't have the latest." So Arbitron/SAMI launched its ScanAmerica service in Denver, with a panel of 600 households metered for TV viewing as well as for purchases. In the summer of 1990, Executive Vice-President Ken Wollenberg of Arbitron/SAMI promised that by the end of that year his service would be tracking a thousand homes in five markets, en route to 18,000 in the 209 mapped areas where Arbitron measures television audiences. In fall 1990 these plans were abandoned, and Arbitron worked out a joint venture with IRI, contributing the Denver panel to the mix. Arbitron claims one interesting advantage over its rivals: because it is also the proprietor of Broadcast Advertising Reports, it knows uniquely what commercials actually ran (rather than what commercials were scheduled to run) at the time the households in its panels were watching.

Like IRI, Nielsen gets data from store scanners, but it also runs both national and local household panels through its NPD (National Panel Data)/Nielsen joint venture. In the national panel of 26,500 homes (as of summer 1990), about 40 percent keep diaries of their purchases, and the other 60 percent have their own home scanners, in the form of a wand that is to be passed over the packages unloaded from the bags when the shopper returns home. The shopper is supposed to tell the wand by pushing buttons on it which member of the household did the shopping today and which stores were shopped; then Nielsen gets the prices from its store contacts. (If the store is not one from which Nielsen gets data, the householder in theory punches in the price herself.) Each week at an appointed time, the householder dials a Nielsen number and pushes another button, and the wand squeaks for about fifteen seconds to unload its data. Arbitron/SAMI's ScanAmerica was entirely a wand service, but the Arbitron wand is lighter in weight than Nielsen's ("The thing Nielsen has," Wollenberg said, with the cattiness that is endemic to the market research business, "you need help picking it up"). And it plugs into a holder Arbitron's computer polls by telephone *every night* to pick up whatever information has been gathered. IRI will continue to use the technology, at least in Denver.

All these services are alike in one other respect: they are hugely capital-intensive. The complexities of gathering and categorizing and preserving and recalling these data are far beyond what any manufacturer — let alone an advertising agency — could undertake solely for its own use. IRI's dictionary of Universal Product Codes includes more than 2,000,000 "names." Each size of package has its own code for each brand. Watching the carbonated beverages market for Pepsi-Cola, IRI must be able to identify no fewer than *10,000* different UPC's printed onto labels for this product category alone. Getting the prices right is a giant job in itself. Safeway has seven different "price zones" in different neighborhoods in Seattle; Dominick's has four price zones in Chicago. The scanner company cannot rely on a separate communication from Dominick's for its pricing data, because Dominick's sends out the *average* price. "Every week," says Fulgoni, "we get thirty-five million pieces of data that have to be verified and cleansed." IRI claims to have designed a "neural network" of computers employing techniques of artificial intelligence to improve data quality. (Nielsen says this is nonsense.) Meanwhile, the variable costs of providing the service — hiring hundreds of people to visit the supermarkets and check on the promotions and displays and price cuts and in-store advertising for each product category — steadily increase as the researchers reach out for greater coverage.

"In the old days," says Ben Lipstein, "if you were knowledgeable and had a telephone, you were in the research business. Today, it takes a great deal of money." NABSCAN couldn't raise it. MediaMark's Timothy Joyce explains why he abandoned NABSCAN: "Bogart had got his data for nothing. By the time we came, the stores were charging $600 a year. Nielsen upped the price to $6,000 a year." To Lipstein's fury ("To save a million or two million in annual losses, the MediaMark people gave up the chance of selling the service for perhaps one or two hundred million"), the new English owners of NABSCAN simply closed the operation down.

But even Nielsen couldn't pick up costs of these dimensions. Among the companies interested in moving into the scanner data business was Dun & Bradstreet, which had one subsidiary (Donnelly Marketing Information Services) that provided demographic data on the customers of different stores around the country, and another (Carol Wright) that was the nation's largest deliverer of "cents-off" coupons. D&B first talked with IRI, but couldn't make a deal; and in 1987 it bought Nielsen.

SAMI was absorbed by Arbitron, which was already a subsidiary of Control Data Corporation, but Control Data was no longer a deep pocket, which is why ScanAmerica never made it out of Denver. IRI built up debts in the tens of millions of dollars, and its 1989 operations showed a loss that was 10 percent of its revenues. Then, in early 1990, a new giant on the block in the market research business, itself deeply engaged in gathering, processing, massaging, and retrieving scanner information, gave IRI an infusion of money and a shot in the arm.

This was Citicorp, the largest bank holding company in America, with more than $200 billion in assets and roughly 80,000 employees around the world. The man who had sold Citicorp on plunging into this business was Peter Engel, yet another Englishman, a soft-spoken but eloquent venture capitalist, president of the Porosan Group of Stamford, Connecticut, who at various times has made his living as a business consultant and as a writer of popular fiction. Engel had run into scanner data while advising packaged goods companies on how to keep track of their increasingly costly but chaotically organized promotions to retailers and consumers. Gerald Saltzgaber, who had worked for General Foods and the Little Golden Books division of Mattel toys, was Engel's partner. What intrigued the two of them was the close fit between the emerging marketing philosophy of narrowly directed messages and the data-management capacity of a system based on scanners and ID cards. Richard Braddock, also an alumnus of General Foods, had become one of the vice-chairmen of Citicorp, which had (rather unwisely) acquired Quotron, then the leading provider of bid-and-asked quotations to brokerage houses and others, and was recasting itself to be less a bank and more an information services company. Saltzgaber and Engel went to Braddock. Rather to their surprise, it was a hard sell. "We'd spent a generation brainwashing businessmen on the accuracy of sample research," Engel says. "They had entirely lost their capacity to understand the difference between a sample and a census."

By midsummer 1990, Citicorp P.O.S. (for "point of sale") had arrangements with 2.3 million customers carrying special ID cards, and was keeping records of their purchases at about 800 stores. To clean up the noisy data, Citicorp had installed its own jiggered PC's between the scanner and the store's computer (Nielsen was in process of doing the same), and the information from the scanner went off to the Citicorp computers even before the store knew about the sale. Saltzgaber, who left Engel's shop to become the head of Citicorp P.O.S., projects that by the mid-1990s — I kid you not — his division will be keeping track of the purchases of *forty million* American households, processing information on *thirty billion* transactions a year at *fourteen thousand* retail outlets (convenience stores and drugstores as well as supermarkets), through computers with memories reaching into the *trillions* of bytes of data. And analyses of these data, differently skewed to meet the needs of manufacturers in various product categories and of retailers serving various communities, will be reported to the customers on a *daily* basis. Machines capable of such tasks do not yet exist; Citicorp has commissioned Teradata, Inc. (a terabyte is a trillion bytes), to create one.

In spring 1990, Citicorp spent about $14 million to buy

just under 5 percent of the shares of IRI, with warrants to buy another 10 percent. As part of the deal, Citicorp paid an additional $9 million for the use of IRI's proprietary software. Gian Fulgoni, now C.E.O. of IRI, cleaned up the rest of the company's debt by doing a sale-and-leaseback of its handsomely appointed converted warehouse just across the Chicago & Northwestern tracks from downtown Chicago. IRI continues to operate and sell its InfoScan and derivative services independently of Citicorp, but the two will clearly cooperate rather than compete in the future. The feeling in the trade is that Citicorp will concentrate on services to stores while IRI handles services to advertisers. In any event, IRI clearly will have access to whatever resources may be necessary in its battles with Nielsen. Even before the Citicorp connection, it was winning a surprising share of them, having taken the Nabisco and PepsiCo accounts away from the old established house. The match with Citicorp is a good one, both companies regarding themselves as smarter than their competition and faster on their feet ("slicker," said SAMI's Lipson with some distaste). But Nielsen's development laboratories may have some surprises in store for them. And Citibank in late 1990 hit a brick wall of losses in the real estate portfolio that put all new projects more or less on hold: Citicorp P.O.S. lost about forty employees.

"We are moving," says John Costello, who left PepsiCo to head Nielsen Marketing Services, "from persuasive selling to fact-based selling." The buzzword among the researchers is "single source." Instead of comparing the demographics and psychographics of communities that buy products with those of communities that receive advertising messages, the advertiser will know the consumers one by one. The ID card in the supermarket identifies the purchaser as the same fellow who subscribes to *Road and Track* and watches *L.A. Law* through a cable system that keeps track of tuning. Sears knows what tires he buys — "we have 68.7 million unduplicated American households in our files," says the information services director, Jim Carter, "and we have scored forty-million-odd for things like their purchases of automotive supplies and baby goods." All the credit card companies have records of what each cardholder buys with the card, and those records can be merged into other data bases. "Single source," says Laurel Cutler of FCB Leber Katz who follows these matters for accounts as varied as Nabisco and Chrysler, "will be able to tell me the name and address of everybody who buys my product, so I can target an individual message."

As Peter Engel found out, census-based marketing offends the advertising community, because like "direct response" it seems to devalue the creative skills of the advertising agency. The industry was already under siege from midlevel brand managers who could see that this-week-only price cuts and displays at the end of the aisles in the supermarkets moved merchandise on any week more surely than ads, and that money taken out of ad budgets fell right down to the bottom line. There might be losses to the brand franchise over the long run, but as John Maynard Keynes pointed out, in the long run we are all (especially brand managers) dead. Now the first scanner studies indicated that price promotions and in-store displays were *much* more effective selling tactics than advertising on television and in magazines (which was, one notes, OK with Bogart and NAB, because the price promotions themselves worked best when advertised in the newspapers).

These studies, however, were not as conclusive as the

trade assumed. IRI's finding that people exposed to thirty TV commercials for a brand were no more likely to buy it than people exposed to four commercials, Frank Stanton of Simmons Research points out, is very close to meaningless, because the former are by definition heavy viewers and are thus also exposed to thirty commercials for the competing brands. Back in the days when Nielsen was still fighting against scanners, its director of statistical research had presented a paper showing that movements of brand share calculated from the same data could appear significantly different depending on what you picked as the starting point — and even with the same base-line date were different if measured on one-week, two-week, or four-week intervals. Most brands move less than a case per store in any week, which means that a couple of units' difference shows up as a big percentage change. And ever since a series of studies for *Progressive Grocer* magazine in the 1960s it had been part of the background wisdom of the trade that placement on higher or lower shelves, and displays at the head or back of the aisle, would have greater influence on a week's sales than almost any advertising expenditure.

Even if the IRI data were new and important, various explanations were possible. IRI, the source of the most negative studies, eventually came along with the happiest explanation from the agencies' point of view: the time horizon on which the scanner pioneers had measured was too low. In any one year, promotions were a more efficient way to sell than advertising was — but if you extended the measurement time to two and (even better) three years, the residual effects of brand-building made advertising the more economical tool. "We find," says Andy Tarshis, who runs Nielsen's panel-based service, "that advertising works the way the grass grows. You can never see it, but every week you have to mow the lawn." Another explanation comes from David Ogilvy, mostly retired but still the inspirational leader of the agency that bears his name, rumbling more often than erupting but still glowing. "IRI data make advertising look bad," Ogilvy said the other day, "because most advertising *is* bad."

Still, the importance of "understanding consumers" is greatly reduced when messages are to be targeted to individuals whose buying habits we know. "In the future," says Tarshis, "media buying will not be done according to the old age and sex patterns but by actual buying habits." Providers of scanner data do not deny that high fractions of customers for a brand fit into the agencies' pet sociographic groupings, but they find the correlations insufficient. "We do demographics and psychographics and zip code," says Citicorp's Saltzgaber, "and they leave you with a major league guess. We find that ninety-five percent of households are unique. What you really need to know is what the hell the people purchase."

Attention then moves to what Don Pepper calls "transactional segmentation." Customers become classifiable in what Pepper calls "image tribes," bound together by no characteristic other than common consumption of this brand of soap. Advertising becomes "addressable," as foreshadowed in 1990 by *Time* magazine's adoption of "selective binding," which permits an advertiser to buy a page in only those copies of the magazine that will be sent to individuals plucked from the subscription list. The new data bases are to some degree transferrable — "drivers of imported cars are more likely to drink imported beer," Pepper says; "I can give you a thousand of these" — but mass marketing is impossible.

There is, of course, no guarantee that these new and enormous research services will be cost-effective in generating strategies or tactics for more than a handful of giant packaged-goods advertisers. "What we're doing," says Paul Gerhold, who used to be research director for Foote, Cone & Belding, "is making the needle smaller and the haystack bigger." None of it comes cheap. William Rubens, formerly research director for NBC and now an independent consultant, told a roundtable of the Advertising Research Foundation in early 1990, "The amount required to really make effective single-source systems is like sending a man to the moon." Gale Metzger, a former ARF chairman, picked up the argument: "I'm not saying it's conceptually impossible. I'm saying it's going to get more expensive, and the relative value for the decisions we are trying to make, marketing decisions, will not warrant our undertaking a campaign equivalent to going to the moon."[21]

Over time, the manufacturers' and the retailers' interests may not be identical. Josh McQueen is research director for Leo Burnett, which has probably spent more time and money on scanner data than any other agency. He feels that advertisers who rely on scanner services may be setting themselves up for dangerous disappointments. "Long-term," he says, "are retailers going to be happy to have information they ultimately own going to a manufacturer? The competitive advantage a store has is its information about its consumers. Citicorp has a race against time. Can they get their services into the stores faster than the retailers can build their own capacity?"

There could be conceptual flaws here, too. The intuitive researchers who were half-salesmen themselves, now pushed out of both the agencies and the corporate marketing departments, may have known things the computers cannot learn. "There's a lot going on the market," said SAMI's David Lipson, "that we can't measure and we don't understand." The dramatist and producer David Belasco liked to say that the art of being a successful showman was giving people what they wanted just before they knew they wanted it. Alex Kroll of Y&R said recently, in a moment of impatience with his own agency's research, "I am sick and tired of trying to steer this ship by its wake."

And there is an obvious political problem: Will the American people *like* the idea that their every purchase is being registered, under their names and addresses, inside a computer file? A man who works for Porsche in the United States says that his company estimates there are only 300,000 possible Porsche buyers in the country — "and we're frightened they'll find out how much we know about them." Ben Lipstein says, "Dun & Bradstreet and Citicorp are octopuses that can keep more information about Americans than the census bureau or the IRS can keep." The people who participate in these data-gathering programs get small rewards. Citicorp arranges for people to get discount coupons at the cash register on the brands they usually buy. (A man from a large advertiser who has looked at this phenomenon says it works much less well than its publicity: "The coupons pile up on the floor: it's too much trouble for the checkout clerk to give them out.") IRI gives an annual gift worth about $25 to cardholders, and every time they use the card they get a chance in a monthly lottery that rewards its winners with prizes ranging from a small appliance to dinner for two in a local restaurant to a trip to Las Vegas. Arbitron paid panel members as much as $300 to $400 a year for cooperating. "We've tried various prompts," said Wollenberg, "and we find that nothing works like cash."

Saltzgaber, who clears virtually everything Citicorp P.O.S. does with the White House Office of Consumer Affairs, insists that "consumers are *not* concerned about people knowing about their grocery purchases. They *do* want to know what's going to be done with their data. We tell them it's going to be sold, and we offer them the opportunity not to have records kept. We promise that we will never release an individual's history to anyone, and never sell the list for distribution. Pepsi says, I'd like to send one message to Pepsi users, one to switchers, one to Coke users, we pull the names and addresses out of the data base and give them to bonded third parties who do the mailings. Pepsi never sees the list, and the mailer can use it one time only — we have it seeded so that we know if they violate the one-time use sale. Under those circumstances, the consumer stays cool about the use of the list." Once credit card users come into the mix, this purity will be more difficult to sustain, and temperatures may rise.

The agencies already have a hard time staying cool. The move to scanner data seems likely to be accompanied by a move to greater in-store advertising as distinguished from advertising in media. (Indeed, the IRI founder, Malec, has left to promote a "Videocart" system to deliver advertising messages to screens on grocery carts, different messages for different aisles of the store.) Agencies fear that in-store advertising will not be "commissionable," and that all this short-term data will reinforce the modern corporate client's low time horizons and bureaucratic organization. Yet the future of the advertising agency must lie in its ability to understand and coordinate the various means of selling. "If the advertising industry insists on bashing all other kinds of promotion," says Keith Reinhard, "it will go out of business."

One piece of information that jumps out of all the scanner data is that promotions have a much greater impact on the sales of well-established brands. Price cuts on the store's own labels or marginal brands have little (sometimes no) effect. Bill Moran notes sadly that the agencies in their hostility to these data have missed what may be the most valuable lesson they teach: that there really is a brand franchise, created by advertising; and the stronger the franchise, the greater the benefit the advertiser can hope to gain from any marketing strategy. Meanwhile, the research function continues to slip away from the agencies. In summer 1990, the A.A.A.A. built a campaign for the industry around work done by The Ogilvy Center in San Francisco to prove the effectiveness of advertising. At the end of the year, WPP, pressed by its creditors, closed down The Ogilvy Center.

CHAPTER SIX

The International Scene

MY WIFE was born in Sweden, and some member of her Swedish family — we've never found out which — has given her a subscription to a very middlebrow magazine called *ICA Kuriren.* One of the ads in a summer 1990 issue was a double-truck color spread with an immense moose occupying about a page and a half, and a Volvo sedan occupying the remaining half page. The moose and the Volvo were face-to-face. The headline on the ad said (in Swedish, of course), "There are no moose in Japan." I mentioned the ad to Ed Meyer of Grey Advertising as an example of how a product benefit which is the same for all cultures (the sturdiness of the Volvo) can be presented differently according to the customer's location. He was amused. "You know," he said, "our agency in Stockholm has the Volvo account. We must have done that ad ourselves."

"For the Chinese," said the DDB Needham research director, Bill Wells, "what they call Fong Shui, wind and water, is a very powerful idea. To build a house in the crotch of the hills, where there's lots of water and you're sheltered from the wind. When you're building an office, the Fong Shui man tells you how to orient the desks and the goldfish bowls. It doesn't exist in Europe. Having the right number of goldfish in the tank is a matter of importance. I was in a man's office in Taiwan, and I saw there was only one goldfish in the bowl. He said, 'One died.' A couple of days later in Hong Kong I got a fax from him — he'd got another goldfish."

Phil Geier, chairman and C.E.O. of Interpublic, the holding company for McCann-Erickson and Lintas, among others, a large, overworked man who runs on nervous energy, walks up and down in his office while talking. He was in a terrible state the morning I interviewed him. He had a nasty cold with a runny nose, and he had just found out that Interpublic's two agencies in Belgium (respectively the second and fourth largest in that country) had accepted clients that competed with each other and didn't hold with Interpublic's philosophical position that its subsidiaries also competed with each other and thus did not have to concern themselves with client conflicts. At least one of these two companies, I gathered from listening to conversations that swirled around our conversation, was a client in other countries, too, and wanted this situation resolved, quickly. The whole thing had blindsided Geier, who'd had no reason to keep tabs on what accounts were taken or refused by his agencies in Belgium, which were two of his group's 235 offices in 75 countries. "I was shocked," he said to his uncomprehending interlocutor, "to find I didn't know we had Main Meal from Unilever's Frozen Foods in our Brussels office."

Dan Chew, advertising manager for Levi Strauss, says that domestic and international strategies must be different in blue jeans. "The markets are different. In the United States,

Levi's is both highly functional and fashionable. But in the United Kingdom its strength is as a fashion garment. We've tested UK ads in American markets. Our primary target market at home is the sixteen- to twenty-year-olds, and they *hate* these ads, won't tolerate them, they're too sexy. Believe it or not, American sixteen- to twenty-year-olds don't want to be sexy." But it was only after the creative team from London's Bartle Bogle Hegarty came to San Francisco to see what Mike Koelker of Foote, Cone had done to revive the original "501" jeans in America that the British agency found the British version. (One notes that the role of the American campaign in starting the process is not mentioned in the tribute paid to the local Levi's 501 campaign by British advertising practitioners in the 1988 awards book published by the Institute of Practitioners in Advertising.)[1]

Chew continues: "We make in the country where we sell. The one exception is Japan, because in Japan the fact that it's American-made is crucial to the success of the product. The emotional appeal comes from their fascination with the fifties and sixties. The counterculture. James Dean and Marlon Brando. When you ask people about Levi's here, it's quality, comfort, style, affordability. In Japan, it's the romance of America." Dockers, however, Levi's brand of casual slacks with what the stylists call a "reverse silhouette," was first produced by the company's subsidiary in Argentina, and the brand name was a corruption of the Japanese word for slacks. Foote, Cone & Belding then gave the brand a nautical flair (don't say verbal cleverness doesn't count anymore). "This is a product,"says Chew, not without awe, "that was launched in 1986 and if you'd judged it on the basis of the first year's sales you'd have dropped it — and in 1990, all by itself, without the rest of Levi's, it would be a *Fortune 500* company."

Everybody has to sell to the Japanese. They spend as little as they can on housing, because even if you spend a lot you can't buy much of it, which leaves them all but endless disposable income. Al Achenbaum of Backer Spielvogel Bates remembers back to his days as a consultant, when he was retained by Alfred Dunhill. "They were big in the pipe and cigar business, and going down the drain. Their biggest product was a gold cigarette lighter, eighty to ninety percent sold to Japanese. It was made in Switzerland and marked 'Swiss.' The company that made it was closing down, and the only other people with the precision tools for this purpose were Japanese. But if the lighter was stamped 'Japan,' they couldn't sell it to the Japanese tourists in the United States. So we made a plan for them to convert to clothing stores." This worked to some extent in the United States, though the Dunhill name never did become synonymous with elegant clothes, but it went like gangbusters in Japan, where Dunhill adopted a "shop-within-a-shop" technique to get into (rather than compete against) the big department stores.

David Ogilvy told a story about just how careful a man has to be these days when he speaks for an agency with a worldwide business. No longer active in the creation of advertising, Ogilvy is still listed as nonexecutive chairman and spokesman for The Ogilvy Group, which is now controlled by an English bookkeeper turned adman named Martin Sorrell. In that capacity, Ogilvy one day in 1989 met with financial analysts to talk about the income-producing possibilities of various members of The Ogilvy Group. He said, "When we bought the London agency back in the 1960s, Mather & Crowther, it came with all these little Asian branches. We didn't pay any attention to them at all, we didn't know we had them. Now they're enormously profitable. You can't *imagine* how much money we're making in Malaysia."

Less than two weeks later, Ogilvy relates, the telephone rang in the Ogilvy office in Kuala Lumpur. It was British-American Tobacco. The man said, "I understand Ogilvy tells people they can't imagine how much money the agency is making in Malaysia. We are a third of your business. We want to come in and have a talk with you about compensation."

Ogilvy's initial reaction to Sorrell as acquirer of his name had been extremely negative. According to *The Financial Times,* he called Sorrell an "odious little jerk." ("Shows you how inaccurate the reporting is in the *Financial Times,*" Ogilvy said the other day. "What I really called him was 'an odious little *shit.'*") Quite apart from his origins as an accountant, which enable him to report profits from an increase in Ogilvy's business in a year when the people who work at Ogilvy were all moaning about shrinkage. Sorrell's capacity to make lemonade from lemons derives, says the researcher Alex Biel, from the fact that "other people in the ad business have a penchant for looking on the rosy side of things, while Sorrell looks at the dark side. It gives him credibility." In the end, it gave him credibility with Ogilvy, too: "If I'd known thirty years ago what Sorrell knows," Ogilvy says ruefully, "I'd be a much richer man today."

Most large American advertising agencies now have networks of branches and subsidiaries and partners abroad that account for at least a third (Burnett) to more than half (Lintas, DDB Needham) of their revenues. The British agency Saatchi & Saatchi has gobbled up seven of what had been leading independent American agencies — Compton, Dancer-Fitzgerald-Sample, Backer Spielvogel, Ted Bates, Campbell-Mithun, William Esty, McCaffrey & McCall (plus a huge collection of non-advertising enterprises, including a service that under the name "Litigation Sciences" helps law-yers track the backgrounds of prospective jurors; but some of these are now being thrown back into the pool in Saatchi's financial agonies). Sorrell, who started with the Saatchis, owns J. Walter Thompson as well as Ogilvy. French, German, and Italian agencies have acquired U.S. franchises. Foote, Cone & Belding has exchanged major pieces of share ownership with Publicis in France. One can, of course, exaggerate: the 1988 *Report on the Industrial Outlook* by the European Association of Advertising Agencies found only 22 "multi-national agencies" in Europe out of 1,500 advertising agencies on the continent.[2] But the global mar-ketplace is real enough to have changed out of all recogni-tion the corporations that own the advertising agencies.

1.

The first American agency to open an office abroad was J. Walter Thompson, which went to London in 1899, but Stanley Resor closed it down to save costs when he took over Thompson in 1916 (he was still running it when I pub-lished *Madison Avenue, U.S.A.,* in 1958). Resor reopened his London branch in 1923, because Henry Ford had begun moving cars off assembly lines in European factories and wanted his U.S. agency to do the work there, too. Sam Meek went over to take charge in 1925, and remained the boss of Thompson's international operation into the 1960s. He was a classic American apostle of progress, wearing bright striped shirts and keeping his hands in his pockets. "People are very much alike the world over," he said in the 1950s. "You try to take something away from them, they resist. They all want some security. They're all a little lazy. And there isn't a housewife anywhere who doesn't want to look presentable — or who wants to hear the truth about how she really looks."

For Meek, the world of the 1950s was already an international market, with international commercials running on television worldwide. His favorite example was Danny Kaye's show about children, presented by Pan Am, then the nation's flagship air carrier around the world, on television stations in every world capital that had commercial television. The celebrity testimonial for Pan Am in those days was Ernest Hemingway. By the 1960s, Thompson in London had become what Ogilvy was the first to call "a teaching hospital," where the researcher Stephen King developed philosophies of branding that were carried to America by John Philip Jones and Timothy Joyce, and creative groups were organized around "planners" with research backgrounds, who in principle understood consumers better than the wordsmiths or the wrists or the suits.

McCann-Erickson was the next to travel, also in the 1920s, carried overseas by what was then Standard Oil and became Exxon. Gasoline advertising that works in one country will almost certainly work in others, too. Exxon's Tony the Tiger was all over Europe for years. For Mobil, Keith Reinhard says, "we created a commercial in New York, made it in London, and it's running in twenty countries." This was the man in the asbestos suit — no face shown, so no nationality implied — who came through the fires of hell like Mobil 1. In 1956, McCann created an insurance policy for its overseas branches by persuading Coca-Cola to give it the worldwide advertising task for Coke — and later made the worldwideness of its representation the theme of a campaign, with the lovely "teach the world to sing" commercials.

American companies expanded rapidly overseas between

the wars — Colgate became the leading toothpaste in Italy, Heinz the leading canned soup (not to mention "ketchup") in Britain, Lux the leading toilet soap *everywhere*. By and large they used the same advertising appeals on foreign soil as they used at home. Hollywood movies were the stellar entertainment all over the world, and Hollywood movie stars were universally known (when stars arose in Europe, Hollywood bought them away); and it was Lux that gave them their complexion. Lou Wasey remembered from a time before World War I "a man named Harry Kramer, who started Cascarets and made an international business out of it. I asked him one day if there was constipation in other countries, the same as in America. He said, 'Mr. Wasey, the whole world is constipated.'"[3] But most such American companies placed their foreign advertising through foreign agencies.

Perhaps the most international of all agencies is Lintas, which was started in 1928 to be a house agency for Unilever in England, Holland, and Germany. (The name stood for Lever International Advertising Services.) Through the 1950s, Unilever expanded Lintas around the world, "because," says the C.E.O., William Weithas, "the state of advertising outside the great capitals was infantile." In the United States, Lintas acquired Sullivan Stauffer Colwell & Bayles. During the sixties, Lever set up training programs for SSC&B people and people from the other agencies the company used in the United States, mostly J. Walter Thompson and Ogilvy. "Some time during the training program," Weithas says, "Lever decided that an advertiser shouldn't try to be an advertising agency, too." In a series of complicated transactions, Interpublic acquired Lintas to run in parallel with, and in competition with, its established

McCann-Erickson franchise. Lever still accounts for almost half the Lintas billings, worldwide, and Lintas is still big on training programs, having established a "Lintas University" for its people, with classrooms in Detroit but the instruction supervised by the University of Chicago.

For Weithas, running an international agency is not something that can be reduced to a rule book. One needs different rules for different countries — and for different clients: "It's basically a different ballgame in every country. The basic creative work is done by the 'drive agency,' which may be Paris, more London, mostly here. Coca-Cola is not a local option business; it's a centrally driven business. Phillips and Nestlé are decentralized, with local decision making. Even when the work is mostly in New York, we don't meet the clients in the Racquet Club for drinks anymore. You meet them in Milan, or if it's Nestlé, in Vevey."

Young & Rubicam went to England before the end of World War II, and some others sought affiliation with foreign agencies that handled the same clients. (Y&R, which now has an all but universal presence, having leaped into Eastern Europe as the wall crumbled, still maintains one immensely important though perhaps eroding affiliation arrangement, with Dentsu of Japan, the world's largest and most insular agency.) Leo Burnett, not usually thought of as an agency that came early to international interests, had a link with the London Press Exchange as early as the 1950s. What took Burnett abroad was Marlboro, a campaign rivaled only by those for Coca-Cola and Pepsi-Cola as the most international of advertising expressions. For reasons probably not unrelated to the Levi's story, the solitary cowboy became the advertising instrument in every country but two: in Hong Kong, where the poster had to include more than one cowboy, because a man alone is a man who has been ostracized; and in Colombia, where a cowboy is a man who cleans the stables, and the poster had to show someone who was clearly the owner of the ranch.

"It was Philip Morris and American Tobacco that dictated the changes in the advertising business," says Bruce Crawford, once chairman of BBDO, now C.E.O. of Omnicom, the holding company that owns BBDO and DDB Needham, among others (he made a stopover between these jobs to be president and C.E.O. of the Metropolitan Opera). "Agencies made unbelievable profits on tobacco. In some years, cigarettes accounted for eighty per cent of the profits of apparently diversified agencies." As the nations of the world relaxed their state tobacco monopolies, the pull on the agencies increased.

Much of this internationalization was very informal in the early years. Ted Bates, around 1960, had a problem with excess retained earnings that would be assessed a penalty corporate tax rate if not expended. At about the same time, Colgate was holding out the possibility of business abroad. On assignment from Bates, the British banking house of S. G. Warburg Co., Ltd., tried to buy Masius & Fergusson (the British agency for Mars candy), but no deal could be struck. Someone from Colgate then told Rosser Reeves that the hot agency in London was Hobson & Metcalf, and Reeves went to London to see for himself. John Metcalf picked up the story:

"I was in the seventh day of a week's fast at Eldon Hall when Rosser arrived maniacally in London, and I was whisked away to a suite at Claridges. I met this absurd phenomenon named Reeves, we looked at each other for about six minutes, and the deal was on from that moment.

"I didn't want to sell one hundred per cent of our agency, but Bates was buying all or nothing, and Rosser convinced me. We were a better buy for him than Masius & Fergusson — we were rising faster, and obviously we were smaller and cheaper to buy. The final deal was made in the U.S.A. Hobson and I came over. Bates was still two hundred thousand dollars below our price, but before we went to the final meeting we decided we would take the offer. We came in, and Ted asked us for our decision. I teased him for a while, then accepted his offer. After I accepted, Bates raised the price to our figure.

"The papers had to be signed and the check given in London, and Rosser and Jim Douglass [then Bates's man for international matters] came over for the closing. There were fourteen lawyers in the room, all the papers to approve. We got through with that, and we were about to have the signing, and Rosser turned to Douglass and said. 'Jim, where's the check?'

"Douglass said, 'Rosser, I gave it to you.'

"'Jim,' said Rosser, showing the strain, 'a lot of pieces of paper come across my desk.'

"I thought, for Christ sake! They kept arguing, and they decided they just didn't have the check. Rosser said, sheepishly, 'Well, we brought you these souvenirs, anyway,' and they took out these hideous cigarette cases, engraved with Bates-type typography, and handed them over. And in each cigarette case was a check."

In general, the agencies went abroad, as the banks went abroad, to service a domestic clientele that was becoming increasingly multinational. As of the late 1980s, 87 of the hundred largest advertisers in the United States were multinational companies. "Multinationals are taking over the world," says Carl Spielvogel of Backer Spielvogel Bates. "They want multinational agencies. We handle Mars [the world's largest candy company, which has historically used the same brand name, like Milky Way or Three Musketeers, for different products in different countries]. We do advertising for them in 32 countries — and they employ two other agencies for the other countries."

Crawford is more skeptical. "It was Saatchi that sold globalization," he says. "Ted Levitt [the Harvard Business School professor who has written extensively about globalization] is on their board. They needed that sort of slogan to justify all the mismatched agencies they acquired." Only five of the top ten advertisers in the United States appear on the *Advertising Age* list of the top 50 outside the United States — and of that top fifty, 26 are Japanese, most of which do virtually no advertising in America. Four American companies on the non–U.S. top 50 list — Colgate, Mars, Coca-Cola, and Kellogg — do not make the U.S. top ten.

When American manufacturers began opening plants in Latin America, the economist Ray Vernon attributed part of the move to the operation of his "product life cycle" theory. These mobile enterprises were assuring their place in the early part of the cycle for this product in places where the clock had not yet started. But as soon as a market leader had gone abroad, the followers in his product category trooped after — not so much because they had done an analysis of the opportunities as because the man making the decision would have no defense if his failure to start up abroad cost the firm profits, while he could easily justify a start-up that lost money on the grounds that he had to do what his competitors were doing. Advertising agencies move for copycat reasons, too. *ADWEEK* editors pulled a boldface extract out of their report on global 1988: "As the pan-European client companies grow, the American agency isolationist could find himself consolidated out of a job." Like manufacturers, agencies setting themselves up on the European continent buy into some problems they had never known existed, especially the social laws that make it all but impossible to fire people just because you're losing money.

A few years ago, attitudes toward internationalization were far less Eurocentered than they became after the adoption of the "single market" by the European Community. Latin America, before the debt crisis disabled its capacity to import, was the largest single market for American manufactured goods and thus well to the forefront in the plans of American agencies. Thompson, Ogilvy, and McCann still have a major presence in Brazil, and most of the larger agencies are at least thinking about all the advertising Mexico will need when the orchards of liberalization now being planted begin to bear fruit. In both countries, agencies based in Europe have become increasingly powerful competition.

And there would also have been more discussion some years back of what the Japanese are likely to do in the advertising business. Unlike American exporters, the Japanese did not seek to take their agencies with them when they entered new markets: the Japanese understood from the beginning that they were exporting goods, not a culture. Jay Chiat reports that Mitsubishi was extremely reluctant to put its name on its electronic exports, preferring the culturally neutral "MGA," and the agency had to persuade its remote client that the time had come when a Japanese name helped rather than hurt the reputation of the product. Though they were highly skilled at analyzing the social trends that would make markets in other countries (they aimed precisely at the youth of the 1960s in the United States, starting their export drives with motorcycles and stereo goods), they left the means for exploiting these trends in the hands of the natives. "Wherever they go," says Y&R's Georgescu admiringly, "they play by the rules they find."

Japanese advertising men understand that employment practices that can be taken onto a factory floor, and to some extent into an investment banking house, will hamper imagination in an American agency. The Japanese agencies do leave home to work on the oriental side of the Pacific rim, but in the United States they have been content to be at the most junior partners in joint ventures. Japanese advertisers appear to choose their U.S. agencies without any reference to the agencies' other involvements with Japanese firms. As the Japanese gained confidence in their ability to conform to foreign requirements and manipulate foreign temperaments, observers expected them to begin acquiring large American agencies, and it might have happened in 1990 — except that the Japanese stock market laid an egg and the Japanese banks found themselves squeezed for capital. But so long as Japanese exports pile up foreign currency that must be spent somewhere, somehow, there remains a possibility that acquisitive eyes will turn toward advertising.

Under the eye of history, the first significant change in American agencies dictated by the international imperative was the conversion from private to public corporation. The apparent and perhaps sufficient reason for these conversions, as an irritated P&G executive said some years ago, was to make old advertising men rich. But what drove many agencies to "go public" was the need for a currency they could use to acquire other businesses, especially other agencies. Bates in 1960 may have had excess retained earnings, but few agencies were cash-rich in the early 1970s or 1980s. Given a market for the stock, a publicly held agency could pay with stock to make an acquisition, because the seller could convert that stock to the cash he really wanted. As the conglomerates that formed through the stock market in the 1960s demonstrated in the 1970s, people who can buy with money they print themselves tend not to be very careful in their purchasing. A number of agencies got in just awful trouble. J. Walter Thompson learned just in time that the project to swap programs for minutes on local stations was booking nonexistent receipts. McCann-Erickson came close to bankruptcy in the 1960s when the broadcasting stations learned that the money clients had given McCann to pay for time had been misappropriated for other uses.

In the 1980s the usual funny money was junk bonds rather than shares of stock, but advertising agencies, for a wonder, were only rarely regarded as suitable issuers of debt paper. Banks tended to be helpful because the fees were good and the interest rates paid were generous. In Britain, the stock market itself was prepared to finance takeover bids through "rights issues," by which existing shareholders in a company are given warrants to buy new shares at a price much below existing market price.

British accounting also favored British firms. One of the follies of modern American accounting is the willingness of accountants sufficiently paid for their trouble to accept the reality of an asset called "goodwill," which expresses the difference between the price paid for a company and the market value of the assets on its books. The "goodwill" asset is balanced by an entry of the same amount in the capital accounts of the acquirer, enhancing its net worth. Abuse of this accounting device, with the consent of the government regulators, was among the sources of the S&L catastrophe in the United States.

In the branded products business, however, goodwill

tends to be real enough. "Brand equity" is not a tangible asset, and does not appear on the books, but what Kravis Kohlberg Roberts bought in its $28 billion acquisition of RJR Nabisco was, obviously, the brand equity of Camels and Winstons, Oreos, and Ritz Crackers. (In the RJR Nabisco that emerged from the deal, more than 99 *percent* of the reported capital was balanced on the asset side by goodwill.) Companies that are acquired by other companies become much more valuable in the process, because goodwill is added to their assets. On the other hand, their apparent profitability diminishes, because in American accounting, goodwill, like any asset, must be depreciated over time. This depreciation is deducted from earnings. Much of the cash flow that supposedly will service the junk bonds acquirers issue to make their purchase will be accounted for as depreciation of the goodwill. The thing works like a watch, provided that the new management can generate enough extra operating profit to pay the difference between the low dividends formerly paid on the stock and the high interest that must be paid on the junk bonds.

British firms under British accounting procedure can value their brand names as part of their assets. This is supposed to encourage the stock market to value the shares more highly (though a rational stock market, as most people who play this market have forgotten, will value a business as a going concern, discounting the future earnings stream to present value, and not as a subject for imminent sale or liquidation). Because the books show the assets already, acquisitions can be financed through rights to buy more stock at low prices rather than through debt. And British accounting does not require companies to depreciate intangible assets. This is probably bad practice: most brands do in fact have a limited life, because either their proprietor or the public gets bored with them — "The whole task of advertising Coca-Cola," says Carl Spielvogel, "is to keep a nineteenth-century product contemporary." But some brands, especially those well nourished by advertising, gain rather than lose value with the passage of time. The top ten brands in British groceries in 1989 had an average age of forty-two years, with Heinz baked beans, introduced in 1901, as the oldest, and P&G's Ariel detergent, introduced in 1966, as the baby.

When an American company acquires another American company, it must reduce the apparent profits of its prey; when a British company acquires an American company, the holding company need not show that depreciation in its annual reports. The rules to some degree cut both ways, because the American company gets a deduction from income for tax purposes the British company doesn't have — but corporate income taxes are low in Britain, and, besides, the accountants, clever fellows that they are, may have other ways to take care of that problem. On balance, the important consideration is that dividends are lower than interest payments on junk bonds, so British companies pay lower capital costs for mergers and acquisitions than American companies do, and can outbid American rivals by paying more for the goodwill — the brand franchises — that is at the heart of the package. The fallacy in using this approach to buy agencies themselves, of course, is that the brand name "J. Walter Thompson" or "Ted Bates" has a limited customer base, which knows perfectly well that the quality of the service given under that label is a function of the people who work in the shop, and they will not necessarily stay in this shop if the ownership changes.

Thanks to British market and accounting structures, Martin Sorrell in 1987, having departed his Saatchi employment and struck out on his own, could issue (and, more significant, sell) more than half a billion dollars of new shares in what was essentially a shell corporation. This money was then available to permit him to pay almost $600 million for J. Walter Thompson.[4] The year before, Sorrell's WPP (a maker of wire shopping baskets when he bought it) had shown revenues of $38 million against Thompson's $649 million. Neither JWT nor The Ogilvy Group, which Sorrell acquired the next year, can truthfully be called a happy ship under Sorrell's captaincy, but there are members of both crews who will admit that the cuts imposed by Sorrell's imported management blokes have improved efficiency a lot more than they have impaired performance. As 1991 dawned on an Anglo-Saxon recession, Sorrell's approach seemed to lose legitimacy. The costs of servicing even the relatively small quantity of debt WPP had taken on to finance its American acquisitions outran the earning capacity of the enterprise, and Sorrell had to request the forbearance of bankers while he searched around for access to cash.

In the early days, when the acquisitions were made mostly by Americans, people were sent across the Atlantic to show the natives how American clients liked to have their advertising agencies managed. ("Jack-booted, a lot of them," Metcalf said at the time, observing others rather than complaining about Bates.) A tour of duty in one of the foreign subsidiaries became in the 1970s part of the career path of every American agency executive who aspired to a marshal's baton in his agency. Now the natives are at least nominally in charge everywhere, though every multinational agency has delegates from the home office in most of its subsidiaries, and people rise to the top through their national stream. It is still true that most of the clients of American agencies abroad are multinational companies with their roots or major operations and major advertising budgets in the United States, and they expect more or less the same service from all the parts of a group. Grey is one of the neatest, with a three-man office in Europe and another in Asia to coordinate the subsidiaries on a day-to-day basis, plus regional meetings every six months and a worldwide meeting every other year. But there's no way the C.E.O. can avoid personal involvement.

"We started buying in 'sixty-two," says Grey's Ed Meyer, "and completed our acquisitions in 'seventy-five. We've had a chance to become a family. Of my thirty-five agencies around the world, thirty-two are run by people who have spent their whole lives in that agency. This is not the Balkans. I've been meeting with the same guys for fifteen years." One echoes the "I've been meeting." Perhaps the most deleterious aspect of internationalization has been that the top management of the agency must spend so much time on the road. "As Rupert Murdoch said," Meyer comments, "the only way you can manage is by walking around." This is a problem, of course, even for the national agency in a country as big as the United States. Asked where he lived at a time when his agency's billings were more or less equally split between Los Angeles and New York, Jay Chiat of Chiat/Day said, "At the airport."

2.

The buzzword through the late 1980s was the "pan-European account," representation of an advertiser through the twelve countries of the Common Market. Most observers expect that this amalgamation of national accounts will become standard operating procedure once so many other national barriers dissolve into the "single market" to be born by proclamation in 1992. The appeal of this approach is, of course, the immense economies of scale if a single creative department at a single agency can handle a multinational campaign — and, perhaps most significant, a single television production company can be paid to make a single television commercial for use throughout the continent.

But it is by no means clear that the same advertising campaign can in fact be used throughout Europe. In April 1989, two new-business officers for J. Walter Thompson described the dilemma of multinational advertising for a conference of the U.K. Advertising Association. They posited a new low-fat diet candy bar named "Jupiter" (presumably not related to Mars), and a commercial with three main selling points: "Your waistline will like it, and you get a free tape measure to prove it"; "It's an after-school treat that won't spoil your evening meal"; and "When your doctor says cut down, reach for Jupiter, with one-third the calories of other chocolate bars." The commercial couldn't be used for anything like all of Europe. In Belgium, commercials may not refer to dieting. In France, premiums can't be worth more than one percent of the sale price, which rules out the tape measure, and children can't give endorsements, which means no child eating a Jupiter after school. In West Germany, any comparison with another candy bar would be illegal; in Denmark, ads can't make nutritional claims; in Britain, candy must be presented as only an occasional snack — and no doctors in the commercial.[5] Some of these differences are to be phased out as part of the reconciliation of national regulations leading up to 1992, but some will still be around for a while. As a witty Irishman put it, "We all know 1992 is coming; we just don't know when."

There continue to be, of course, ten different languages (plus Gaelic) in the European Community, and cultural differences that reach back to the dawn of history and are by no means eliminated. Selling blank videotape to the Italians, the best argument is high color fidelity; selling it to the Scandinavians, the best argument is the durability of the tape, the fact that you can play it over and over again without any loss of quality. Jay Chiat, who rode the tiger of Reebok sneakers for several years, found that in France viewers don't like commercials in which people sweat. "In England," says Y&R's Satish Korde, "hunting is an upscale activity. In the United States it's a downscale activity." Heinz can't make money with Weight Watchers in England — "there's more of a stigma attached to Weight Watchers," a twenty-five-year-old shopper in a London suburban supermarket told a *Wall Street Journal* reporter — but Nestlé can do well with Lean Cuisine.[6] Allan Morgenthau of Ayer/Barker in London cited "a recent commercial for an indigestion medicine in which a person is 'farting in a lift.' This, he warns, would not be acceptable in many European countries."[7]

Products are differently positioned in different markets. Badedas gel, a bubble bath, was a luxury product in Britain, but a middle-market brand in Germany. The products themselves may be different, too. John Bernbach of DDB Needham (first president of the European Association of Advertising Agencies) notes that Cadbury chocolate bars, manufactured in England, sold in Australia and New Zealand, taste quite different from Cadbury chocolate bars, also manufactured in England, sold in New York. Hershey chocolates have never done well in Europe, because the product isn't sweet enough for European tastes and the company won't reformulate. As late as 1988, and maybe later, Colgate was differently formulated for the different countries of Europe. "If we were taking Tropicana to Japan for Seagram's," says John Bernbach, "the first thing we'd have to tell them is that there's a big difference between the United States and Japan in what people consider the right taste for orange juice." Grapefruit-flavored Gatorade doesn't sell at all in Italy, but it's the best-seller in Germany. The French like top-loading washing machines, and the British want front-loading washing machines. "Philips," said David Pringle, chairman of BBDO Europe, "is required to manufacture seven varieties of television sets and employ seventy engineers solely to adjust new models to extant local requirements — all within Europe."[8]

The universality of advertising has natural limits. "I think you can launch an international campaign from a single idea source," says Jay Chiat, "but you can't manage it centrally. You have to manage from inside local cultures. Couture is the same all over the world: you see the same brands everywhere. Does that mean you can use the same advertising? You can, but what you get is a level of mediocrity. It sounds like a boring way to make money." Some limits are dictated by the nature of the campaign. Backer Spielvogel Bates has Mars's Pedigreed brand of pet food across a number of markets (one notes in passing that two of the top ten brands in British groceries, measured by sales value, are Pedigreed's Whiskas for cats and Chum for dogs). The agency uses the same slogan to sell dog food in all of them: "The world's best dog breeders recommend Pedigreed," with pictures of the breeders and their prizewinning dogs. In each country, obviously, you want that country's best breeders and their individual dogs. You have to make arrangements in each country to get the people and have the commercials filmed.

Beyond that, there may be legal constraints. Countries may require that producers of television commercials use local talent, and local talent is always required, of course, to speak the voice-overs and, where appropriate, the dialogue.

Dr. Ronald Beatson, executive director of the European Association of Advertising Agencies, told a meeting of Euro-marketers in 1989 that products with "the same formula, the same name, the same positioning, the same pack design and the same advertising across the EC account for less than 5 percent of the sales value of branded products. These are products like Head & Shoulders [shampoos are among the most universal products, and pictures of women's hair ben-efitting from them are the most universal sales pitch], Martini, Michelin, Pampers, Rolex, etc." Their share, he added, would probably rise to 10 percent by the middle of the nineties. In fact, there may then be more such brands than Dr. Beatson projected. Gillette very spectacularly joined the group in 1990, launching its new Sensor razor with identical advertising in Europe and the United States. Whirlpool, having acquired 53 percent of the Philips world-wide white goods business, launched its brand name in ten European countries with a single pan-European campaign, spending $40 million in the process. One notes sadly, speak-ing of perceived values, that research told Whirlpool not under any circumstances to stress its American origins. Nick Mote, the coordinator of the campaign for the Publicis agency, said that people in Britain and Austria especially "associate technology and innovation with Germany; they do not associate it with America." The U.S. was seen as a fast-food, throwaway society "where consumers lacked dis-crimination and would buy anything."[9]

While fully identical Eurobrands accounted for only 5

percent of sales in 1988, Dr. Beatson continued, "Semi-standardized and 'developing' Eurobrands, whose marketing may be similar across the EC but is not yet the same because of differences in formulation, positioning, packaging, or even the brand name, account for about forty percent of sales' value. These brand categories may grow to sixty percent of the sales' value of branded products over the next five years." At least some of these developing Eurobrands will be brands that were purely national as the decade began. Product access across national boundaries will be smoothed by the great collection of codes and specifications being prepared by the bureaucrats and politicians of the European Community to supersede the codes and specifications now imposed by the national governments. The Germans have even been persuaded to relax the notorious "purity" regulations that in effect said only German beer was pure. Nurturing the growth of local and regional brands into Eurobrands — and perhaps, who knows, world brands: Oil of Olay started somewhere — will be the exciting and profitable task of the multinational agencies as the decade progresses.

In 1988, the satellites flew, equipped to bring European households access to channels not owned or licensed by their governments. As of 1990, there were nine satellites in the sky, transmitting about forty channels to a pan-European footprint. Most of the programs, of course, are beamed at homes where the language of the program is not spoken. Salacious movies, of course, know no nationality. The number of satellite dishes turned on in the backyards of British households passed the million mark in 1990, and Nielsen projected that by 1995 about a quarter of all British homes would be able to receive programs via direct broadcast satellites. All these channels are heavy — perhaps dangerously heavy — with advertising, and some have returned to the sponsorship models of the 1950s (*The Ford Ski Report, The Coca-Cola Eurochart Top 50*). Annie Read of the Parallel Media Group in England suggests that in buying time for Europe, advertising agencies will come around to choosing a single program as their vehicle rather than the channels selling the time.[10] Others have suggested that with the internationalization of media ownership, advertisers can deal with a single organization — Rupert Murdoch's could give you newspapers, magazines, and television in Europe, the United States, and Australia — for the placement of an entire campaign.

As long ago as 1987, Alex Kroll of Y&R made the point that certain marketing wars had been won and lost in certain countries even before the product was available to most (or even any) consumers: "In India, Colgate has a lock on the toothpaste market. Maybe forever. Lux has it in soap. Gillette has won the battle of the beards and blades, even though they don't have a plant there — their share is built on smuggled blades from Saudi Arabia. The cola wars are over in the USSR. . . . Pepsi is preferred. . . . The Japanese have all but conquered China in electronics and autos: Toyota is preferred to a Rolls, regardless of price." A Nielsen study in East Germany in early 1990 reported that "GDR [German Democratic Republic] consumers know some western brand names better than do consumers from the FRG [Federal Republic of Germany]."[11] When the wall came down, East Germans poured into West German Kaufhausen demanding products by brand name. In 1990 and 1991, advertising in Eastern European countries was entirely an investment for the future, because any western goods that come in are bought immediately, at premium prices, whether advertised or not. As Kroll pointed out, you can win the battle for share of mind before the market opens.

3.

For almost fifty years after the end of World War I, Americans supplied the rest of the world with popular culture and the advertising that related to it: movies (especially spectacles, Westerns, Chaplin, Laurel and Hardy), Gershwin-Porter-Kern-Youmans-Rodgers, flappers, gangsters, picture magazines, television comedies in gray kinescope, Elvis. As late as 1980, I saw a wedding party in Turkey let their festivities wait a while so they could watch *Dallas*. But by then we had begun importing — James Bond and the Beatles, Twiggy and *Till Death Us Do Part* (known domestically as *All in the Family*), an appalling sadomasochistic Japanese serial that became *Charlie's Angels,* songs from the San Remo Festival, Brigitte Bardot, Andy Capp. The Saatchis and Sorrells may have been assisted by accounting and capital formation rules in England, but they could never have moved as they did without the admiration and even envy of modern British advertising felt by American practitioners.

Andrew Ehrenberg of the London Business School explained to Randall Rothenberg of *The New York Times* in April 1989 why American and British advertising were so different: "There is a public view in the US that advertising is a very powerful force, so the hard sell is more common there. Here it is widely accepted that advertising is a very weak force and exists to reinforce existing attitudes rather than to persuade people of things they didn't believe before. That's why it tries to be so entertaining." Peter

Cooper of the International Qualitative Research Group drew a series of dichotomies between the European and U.S. attitudes. Toward science and data collection:

EUROPE	US
Humanism	Logical Positivism
Subjectivism	Empiricism
Phenomenology	Behaviourism
Eclecticism	Pragmatism
Feeling-based	Data-based

Toward the activity of advertising:

EUROPE	US
Holistic	Linear
Symbolic	Measurable
Complex	Assertive
Rapport	Control[12]

Interesting examples of what the Europeans like in the way of advertising come out of the *concours* for the year's best commercials, held at Cannes in the same theatre that holds the film festival. One American winner was Phil Dusenberry's commercial for Pepsi-Cola, featuring an archaeologist from the third millenium digging out a midden near New York and explaining all the artifacts to his assembled students until he comes to the distinctively shaped Coke bottle, which he can't explain at all. This is a pleasant piece of entertainment, and probably worth Pepsi's money because it makes the bottlers feel happy, but it is of course an in-joke for people in the advertising business and the cola wars. European Pepsi drinkers who saw the joke may perhaps have felt reinforced in their choice, but it's hard to imagine an American to whom this commercial would have sold a bottle of pop.

Alex Biel of the Ogilvy research operation had a practical explanation of why European advertising has been on the whole more imaginative than American advertising during the past fifteen years. "It's because corporate structures are smaller," he says. "The head of the agency deals with the president of the company. It's the chain of nay-sayers in the United States that gives us such bland advertising." The head of an agency who would not like to be quoted saying it commented sourly that because compensation in Europe is from fees rather than commissions, "you don't automatically put everything on television, which means you think to more purpose." Another possible practical reason makes for a cheerful thought. The top ten food store chains account for more than half of all food store turnover in more than half the Common Market — in Germany, Denmark, Netherlands, Belgium, Britain, France, and Ireland. Establishing a brand image that makes a difference in sales is much harder when the retailers are in control; only persistence and delicacy can do the job. The United States, in this respect, is well on the way to become Europeanized, and maybe American advertising will follow on a similar path.

Not the least of the paradoxes in the advertising world of the 1990s is the simultaneous insistence on segmentation in national markets and universality in markets across borders. What this means, mostly, is that advertisers have set their agencies different problems in the American and European markets. But there is also a good deal of intellectual excitement in the concept of a nonverbal communication that cuts across language barriers. "I'm studying semiotics," said Bill Wells of DDB Needham with the enthusiasm of a man in his sixties learning something new and important. His boss, Keith Reinhard, talks about making a presentation to a meeting in Europe, almost half an hour of film clips without a voice in any language. "The technology of global advertising," says Laurel Cutler, "is ahead of the practice. Sight, sound and motion are the future — words will become very much less important, especially if your product is standardized, like Coca-Cola or Levi's or Marlboro, which have their own imagery and symbolism." Even if they are formulated differently, brands now look alike wherever they are on sale: love and money have been expended on distinctive logos. The argument that nonverbal messages will do the trick does not, however, find universal acceptance. "I do not believe," says BBDO's Allen Rosenshine, "that visualization transcends culture. But it's easier to produce the commercials. If you have to use words, saying it in German takes twice as long."

Technical and another set of legal differences may direct attention in different directions in different countries. You can't build a data base out of direct response to telephone numbers presented in TV commercials in Germany, for example, because German law forbids telephone orders. Neither Germany nor Denmark permits privately operated "800" numbers. In Germany it is illegal for an advertiser to sell the list of his customers to another advertiser. In both France and England, however, lists and their use are well developed. Drayton Bird of Ogilvy Direct told a charming story of the British launch of a line extension of Impulse, described here as "a fragrance," elsewhere as a "female body spray." Bird hired list makers, who found lists of purchasers of romantic novels. The mailing piece offered its recipients "a special gift for your skin," and a chance at a free trip on the Simplon-Orient Express — "A Touch of Romance" — from London to Venice. "The interesting thing," Bird wrote, "was not so much the great success of the mailing (on some lists it got over 50 percent response) but the *letters* that came with the replies to the offer. A very high percentage of these letters had actually been sent on notepaper with pastel colors or floral designs, very similar to the notepaper we used for the mailing. That was how accurately we had gauged the *group* which represented our target market."[13]

The future, then, seems to hold "convergence" across national borders. The corporate proprietors get bigger and fewer as European companies merge or buy each other out, and they tend to consolidate their advertising in fewer agencies to achieve economies of scale. But a relatively minimal state of alert in the governments to prevent anticompetitive mergers will permit market forces to deconglomerate the conglomerates — especially, one suspects, the grouped advertising agencies, which are subject to sclerosis. The rules of the game will be similar from nation to nation, and the policing of content will probably diminish as societies become more market-oriented. In the context of constitutional law, Judge Learned Hand once argued that "a society so riven that the spirit of moderation is gone, no court *can* save; that a society where that spirit flourishes, no court *need* save; that in a society which evades its responsibility by thrusting upon courts the nurture of that spirit, that spirit in the end will perish." Similarly, a capitalism in which a substantial fraction of the population believes for any length of time that oat bran prevents cancer cannot be rescued by mere political action, and except where necessary information is expensive to get (that is, whether the scale gives true weight or the ingredients are as advertised), or where products are demonstrably harmful and addicting, the market will dispose of false values at least as rapidly as the legislature can.

Sales are stubbornly local even when the retailers and the producers are global, and the fragmentation of the mass media is happening everywhere. There are dangers here: the educative function of the mass media has been much underestimated by the vocal fraction that is already educated (more or less). The efficiencies of data-base marketing may indeed reduce opportunities for innovation — and capitalism in the end, as Joseph Schumpeter stressed, succeeds only through innovation. The ultimate social justification for advertising, as I shall argue in the next chapter, is that it facilitates innovation.

Fortunately, the antibodies are strong, and spread even more rapidly than the diseases. In Europe and Asia as in America, advertising is a business where intelligence can never entirely substitute for talent. Successful advertisers over time will be those who use the thrusting small shops to slash the tails of the dinosaurs. "There's no barrier to entry in the advertising business," says Alex Biel. "You can open a shop across the street, and if you do good work you can still do what David [Ogilvy] and Bill [Bernbach] and Leo [Burnett] did. The key is that you want to make advertising, and if you get paid well for it, that's so much the better."

Advertising in the 1970s and 1980s grew most rapidly in Europe most obviously because it penetrated new media — neither radio nor television had much commercial content outside the United States until well into the 1960s. But an even more important factor may have been the ease of entry, for new nationalities and new social classes. The spread of the American agencies to other countries offered grand inducements to talent to get into this work and build something that could be sold for what would have been unimaginable prices only a few years earlier. As new people came into advertising, perspectives changed, and everybody became less parochial. The process continues, though often frustrated by risk-aversion and overreliance on research.

This continues an American pattern, for just as the advertising business spread across the globe in the 1980s, it spread across the American continent, into the cities of the hinterlands from which aspiring professionals used to depart (like Earnest Elmo Calkins) to seek their fortune in the big town. Agencies won national recognition and national accounts from places like Richmond, Virginia, Minneapolis, and Portland, Oregon. In the economics of the industry, they were inevitably minor factors, but they did much to maintain the self-image of the creative community.

"The nineteen-seventies had been a dreadful time," says Harry Jacobs of The Martin Agency in Richmond, "the era of the stand-up commercial. But in the eighties we got through consumerism, stopped worrying so much about what you could say, and we had a wonderful decade. Regional agencies weren't confronted with the bureaucracies in huge client companies, didn't have to satisfy all the testing that depressed creativity. The regional agencies came up through the advertising shows — shows like the One Show, and CA on the West Coast, where the winners were not the branches of the big agencies but the regionals: we dominated the shows. We began to be the definition of what was considered good work; people talked about Tom McElligott in Minneapolis and our Mike Hughes.

"We're beginning to pick up work that has numbers as the criterion," Jacobs adds in a soft Southern accent. "But in most cases we are still close to the top people in the client's business, which means we don't have to walk around in mud the way they do in New York." It's easy to be too sanguine in these matters: The Martin Agency is owned by Scali, McCabe, Sloves, which is in turn owned by The Oglivy Group, which is owned by WPP; and Fallon McElligott through a different chain has the same ultimate ownership. As agencies show increasing promise, in the United States or elsewhere, they tend to be gobbled up by the international conglomerates. The purpose of selling stock in advertising agencies is to make old ad men rich. . . . But especially as their troubles mount in the more austere 1990s, the conglomerates may learn that they really have to leave these fellows alone to do their work. "The only thing I know that's consistent about this business," says Jacobs, "is that there's some degree of creativity in it." Both at home and abroad.

Futures, and Options

A LOVELY OLD STORY tells of the man who came to town with a pushcart, and opened a shop, and by offering fair prices and good service built that shop into a department store, a veritable emporium eight stories high and a full block square. He had an only son, a bright boy whom he sent to college and then to business school, to take over the department store. After completing business school, the young man became a C.P.A., learning the innards of many businesses and their organization. Finally, he was ready to return home.

His father welcomed him, and told him that the first thing the store needed was a business plan, for it had grown like weeds. He ordered everyone to open all the books to his son, and gave him the keys to every room but one, a corner of the eighth floor that had long been sealed from prying eyes. The young man took his portable computer with him to every floor and every department, went through the files, analyzed the statements with his father's accountant, and at the end of the year came back to his father's office white-faced. "I think we're bankrupt," he said. "We're losing money all over the store. Frankly, Dad, as I go through the books, I don't think this place ever made a profit."

The father took a last key from his key ring, and gave it to the son. "Go to the eighth floor, my boy," he said, "and look in the secret room."

The young man was back in a few minutes, bewildered. "There's nothing in that room," he said, "but a battered old pushcart."

"Yes," his father said. "Everything else you see in this building is profit."

1.

In 1960, American business spent not quite $12 billion on advertising, which was 2.32 percent of the U.S. gross national product. In 1990, nominal GNP was about ten and a half times what it had been thirty years earlier, and "advertising" expenses were eleven times as great, more than $130 billion, about 2.4 percent of GNP.[1] In Japan, advertising takes about 1.1 percent of GNP; in Europe, about 0.7 percent.

In 1960, "Madison Avenue" stood for elegance and power, gray flannel suits but also a certain roguishness, expense accounts used for all sorts of things, hucksterism, "hidden persuasion." As a result, three of the four then-giants — J. Walter Thompson, Young & Rubicam, and McCann-Erickson — cultivated an image of great dignity. At Thompson every senior executive had a budget to decorate his own office in anything from Louis Quinze to Mies van der Rohe. Young & Rubicam went (and still goes) for the color green, with overstuffed green leather couches and chairs, wide hallways, open spaces around the secretaries, like the platform of a small-city bank. McCann was very modern but restful, with pastel colors. Only Batten, Barton, Durstine & Osborn, perhaps because Bruce Barton was the lay preacher of American capitalism and needed no further dignity and perhaps because Bruce Barton was cheap, housed senior employees like junior employees in a rabbit warren of cream-colored corridors and closets. Even today, housed in one of those utilitarian buildings that extended Rockefeller Center across Sixth Avenue, BBDO is a little less decorated than its rivals.

Thompson, the biggest agency, employed about 2,500 people in its U.S. offices in 1960, but most of them were engaged in scutwork of one kind or another, punching keys on typewriters and adding machines, detailing layouts sketched by other hands, calling respondents to question-naires, billing, filing. There was no table of organization. When a consulting firm prepared one for the agency, its chairman, Stanley Resor, welcomed the chart enthusiasti-cally, and said he wanted only one change in it. He then took an eraser and erased all the lines that connected the boxes.

Resor's Thompson had grown organically, by the growth of its own clients and of the packaged goods industry from the Great Depression to the 1960s. Most large agencies were dominated by the people who handled, and in a sense owned, the client accounts — just as Wall Street brokerage houses were dominated by the "customers' men." Good "account executives" took their clients' businesses very seri-ously indeed (just as good customers' men lived or died by the investment success of those who used their services). Proper performance of the account service function was the fulcrum on which the successful agency moved the world. "A lot of clients trusted agencies to look after their affairs," said William Phillips, retired C.E.O. of The Ogilvy Group.

"Then the clients became more marketing oriented and hired better marketing people themselves. If the account people weren't qualified, the agency got on slippery ground. If your account person isn't smarter or more experienced than the client, you lose control. And when you lose control in a service industry, you can't manage your expenses."

Today's big agencies, except for Leo Burnett and Young & Rubicam, are in large part the result of mergers and acquisitions. Well over half the magazine ads and commercials the consumer encounters are made by a large organization, with several thousand employees flung far over the globe. There must be a management information system that permits a top management to control expenses and allocate resources, and the almost inevitable tendency is for the people who acquire these powers to run the agencies — or for the people who run the agencies to become absorbed in the internal problems, like Phil Geier fretting about client conflicts in Brussels. "When you get that big," says Hal Riney, "your interests in preserving the company transcend your interest in the longevity of the client business." Daniel Yankelovich, who was making money by taking the market strategy business away from agencies, saw the difficulty as long ago as 1981. "There's been a great loss at the agencies," he said. "The work has been routinized." Yankelovich didn't sell his research and consulting services to advertising agencies. "We're not interested in dealing with the *parts*," he said.

The difficulty is generally recognized, and worried about. "In any advertising agency, you have the inside people and the outside people," says Roy Bostock of D'Arcy Masius Benton & Bowles. "The outside people create the ads and solicit new business. You've got to have somebody on the point, a linebacker who puts his nose in every day. The inside should be done by a CFO, by internally focused people. I should be outside, because this is a service business, a hands-on business, but much of the time I can't be." And D'Arcy, with $4 billion in billings, is one of the three large agencies that never went public. Elsewhere, the situation is worse. Backer Spielvogel Bates's brochure for itself proclaims, "This is the only truly global agency where two of the names on the front door still signify individuals who actually work with clients and create advertising."[2] But Saatchi & Saatchi owns BSB Worldwide, and the idea of absorbing Bates and Rosser Reeves's old "Unique Selling Proposition" was neither Spielvogel's nor Backer's, though they have to live daily with the fallout.

From 1960 to 1975, with the single exception of 1972 (when the Federal Reserve loosened all the restraints on the money supply, in part to help Richard Nixon beat George McGovern, and all businesses had some unanticipated cash to spend), advertising's share of GNP declined, bottoming out at 1.75 percent in the recession year of 1975. Then came the greatest boom the industry had ever known. In the nine years 1975–1984, expenditures on advertising rose by an average of 13.5 percent a year, from $28 billion to $88 billion. There was a more-than-threefold increase in agency revenues. Some of that was attributable to inflation, but for most agencies costs inflated much less than revenues. They had long-term leases on their office space, the electronic revolution was cutting their costs (a report from the European Association of Advertising Agencies noted in passing that in 1970 a computer cost the wages of twenty people, while in 1990 you could buy twenty computers for the wages of one person). Because there was more money to spend, agency leadership passed from the cost controllers at the gateway between advertiser and agent to the creative department.

Conglomeration began in this heady time. "There's no question but that the largest agencies, as a group, are continuing to increase their market share at the expense of the medium-size agencies," Doyle Dane Bernbach president Neil Austrian told the company's annual meeting in May, 1982. "This is happening because most of the large budget increases are coming from multinational clients who are assigning their accounts, with increasing frequency, to the large multinational agencies."[3] Then the roof fell in: from 1985 to 1990, an industry accustomed to double-digit growth fell back to a rate consistently below 8 percent. "Everyone said the problem was costs," said Bill Phillips. "But, really, it was revenues." And it was in those years of economic pressure and low margins — not in the glory years of 1975 to 1984 — that the megamergers and takeovers rocked the advertising business.

Almost by definition, mergers and acquisitions are not driven by the creative side of the business. And the money men, in the modern world, have no interest in the future. David Ogilvy was one of the first to take an agency public, and is now ashamed of it: "My excuse is that I'd been a poor boy. I'd never even owned a house. A million dollars seemed like an immense amount of money to me." Bill Bernbach, another poor boy, also cashed in early, to his son's later discomfiture. The fact is that going public substantially disabled the agencies in terms of their ability to recruit and keep talent. The price the sellers got for their interests reflected estimates of the cash flow the agency would generate in future years. Simply, they took for themselves the discounted value of an income stream that others would in fact earn. These transactions often involved taking on debt, and even when purchasers of the stock paid the full price, the agencies now became accountable to the people who managed the money of the nation's pension funds, universities, and hospitals and got paid for their results, quarter by quarter — an avaricious collection of market manipulators with the time horizon of a caterpillar. The agencies became much less flexible in their ability to respond to the changing economic environment. And the years when the mergers and acquisitions were making news in the advertising industry were years when the underpinnings of the business were growing increasingly shaky.

Agencies had risen historically with' the growth of national media and the conquest of the distribution system by large, nationwide manufacturers. A lot of what had made advertising "work" in the postwar years had been the power of television. When brands sponsored television programs, the network by contract had the right to preempt an advertiser's time twice or three times a year to show some special presentation. As noted, it was the all but universal observation of the packaged goods companies that when your show was preempted, you felt the reduced sales all the following week. Efficiencies in buying spots on local television stations counted for a lot, because everything on television was effective to some degree. Some advertising, of course, worked much better than other advertising, but money spent on television was almost never wasted. The situation was tailor-made for the Procter & Gamble approach to marketing — hang a sample of a new product on every doorknob and then run commercials that simulated word-of-mouth.

In the 1980s, the national media began to fragment: network television lost almost a third of its share of the national audience. Cable channels grew unbelievably in number, profiting by the desire of advertisers to target messages to narrow audiences. "The difficulty now," says Reginald Brack of Time-Warner, which owns lots of cable systems plus Home Box Office and Showtime, "is channel availability. I never thought I'd live to see a day when eighty-five channels wasn't enough." When interviewed in early 1990, Brack was trying to clear space on cable systems for a "courtroom channel" to be managed by *American Lawyer*. The specialization of cable channels meshes well with the increasing specialization of magazines. Brack reports that cable has become the largest source of new magazine subscribers, while magazines and book clubs have become the largest advertising customers for cable.

Absent such specialization, however, the effectiveness of the medium plunged. Thirty-second spots had taken over from one-minute commercials in the 1970s, and as the 1980s proceeded the fifteen-second spot became common. In the last years of the decade, the networks were broadcasting more than *six thousand* commercials a week, more than a third of them in the form of fifteen-second spots (one-minute and longer commercials constituted only 2 percent of all the commercials broadcast). And the agencies were hooked on television — it was part of the routinization, and part of the way the compensation structure worked, because both television time *and television production costs* had remained commissionable. Negotiating with clients about compensation, Burnett's Fizdale wants commissions on everything the client spends, to protect the quality of his people's advice: "We want to be neutral about how you spend your money. We want to tell you that the best thing you can do is put your name on a race car, and get paid for it the same as if we had said, 'Put your money in network TV.' The wonderful thing about the commission system is that you don't charge them when you get an idea." But the decision as to what is and what is not "commissionable" inevitably resides with the client.

Meanwhile, retail outlets were consolidating. In hindsight, it seems obvious that the arrival of the computer would dictate a move to centralized information control in retailing. Charles Peebler, Jr., of Bozell argued as late as the spring of 1990 that it hadn't happened yet: "Of the 25,000 supermarkets, scanners are being used in maybe two hundred to control and replace inventory. All that money has been spent and they're only glorified checkouts. In one store we are aware of, there were twenty thousand items, and only eleven thousand, six hundred of them were scanned in a given week. Eighty-four hundred never sold at all, and of the eleven thousand, six hundred that did sell, four thousand sold less than four units. This gives advertising agencies a chance to assume a different kind of relationship with manufacturers and retailers."

But Peebler was out of date: from Vons to Jewel to Safeway to Publix, the big supermarket chains had bought their IBM systems and with or without help from Nielsen and IRI were busily evaluating the profitability of every inch of shelf space in the stores. They had already flexed their muscles with the food manufacturers by demanding "slotting allowances" and "cooperative advertising" beyond what the space actually cost them, fees for setting up displays, rights to return new products that didn't sell, and much else. "There's no question," said Grey's Ed Meyer somewhat uncomfortably, "that today the advertiser has to spend more of his money against the trade." By 1990, trade promotions — promotions for the benefit of the stores, not the consumer — had become not only an occasional substitute but an absolute precondition for an advertising campaign.

The impact on brand equity is severe. "For ten years, American business has been in the business of destabilizing brand loyalties," says Lester Wunderman. "That's what promotion does: it turns stores and consumers into disloyal husbands who chase everything that comes along." In July 1990, General Motors announced significant price increases for the 1991 models. In August, they announced rebates, to be offered by dealers even before the cars officially went on sale. "At age five," says Larry Light scornfully, "I had an image of a Chevrolet or a Pontiac or an Oldsmobile. There are now three hundred and fifteen nameplates on cars in the United States, but these brands don't exist anymore. It's a cancer. You don't think about the brand, you think about the price. Not because the consumer doesn't want them — the consumer desperately wants them — but because the marketing people have destroyed the brands. It's a test-tube case of how an industry can do it all wrong." Almost fifteen years have passed since Henry Ford II said, "Agencies are in the caddy shack." They have not been good years for the franchise value of American automobile brands.

Worse lies ahead for the agencies that live by packaged goods advertising. "In-store advertising" of one sort or another is obviously going to be a major feature of the 1990s. Some such has long been there — end-aisle displays and counter cards are of great antiquity. Now there are background music tapes with commercials to play in the stores, and electric signboards with messages running along them wherever the shopper looks up. The fanciest form of in-store advertising is the Videocart (mentioned earlier), a screen built into a shopping cart to carry advertising messages triggered by transponders in the section of the store to which the cart has been pushed. This gizmo was originally developed by IRI, the research house, but has now been spun off to independent status — and the founder of IRI has abandoned his own company to run it. Several of the largest packaged goods advertisers have already decided that the creative departments of advertising agencies have no contribution to make to in-store advertising, which should therefore be noncommissionable.

Except for Bill Bernbach and his image-building ads for the downscale Ohrbach's thirty-odd years ago (and Ohrbach's went bust anyway, some years later, because the merchandise didn't validate the ads), agencies and stores have never had very happy relations. Sears is notoriously the worst large client. The Gap started as a store to sell Levi's jeans (plus records and tapes), in part because its owner couldn't find his size when he went shopping. Levi's became a discount item, and The Gap bought Millard Drexler away from Ann Taylor to change the chain's image and appeal. "I had decided before I got here," Drexler said in the company's headquarters building, a converted loft by the piers in the unfashionable side of San Francisco, "that I wanted a different vision of what we had. Before, every ad this company placed had been promotional. Every TV ad said, 'Levi's on sale.' I thought that what drives this business is the top five percent, the people with taste. We had to go from a schlock discount business to a high image. As at Ann Taylor and Brooks Brothers, which had the same ownership, we had to create our own brands and control our product. Except for Levi's, everything is our own label; we sell nothing that's not concepted and produced by the store. Good taste is a rare commodity in America. Everything is concept: no one piece can be separated from any other piece. We had ad agencies come here, sat through these tortuous presentations, and none of them got it."

So Drexler brought over from Ann Taylor, Maggie Gross, a young woman with frizzy red hair, who had been his advertising manager there (after ten years of experience as a buyer). "I don't consider myself in advertising," says Ms. Gross; "I consider myself in retailing. We start from the merchandise, not from some great idea for an ad. We're in a business where gut reactions are much more important than focus groups. With eight hundred stores, accessibility to the company is pretty easy, and there's one factor that defines our market — there has to be something about your life that takes you out of a business suit." Gross's staff of twenty-five does all the advertising — "everything except taking the pictures and posing for them" — for the national chain, and, where desired, for the more than 800 individual Gap stores. Plus Banana Republic. Agencies still pitch the account once in a while, and Gross hears them through. "I've seen thousands of presentations, but there's not one agency that could interpret the vision."

What the advertising agencies must face in the 1990s is a still-growing feeling among advertisers that advertising is no longer the central element in the marketing of branded products. "We have 'techie' management," says Peter Georgescu, meaning technologically oriented bureaucrats, "who don't feel the power of advertising in their gut, as their predecessors did." But the skeptics are not doctrinaire nor naive. Most of them are people who used to work for advertising agencies and now work for clients. They know perfectly well that the best advertising sells vast quantities of whatever it is they have to sell, at very low cost per sale. "Every so often," says one of them, "we see a brand take off for no reason other than advertising. We're very interested when that happens." But they also know that routine advertising is not cheap per sale. They have been taught, rightly or wrongly, that market share drives profits, and they see too many experiments where heavying-up the advertising budget does little for market share, while other elements in the marketing mix produce dramatic (if short-term) effects. "Knowing my share of market is useless unless I know the price," says the PepsiCo C.E.O., Roger Enrico, a good client, whose company has been with BBDO for 32 years and who credits the agency for many of its victories in the cola wars, "because price [meaning the comparison between your price and competitors' prices] drives share."

IRI has recanted its initial scoff at the relationship of benefits to costs in advertising. And strong arguments for the longer-term efficiency of advertising, backed by computer-generated three-dimensional graphics, have been generated by the PIMS study (Profit Impact of Market Strategy), sponsored initially by General Electric, Scott Paper, and Armstrong Cork. But at best that's averages, and a lot of it is tautology, because advertising expenditures track sales: if greater advertising over time doesn't generate greater profits, there's something seriously wrong with the fellows who make up the budgets. Keith Reinhard of DDB Needham notes grimly, "I have a client who says, 'Don't waste your breath telling me how advertising built brands. I know that. What can you do for me *today?*'" And the answer had better be something more than "I can make advertising for you that will jump the hurdles raised by the copy-testers who work for you."

Perhaps the most level-headed evaluation of modern advertising has come from the British researcher Simon

Broadbent, whose conclusions are summarized in *The Longer and Broader Effects of Advertising,* a pamphlet assembled by the Institute of Practitioners in Advertising.[4] "Branding" he writes, "is part of the reason consumers buy one product rather than another.... Advertising is usually the major contributor to branding.... The brand image is a mass of great momentum which is slow to alter direction, and often we are dealing with unquantified effects. This does not mean that they are unreal. True marketers have the instinctive and correct feeling that the brand is their most valuable property, that it will evaporate slowly unless supported, and that long-term effects are the main justification of the advertising investment."

The half of the advertising dollar that is *not* wasted supports not only consumer attitudes but also trade enthusiasm — Broadbent points to a case where the loss of sales following a cessation of advertising seemed far more the result of dealer discouragement than loss of consumer support. For the results of advertising to be measurable in the marketplace, Broadbent notes drily, "the advertising content must *be* sales effective (this cannot be assumed)." Good advertising, in other words, pays out: advertising that is not good advertising doesn't pay out. The conclusion is far from surprising, but it leads quickly to a further question: are the conditions right in the industry for the creation, recognition, and support of good advertising? And the answer here is by no means certain. Risk aversion and low time horizons may work their worst harm here — and the national tolerance for high greed levels may have wrecked the industry's natural resilience. It is hard for people to argue that their clients should take a long-term view when they have themselves sold for their own benefit today the cash flow that will come from the work of their successors.

2.

"On the marketing side," says Enrico, "I can't see what the agency brings to the party. Why should great marketing minds go to work for an advertising agency?"

The future of the industry resides in its ability to find an answer to Enrico's question. If advertising is merely a way to execute a marketing strategy developed by the client, the advertising agency will indeed become a vendor of technical services and nothing more. And because the client has so many things to think about other than the relationship of his brand and its customers, the value of the brands themselves is likely to decline.

Agencies can flourish only to the extent that they establish themselves as the custodians of the brands. Though I thought some of the customs of the industry degrading a generation ago, there were odd symbolic virtues about the old ways. When Leo Burnett demanded that the employees of his agency use the brands it advertised, he was demanding of them a gesture of faith that their brands were better than other people's brands. When brands sponsored radio and television shows, the people choosing the shows were guided by some sense of the personality of their brand. The copywriters visited the factories to be sure they had a grip on the qualities of the brand and how those qualities got into it. The consumer research the agencies performed was directed at how customers ranked this brand and why, what they liked about it, and what they disliked about it.

The attitudes involved went back a long, long way. "The brand is a concept that goes back to the medieval guild," says Larry Light, a stout man of forty or so with fire in his eyes, who was bought out of Ted Bates when the agency was sold to the Saatchis. "It began with silver, pewter, and cloth. The tradesman put a mark on it. His mark was a promise that he would make the same thing to the same quality next time. He called that mark his 'trademark.' A trademark is not a brand. A trademark is a name. A brand is what you do with the name. It means the quality of the product will be there next year: quality is in open stock. The Europeans understand this. That's why the luxury products come out of Europe today, why the Japanese buy European rather than American. We sell products. They sell brands."

The conventional American wisdom these days is that advertising agencies work in conditions of "parity products." This attitude, too, is not entirely a novelty. A generation ago, Rosser Reeves said that his clients came into his office with two half-dollars, threw them on his desk, and said, "Mine is the one on the left. You prove it's better." Even a genuine product advantage, Reeves argued, couldn't last very long, because it would be copied. Reeves, however, took this as a challenge to find something in the product or the manufacturing process that was not being *advertised* by anyone else (and that was of some importance to consumers) to create a "Unique Selling Proposition." By getting there first with the claim, his client would secure possession — especially if he kept advertising it. Anybody else who made the same claim, true as it might be, would in large part advertise the brand that had got there first.

Today, by contrast, the copywriters rarely visit the factories, and the "planners" who advise them are experts only in consumer attitudes. Focus groups tell the people who prepare the ads what consumers want from this sort of product, and the ad then seeks to tell what looks like the largest identifiable group of prospective customers, within the bounds of a legality greatly stretched in the Reagan years, that this product offers what they want.

Peter Georgescu says that the answer to Enrico's challenge will come when advertisers realize that modern technology has made the consumer king, and that the advertising agency is much closer to the consumer than the advertiser can be. But the argument is less than self-evident. It's at Procter & Gamble, not at the agencies, that every employee up to and including the C.E.O. is supposed to take fifteen minutes once a year manning the consumer-complaint hot line. Though there are clearly exceptions (Keith Reinhard being among the most obvious: all the campaigns identified with his name relate to a personal understanding of what eliminates consumer worries about a product), the people who work for advertising agencies are even less likely than the people who work in consumer-oriented corporations to have a natural fellow feeling for Joe Sixpack or Harriet Homemaker. Remember Bill Wells's life-style questionnaire. Time in the office will not effectively substitute for time spent walking up and down the world and looking around; "qualitative research" in sterile surroundings may yield insights to the insightful, but not strategies.

Since some time in the 1970s, the buzzword has been "positioning" — the goal of the advertising is to "position" the brand. Shortly before his death, Reeves made fun of "positioning." He said, "That word is so used today, I have been in no advertising discussion in the last ten years in which the word positioning wasn't used in every other sentence. So I went to one hundred advertising men and asked them to write a definition, and no two of them agreed." One could make fun of the Reeves approach to argumentation ("One hundred advertising men," and "no two of them"). And the Reeves view of advertising, the notion that "USP" was a science, was an easy target, for much the same reasons. So were the ads Reeves wrote and inspired, which ranked every year among the most offensive. But because the people who worked under his direction looked first to the product they were advertising, USP produced unusually *durable* campaigns. Indeed, BSB Worldwide is still claiming "USP" as the reason a client should shop here.

Looking to what the consumer wants rather than to the product has generated some of the most effective advertising — "less filling" for Miller Lite, "good neighbor" for State Farm — and it fits well with the instincts of many high-quality creative people. ("Jay Chiat and Hal Riney," said Y&R's Peter Georgescu very generously, "have a research department in their own souls, but the rest of us have to intellectualize it.") But because it rests on what may be the shifting sands of consumer taste rather than the enduring qualities of the product itself, such advertising may do less to establish the brand for a long haul. In the end, brands do not seek their customers; customers seek their brands. Apart from its purely informational function (most often used to convey the news of price promotion), advertising adds a value, and carries the existence of that value to the attention of those who will be motivated to find it. Consumer research is essential to find the benefits people hope for when they buy the product and to choose media for the advertising message, but it can't tell you what value can most effectively be added to the brand. That's what the creative folk create.

And consumer research, of course, may be very seriously misleading. All the consumer tests showed that people preferred Seven-Up to Slice. IBM decided not to help the Haloid Company make its new Xerox copier because an expensive Arthur D. Little survey of businesses indicated there wouldn't be enough demand for the product. "Invention," in Sol Linowitz's nice phrase, "was the mother of necessity." It often is, in a capitalist economy where law prevents undue concentration. In a fair proportion of cases, people don't know what they want until they've had some time to try it.

Bill Phillips, recently head of Ogilvy, says that the "parity products" argument is itself disabling: "If a client comes in and tells you his brand is like the others', you know he's going to be a bad client." But worse than that is on the horizon. At both IRI and Nielsen, the word is that the most common single request from advertisers testing changes in their product or marketing mix is for information about what happens when you knock an ounce off the package or an ingredient out of the product. Do consumers notice? Or can you charge the same price for 23 ounces of cereal that you've been charging for 24 ounces? What can advertising do when the client comes in and says, in effect, "My brand is now less good than its competitors. You get consumers to believe it's better." The second most common demand made of the research houses relates to price. If we bump the price up by 20 percent and then advertise 10 percent off, does anything happen to sales that argues people have noticed that they're paying more than they did before the "price reduction"? Of course, we don't need an advertising agency to do that.

Phillips in 1985 made a blunt speech to a conference of the General Foods Post group, which had been an Ogilvy client for 27 years. Its title was "Why Your Advertising Agency Needs a Better Product." He picked up from the PIMS study not the argument that corporate profitability from branded products is directly correlated with advertising expenditures (which is what the American Association of Advertising Agencies chose to feature five years later) but the evidence that "the variable most closely associated with good financial performance over the long haul is *relative, perceived product quality*."[5] Hal Riney is even more blunt. "The truth is what it all comes down to," he says. "Advertising today is supposed to make up for product weakness, which it was never designed to do." One of the most brilliant campaigns of the late 1980s was Leo Burnett's series of vignettes featuring the children of celebrities, proclaiming "the new generation of Olds." But the car, unfortunately, *was* "your father's Oldsmobile," and the campaign did not do much for sales.

An internal memo from another agency, which would not enjoy being cited for it, spoke of "the Schlitz example, where the manufacturer cut the actual quality of his product and realized a short-term profit but a long-term disaster. The fact is, it often takes a while for a change in actual product quality to be perceived by the consumer. Buried somewhere in my long-term memory are research projects where the manufacturer has made a minor cost-cutting change in the product and 'tested it' via consumer research to see if consumers noticed the difference. And often they didn't . . . according to the research techniques used. And later on they did it again, and indeed, consumers couldn't tell the difference between this newer formula and the last one. But somehow after a while the brand lost share. Maybe if they tested the second cost-cutting variant against the *original* formula, the consumer could have indeed perceived a difference between them.

"But that was in another country, and besides, the brand is dead."

I leave to others discussion of the question of what will

happen to American competitiveness in the world market if the makers of American brands seek their profits by substituting inferior ingredients or giving short weight. For present purposes, I need note only that an advertising agency confronted with such a situation would do well to resign the account, for the client will ultimately blame the agency when the brand fails, and the reputation forfeited by an agency that serves such a strategy is probably worth more than the commissions lost by refusal to do so.

There are interesting questions of intellectual property here, rarely raised. Rick Fizdale of Burnett reports soliciting an account from a client who said that he felt an agency should no longer receive commissions on a campaign that had been running for two years. "Do you mean," Fizdale asked, "that Philip Morris should have stopped paying Burnett for the Marlboro Man in 1948?" And the prospective client said yes, at which point Fizdale told him Burnett was no longer interested in his account. Whatever Philip Morris pays Burnett for the Marlboro ads, the agency's contribution was cheap at the price, for the value of that brand rests primarily on the advertising. In a well-ordered world, clients would continue to pay the creator of the campaign some fraction of the commission on commercials or ads for a brand as long as the campaign survives, even if the client drops this agency and signs up with another.

If an agency is going to perform effectively as the custodian of the brand, it must have some degree of say on the packaging of the product, the other uses of the name (to what extent will line extension weaken or cannibalize the original, as Miller Lite did to Miller High Life, or Orange Slice did to the original Slice), the consonance of the distribution and the brand character (Jay Chiat urged Mitsubishi not to sell its television sets to discount stores), and the extent to which the existing franchise should be risked by advertising designed to induce switches by people not now consumers of this brand. "Brands deserve that messages on their behalf be internally consistent and mutually reinforcing," Lewis Pringle of BBDO Europe told a meeting of the European Marketing Council in 1988. "A customer ends up with one impression of a brand's identity. How much of that impression results from advertising, point of sale, packaging, collateral materials, a salesman, direct marketing stimuli, sales promotion, sponsorship, customer motivation techniques, delivery vans, service engineers, match books, telesales or sky writing isn't relevant and is usually not recalled. The customer has one net impression. And somebody had better be managing the overall process by which that impression is created. That someone has and will continue to be the client. But, as the next five years unfold, clients will need help, a partner, and the ideal agency had better be prepared to provide that help and be that partner."

Advertising agencies understand as advertisers often do not that you can't sell everything to anybody, and you can't sell anything to everybody. "There's this great big market out there called the United States," says Jim Carter of Sears's information services. "If you go after that, it's the death knell."

For years, advertisers have asked those who test their campaigns to measure the "switching" — the customers of other brands who buy or say they will now buy this one — that occurs as the result of exposure to the new advertising. If the switchers are light users — or even heavy users whose tastes are flighty — the campaign that tests as a success may well prove a disaster. Advertising for a brand significantly different from the previous advertising may in time lose more sales to current customers, as the image of the brand changes, than it gains from new customers. Simon Broadbent warned British advertising people that the almost exclusive use of short-term sales results as the criterion for their Institute of Practitioners in Advertising awards could be misleading: "Nearly all published IPA papers show that the campaign studied increased sales in the weeks or months after it appeared, and did so economically. Nothing wrong with that. But as so often happens with managers who are given a new aid, they come to believe that there are no others. Once more, a particular objective, this time the achievement of short-term volume return, is seen as all there is."[6] The possible irrelevance of short-term sales results also lies behind Rosser Reeves's boast that mediocre advertising carefully tended for years would beat the whey out of brilliant advertising that a competitor changed every six months.

The challenge and danger to advertising from the scanners is that messages can be delivered individually to prospective customers. At first, this capacity will be used in simple ways, to select for coupons or other benefits only those who do not normally buy this brand, inducing switches without losing revenues from current customers. Or, given the known purchasing habits of the targeted prospect, the advertiser can deliver a simple message geared to his habits. "We are moving," says Nielsen's John Costello, "from persuasive selling to fact-based selling." But individualization can also be used, once this system is in place and familiar, to change the claimed values of a brand only for this one consumer. Your customer can conceivably be switched from your brand by someone advertising another brand — who is not risking the disaffection of his own current customers because this advertising is being delivered *only* to your customers. On the day that such advertising becomes feasible, the commonplace war imagery of the business will no longer suffice to express the viciousness of the competition among the makers of branded products. One cannot even speculate on what schizophrenic brands will do to the affect of communications, and to the morale of business and society, in an information-soaked era.

"Brand managers," said Ronald Beatson of the European Association of Advertising Agencies, "should regard themselves not just as administrators of advertising and promotion budgets, but as custodians of assets that may well be worth more than the factory."[7] But the brand manager is there a year or two: it's a training job. The advertising agency on average will be there a decade, probably longer if the advertising is successful. The agency is a more plausible custodian, but if it is to perform that function it must have a significant in-house research facility, some degree of authority over the marketing function, and some influence in product planning. The research is especially crucial, and increasingly absent. As long ago as 1986, Leo Bogart warned, "The super-advertiser has so much at stake that it becomes more inclined to think it knows best and less inclined to listen to the agency's advice. Advertising research represents sensitive marketing intelligence that becomes a pawn in the game. Competitive considerations might make clients more inclined to concentrate it in-house, more reluctant to leave it within the agency's control. Where agency research, at least in its heyday a quarter-century ago, tended to be feisty, eclectic, and cosmopolitan, corporate research styles tend to be insular, linked to the company's internal politics and dependent on favored research suppliers for intellectual stimulation."[8]

DDB Needham may have been disingenuous but it was not foolish in its proposal that it would accept compensation based on results if it could "orchestrate" the marketing of the brand. How this is to be done is a question that exercises many agencies. Y&R's "whole egg" is one statement: the client is to find it efficient to purchase the range of marketing services separately from subsidiaries of his agency. Lintas has a diametrically opposed approach, offering a variety of services to be performed as needed, costs paid by a single payment to a profit center that allocates the work. But both rest, obviously, on the client's willingness to regard the agency as a partner rather than as a vendor — and that, in turn, rests on the agency's access to the marketing talent Enrico thought would not wish to work for an advertising agency.

Enrico undoubtedly expresses the historic trend: the movement in the industry is overwhelmingly from agency to client. But there could be a different answer to his question. Just as creative talent often finds it more stimulating to work on a range of products, marketing talent might wish to work by brief immersions in a variety of problems stimulating a variety of solutions. To draw such people, however, the agency would have to promise them more money than they make at client companies, and would have to assert a political position vis-à-vis its clients that gave agency marketing people the belief that what they said would count.

The pay problem is by no means insuperable. A recent study by the Wyatt consultancy, *Top Management Remuneration,* indicated that among American companies with gross revenues of $100 million or more, the heads of the marketing divisions made only 36 percent as much as the C.E.O.'s, and ranked sixth (after finance, administration, sales, production, and research) on the pay chart. By contrast, marketing division heads ranked second in Switzerland, Germany, France, and Sweden, and third in Britain — and in all countries their compensation was at least half again as much as it is in the United States by comparison with a C.E.O.'s compensation (largely, of course, because C.E.O.'s are so preposterously overpaid in America).[9] Especially if the agency can promise the marketing man a piece of its action, the price would probably not be imposing. But here, again, the agencies are hampered by their status as publicly traded companies. A courageous board at a publicly traded agency would try to start educating stockholders to the need for substantial and widespread stock options to return an increasing share of the ownership of advertising agencies to the people who work in them. Dilution is a lot better than disaster.

The other requirement is, of course, even trickier. The fact is that the advertising agency's position has grown increasingly servile. Too many layers of brand management separate the agency from top management in a client company. Even if the agency chief does have access to the corporate chief, he can only rarely cut through his client's bureaucracy: "The C.E.O. feels that if he overrules his own people," says Grey's Ed Meyer, "he's going to lose the best of them." The very idea that an agency might have the authority to oppose a client's decision to cut the quality of a product sent a senior officer at a big company into a paroxysm of laughter. "They're all whores," he said. "They do what you tell them to do. The only thing that worries them is losing the account." His reproof is certainly too round: agencies really do resign accounts, without being fired and without knowing what new business can replace what they're giving up. But nobody in the industry would deny that there is something in what he says.

Thirty-odd years ago, I argued that the best of the leaders of the agencies were in truth professionals, and illustrated the argument with the claims of those agencies that they had turned down or resigned accounts because they didn't like what they would be asked to do. They asserted, I wrote, that "advertising is a profession based on the creative intelligence of its practitioners. . . . The future of advertising," I pompously continued, "must lie in this direction." What the future held, in truth, was the decline of professional standards everywhere, so that the most servile advertising person is today no less "professional" than any number of eminent lawyers and accountants. But the custody of brands will require, if not vestal virgins, some degree of priestly vocation. Adding perceived value to branded products implies an assumption of responsibility. If you don't believe that the people who consume the brands to which you add value should be doing so, you shouldn't be advertising them.

The obvious reference is cigarettes. Bill Bernbach, when he took his agency public, announced as part of his registration statement that he would never permit it to accept a cigarette account, because he didn't want to be a party to poisoning people. Investors were entitled to know that he was deliberately limiting his possible profitability because he felt personally accountable for his work. Lots of advertising people who wouldn't say so publicly admired that statement then and would admire similar statements now, if anyone in this business were prepared to make them.

Prohibiting cigarette advertising is doubtless a bad idea, because it is a large camel's nose in a small tent. Even in conditions of dire emergency, it is unwise to give governments the power to prohibit people from receiving encouragement to do things that are bad for them. The Constitution wisely enjoins the making of law for that purpose, because most governments most of the time will want to prohibit what's bad for the government. But advertising people who believe that their work adds value to the brands they advertise must take the next step, and believe also that these values will lure their neighbors — and their neighbors' children — to an addiction that causes sickness and death. Surely, the best talent of an industry should not be devoted to the promotion of such products, simply because the tobacco companies pay well. Sunshine being still the best disinfectant, perhaps the compromise would be to require that the agencies that prepare cigarette ads sign the ads themselves, together with the manufacturer. Your friends and neighbors know where you work. Would I rather, someone asked, have cigarette advertising done by irresponsible cheapjacks rather than the cream of the industry? To which the answer is: Yes.

4.

"To live on the human plane," Frank Knight wrote in 1925, "is to choose." Bill Moran looked back to Sir Herbert Read's appreciation of Greek antiquity, where the same word served for both grace and efficiency. "Read observed," Moran noted, "that our technological civilization divorced grace and efficiency — and thereby diminished the richness of life. He declared that the desirable values are always aesthetic in origin, and he added: 'Where there is choice there is value.'"

Moran proposed that "we should encourage proliferation of choice, that although the new choices will be less price elastic at first, they will pay for the maintenance of the old choices while increasing the number of specific times and circumstances and people which can be satisfied.... There is value added by association as well as by engineering specifications in product design and in advertising.... There is social value in the other person's choice."[10]

These attitudes were always latent rather than conscious among advertising people, but they were, beyond the money and the fun, the ultimate justification of the efforts that built this industry from Earnest Elmo Calkins's pushcart to the giant emporia of words and pictures we see today. There has been a substantial loss of nerve in the last third of a century, a lowering of horizons caused in large part by the fortress mentality of a conglomerating debt-based capitalism that digs itself ever deeper into the trenches of assured cash flow. Choice is not served by line extensions. Imagination is not likely to be highly valued when agencies working for one or more of the three giant advertisers (P&G, Philip Morris, RJR Nabisco) place more than half of all national advertising billings. The idea of added value fits poorly into an ethos where time is money; a mentality that is forever trying to control costs will not stimulate creative efforts that are by their nature highly wasteful.

Those who do not believe there is a mystery about advertising will never be good clients. But mystery does not lie in averages. Once upon a time, clients thirsted for breakout advertising, and the leaders of the industry reveled in the opportunity to slake that thirst, sometimes with Montrachet and sometimes with branch water. For advertising to remake itself, and for American business and society to benefit by advertising's capacity to promote choice, the nation will have to be shaken from its insistence on safety first. That's not the way the world is moving — indeed, it's not the way the leaders of today's advertising industry would like to move — but one of the lessons that can be drawn from the study of advertising, or business, or society, is that change comes when you least expect it.

Some Hails and a Farewell

As NOTED in the preface, this book was suggested originally by Peter Georgescu of Young & Rubicam, and he and John Rindlaub of that agency were helpful throughout its preparation. John O'Toole of the American Association of Advertising Agencies not only introduced me to many of his leading members, some of whom were too young to remember *Madison Avenue, U.S.A.,* but on several occasions actually made the appointments for me, a kindness that cannot be fully appreciated by anyone who has never been a free lance and had to do these things for himself. He was also unfailingly courteous even when he most disagreed with me. Marilyn Bockman of the A.A.A.A. library and her invariably helpful and informed staff put my hands on much material that would have been difficult to find without them.

The greatest help came, as always, from the research community — William T. Moran, Charles Ramond, Frank Stanton, Alex Biel, Larry Light, Rena Bartos, Timothy Joyce,

Bill Wells, Leo Bogart, Ben Lipstein, Gian Fulgoni, Josh McQueen, Satish Korde, and a number of people at Nielsen who can't be thanked by name because they are part of the Nielson machinery. Don Pepper walked me through the most fascinating presentation I have ever witnessed. Among the agency heads, Carl Spielvogel, Hal Riney, Bruce Crawford, Allen Rosenshine, Keith Reinhard, and Lester Wunderman gave me especially informative interviews. It was great fun, and useful, to see David Ogilvy again.

This page is written at a time of deepening gloom in the business, and much of this book turns out to be about the reasons for gloom. But W. H. Auden's Prospero advised his Ariel, "should you catch a living eye/ Just wink as you depart," and perhaps a wink is in order. What has been devastating the advertising industry is the growing feeling among advertisers and retailers that the selling job should be done predictably through the weight of money rather than speculatively through the employment of imagination. In 1991, and perhaps for some time thereafter, money will be scarce, and as a result, the demand for imagination may rise. As the levels of management are reduced, reliance on suppliers must increase. Though it is hard to imagine a future when the advertising agency would become again more than just a supplier to what are now distinctly customers rather than clients, the business *can* become again more fun than it has been in recent years. The sort of wise guy who went to advertising in the 1950s wound up in the 1980s in investment banking, which was not good for banking or for the wise guys. As they drift back to the realm where illusion is legitimate, the irreverent young may give the industry what Bill LaPorte of American Home Products said was all an agency needed: a few more lucky commercials. As producers, consumers, and indeed viewers we would all be the beneficiaries of that.

Martin Mayer
New York
January 1991

Notes

PREFACE

1 Milton Rokeach, *Beliefs, Attitudes and Values.* San Francisco: Jossey-Bass, 1970, pp. 182, 183.
2 Martin Mayer, *Madison Avenue, U.S.A.,* New York: Harper & Brothers, 1958, p. 313.
3 Frank H. Knight, "Cost of Production and Price Over Long and Short Periods," *Journal of Political Economy,* 39 (1921): 304–335; in Frank Knight, *The Ethics of Competition and Other Essays.* London: Allen & Unwin, 1935, p. 213.
4 See U. S. Congress, Office of Technology Assessment, *International Competition in Services,* OTA-ITE-328. Washington, D.C.: U. S. Government Printing Office, July 1987.

CHAPTER 1

1 Earnest Elmo Calkins, "Eliminating the Jobber," *Printer's Ink,* May 31, 1905, p. 8.
2 Jean-Noël Kapferer and Gilles Laurent, "Consumer Brand Sensitivity: A Key to Measuring and Managing Brand Equity." In Lance Leuthesser, *Measuring and Managing Brand Equity.* Cambridge, Mass.: Marketing Science Institute, 1988, p. 12.
3 David Ogilvy, *The Unpublished David Ogilvy.* New York: Crown, 1986, p. 112.

4 John Philip Jones, *What's in a Name?* Lexington, Mass.: Lexington Books, D.C. Heath Co., 1986, p. 32.

5 Frank Knight, "Economic Psychology and the Value Problem," *Quarterly Journal of Economics,* 39 (1925): 372–409; quoted from Knight, *Ethics of Competition,* pp. 77, 98.

6 James Webb Young, *How to Become an Advertising Man,* Chicago: Advertising Publications, 1963, p. 69.

7 George Akerlof, "The Market for 'Lemons': Quality Uncertainty and the Market Mechanism," *Quarterly Journal of Economics,* 84 (August 1970): 499.

8 Lord Kaldor, "The Economic Aspects of Advertising," *Review of Economic Studies,* 18 (1950): 1.

9 John Philip Jones, *Does It Pay to Advertise?* Lexington, Mass.: Lexington Books, 1989, pp. 3–4.

10 Lester Thurow, *The Zero-Sum Society.* New York: Basic Books, 1980, pp. 147–149.

11 William D. Wells, *Planning for R.O.I.* Englewood Cliffs, N.J.: Prentice Hall, 1989, p. xv.

12 John O'Toole, *The Trouble with Advertising.* New York: Times Books (paperback ed), 1985, p. 101.

13 Quoted from John Philip Jones, *What's in a Name?* from *The Art of Writing Advertising,* ed. Denis Higgins, Chicago: Advertising Publications, Inc., 1965, p. 23.

14 Jones, *What's in a Name?* p. 5.

15 Jerry Della Femina, *From Those Wonderful Folks Who Brought You Pearl Harbor.* New York: Simon and Schuster, 1970, p. 137.

16 Leo Bogart, *Advertising: Art, Science or Business?* The James Webb Young Fund Address, Urbana-Champaign, Ill.: University of Illinois Press, April 7, 1988, p. 5.

17 Earnest Elmo Calkins, . . . *And Hearing Not.* New York: Charles Scribner's Sons, 1946, pp. 245, 229–230.

18 Ibid., pp. 225–226.

19 John Martin, *The New York Times,* December 6, 1959.

20 Anna Kisselgoff, *The New York Times,* December 7, 1974.

CHAPTER 2

1 Carol J. Simon and Mary W. Sullivan, *The Measurement and Determinants of Brand Equity: A Financial Approach,* p. 4.

2 Al Reis and Jack Trout, *Bottom Up Marketing.* New York: McGraw Hill, 1989, p. 71.

3 Jones, *Does It Pay to Advertise?* p. 296.

4 IBM and Xerox: Sol M. Linowitz, *Memoirs of a Public Man.* Boston: Little, Brown, 1987, p. 80.

5 Timothy Joyce, *What Do We Know about How Advertising Works?* London: J. Walter Thompson, Booklet No. 25, 1967, p. 1.

CHAPTER 3

1 Earnest Elmo Calkins, . . . *And Hearing Not,* p. 228.

2 Ibid., p. 211.

3 Ibid., p. 248.

4 Ibid., p. 253.

5 Stephen Kessler, *Chiat/Day, The First Twenty Years,* New York: Rizzoli, 1990, p. 215.

6 William Wells, John Burnett, and Sandra Moriarty, *Advertising Principles and Practice.* Englewood Cliffs, N.J.: Prentice Hall, 1989, p. 93.

7 Ibid., pp. 95–96.

8 Roger Enrico, *The Other Guy Blinked: How Pepsi Won the Cola Wars.* New York: Bantam Books, 1986.

9 "Media Buying under a New Aegis," *The Financial Times,* May 3, 1990, p. 14.

10 See John Wicklethwait, "The Advertising Industry," *The Economist,* June 9–15, 1990, p. 14.

11 Calkins, . . . *And Hearing Not,* p. 234.

12 *Broadcast Ratings,* Hearings Before a Subcommittee of House Committee on Interstate and Foreign Commerce, 1963, part 3, p. 1448.

13 Bernice Kanner, "New Bag of Tricks," *New York,* May 28, 1990, p. 20.

14 Enrico, *The Other Guy Blinked,* p. 151.

15 Martin Mayer, *About Television.* New York: Harper & Row, 1972, p. 73.

16 Eric Clark, *The Want Makers,* London and New York: Viking-Penguin, 1988, p. 84.

CHAPTER 4

1 Kessler, *Chiat/Day: The First Twenty Years,* p. 156.

2 FRC General Order No. 32, cited in *Television Network Program Procurement, Report of the Committee on Interstate and Foreign Commerce.* Washington, D.C.: Government Printing Office, 1963, p. 264.

3 In Gilbert Seldes, *The Great Audience*. New York: Viking, 1961, p. 197.

4 Seldes, p. 197.

5 Mayer, *About Television*, p. 28.

6 Calkins, . . . *And Hearing Not*, pp. 228–229.

7 Raymond Sokolov, *Wayward Reporter*. New York: Harper & Row, 1980, p. 3.

8 *Red Lion Broadcasting Corp. v. FCC*, 375 U.S. 367, @ 389–390.

9 Mayer, *About Television*, p. 15.

10 Neil Borden, *Advertising: Texts and Cases*. Chicago: Irwin, 1951, p. 576.

11 Fred W. Friendly, *Due to Circumstances Beyond Our Control*. New York: Random House, 1967, p. 183.

12 *Television Network Program Procurement*, p. 90.

13 Mayer, *About Television*, pp. 62, 63.

14 "Sears Wants to Increase ROP Spending; Asks Newspapers' Help," *Editor and Publisher*, July 5, 1986, p. 19.

CHAPTER 5

1 Quoted in Mayer, *Madison Avenue, U.S.A.*, p. 41.

2 Martin Mayer, *The Schools*. New York: Harper & Brothers, 1961, p. 366

3 Daniel Starch, *Principles of Advertising*, Chicago: A. W. Shaw & Co., 1925, p. 309.

4 Timothy Joyce, *What Do We Know about How Advertising Works?* Booklet No. 25, London: J. Walter Thompson Co., 1967, p. 3.

5 Alfred Politz, "The Dilemma of Creative Advertising," *Journal of Marketing*, 1960. The parable as told here is in the phrasing of Timothy Joyce, *What Do We Know about How Advertising Works?*, p. 21.

6 Politz material from Mayer, *Madison Avenue, U.S.A.*, pp. 253, 186 ff.

7 Calkins, . . . *And Hearing Not*, p. 162.

8 Leo Bogart, *Advertising: Art, Science or Business?*. The James Webb Young Fund Address, Urbana-Champaign, Ill.: University of Illinois Press, April 7, 1988.

9 Joyce, p. 11.

10 "Two Views of Advertising Research: US vs. UK," *Journal of the Market Research Society*, vol. 31, no. 4 (October 1989): 538.

11 John Ward, "Four Facets of Advertising Performance Measurement." In Chris Baker, ed., *The Longer and Broader Effects of Advertising*. London: Institute of Practitioners in Advertising, 1990, p. 44.

12 Charles Ramond, *The Art of Using Science in Marketing*. New York: Harper & Row, 1974, pp. 177–178.

13 Wells, Burnett, and Moriarty, *Advertising Principles and Practice*, p. 140.

14 Mayer, *Madison Avenue, U.S.A.*, p. 45.

15 Ramond, p. 3.

16 Wells, Burnett, and Moriarty, p. 118.

17 Ibid., p. 140.

18 William T. Moran, *Brand Presence and the Perceptual Frame*. Greenwich, Conn.: Longman-Moran Analytics, Inc., 1987.

19 Stephan Buck, "Single Source Data — The Theory and the Practice," *Journal of the Market Research Society,* vol. 31, no. 4 (October 1989): 492.

20 Leo Bogart, "What the Scanners Show," *Advertising Age,* June 8, 1987, p. 18.

21 "Roundtable Discussion: A Creating Exploration of the Future," *Journal of Advertising Research,* February–March 1990, p. 17.

CHAPTER 6

1 Paul Fenwick, ed., *Advertising Works.* London: Institute of Practitioners in Advertising, 1990, pp. 181 ff.

2 European Association of Advertising Agencies, *Industrial Outlook.* Brussels, 1988, p. 10.

3 Both Meek and Wasey are in *Madison Avenue, U.S.A.,* pp. 90–91.

4 Nancy Millman, *Emperors of Adland.* New York: Warner Books, 1988, p. 181.

5 Laurel Wentz, "Pan-European Ad Faces Regulatory Gymnastics," *Advertising Age,* April 24, 1989, p. 44.

6 Joann S. Lublin, "U.S. Food Firms Find Europe's Huge Market Hardly a Piece of Cake," *Wall Street Journal,* May 15, 1990, p. 1

7 Casey Davidson, "Mass Marketing, European Style," *ADWEEK Special Report,* June 6, 1988, p. G28.

8 Lewis G. Pringle, *What European Clients Will Need from Their Advertising Agencies in 1992: A Talk.* Brussels: Brussels, Exhibition Center, May 20, 1989, unpaginated.

9 Clay Harris, "Women of Europe Put Whirlpool in a Spin," *Financial Times,* March 1, 1990, p. 11.

10 Sue Woodman, "Looking at the Eurotube," *ADWEEK Special Report,* June 6, 1988, p. G16.

11 *AIM* (Age of Information Marketing), vol. 2, no. 1, 1990. Northbrook, Ill.: A. C. Nielsen Co.

12 Peter Cooper, "Comparison Between the UK and US: Their Qualitative Dimension," *Journal of the Market Research Society,* vol. 31, no. 4 (October 1989): 512, 513.

13 Drayton Bird, "The Database Demystified," *Viewpoint.* Chicago: Ogilvy & Mather, August 1989, p. 5.

CHAPTER 7

1 Figures and percentages from *Trends in GNP Ad Volume, TV Ad Volume, 1960–1995,* TVB Research Trend Report. New York: Television Bureau of Advertising, 1990.

2 *The Largest Small Agency in the World,* Backer Spielvogel Bates Worldwide, New York, 1990, p. 3.

3 Nancy Millman, *Emperors of Adland,* p. 75.

4 Available from the Institute, 44 Belgrave Square, London SW1 8QS. Thé quotations are from pp. 9, 10, 11.

5 William E. Phillips, *Why Your Advertising Agency Needs a Better Product,* a speech to General Foods Post Division, Battle Creek, Mich., October 10, 1985. p. 12. Emphasis in the original.

6 Paul Feldwick, ed., *Advertising Works 5.* London: Cassell, 1990, p. xv. Quoted from Broadbent, "Wait and Measure," *Marketing,* September 22, 1988.

7 Beatson, p. 22

8 Leo Bogart, "What Forces Shape the Future of Advertising Research?" *Journal of Advertising Research,* February–March 1986, p. 102.

9 Michael Dixon, "US Chiefs a Heap Bigger than Europeans," *The Financial Times,* June 8, 1990, section 3, p. 1.

10 William T. Moran, *Where There Is Choice There Is Value.* Greenwich, Conn.: Longman Moran Analytics, Inc., pp. 7, 14.

Index